The Canterbury and York Society.

GENERAL EDITOR: REV. F. N. DAVIS.

DIOCESE OF HEREFORD.

VOL. I.

CANTERBURY AND YORK SERIES.—VOL. II.

Registrum Thome de Cantilupo,

EPISCOPI HEREFORDENSIS,

A.D. MCCLXXV–MCCLXXXII.

TRANSCRIBED BY THE
REV. R. G. GRIFFITHS, M.A.,
Vicar of Clifton-on-Teme,

WITH AN INTRODUCTION,
BY THE
REV. W. W. CAPES, M.A.,
Canon of Hereford.

London:
ISSUED FOR THE CANTERBURY AND YORK SOCIETY
AT 124, CHANCERY LANE.

MDCCCCVII.

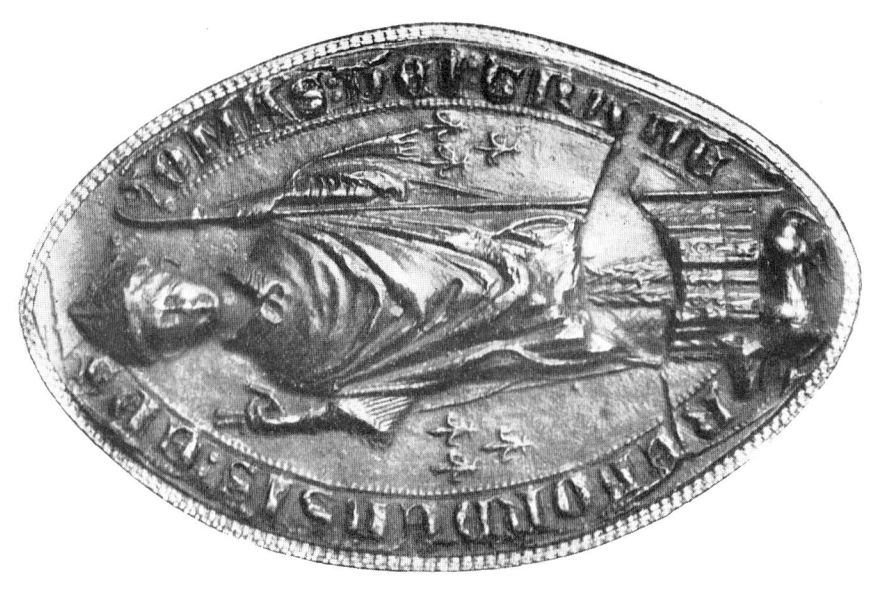

THE SEAL OF BISHOP CANTILUPE.

PREFACE.

THE Register of Bishop Thomas de Cantilupe is issued by the Canterbury and York Society in conjunction with the local Herefordshire Cantilupe Society. It consists of the first seventy-two folios of a volume measuring eleven and a quarter by seven and three-quarters inches, which also contains the Registers of Bishops Swinfield and Orleton. The part belonging to Cantilupe's episcopate is in good condition, and most of the writing is fairly distinct, though the ink has faded in a few places. As a rule the parchment has been well preserved, the exception being that the right hand bottom corners of several folios have been eaten away, apparently by mice. The writing varies in style, some of it is very small and cramped; on the whole the Latin of Cantilupe's scribes is more contracted than that which follows. A number of documents are stitched to the folios.

The work of transcription has been performed as a labour of love by the Rev. Robert George Griffiths, M.A., Vicar of Clifton-on-Teme, in the diocese of Hereford. In the accomplishment of the work he wishes to acknowledge with grateful thanks the assistance he has received from Prebendary Hingeston-Randolph, to whom he is indebted for his ability to decipher many obscure and difficult portions of the Register, and to whose mature experience the accuracy of the text is due. Viscount Dillon, M.A., F.S.A., is thanked for kindly explaining some obscure terms in a passage dealing with mediæval armour, also several friends who have given help in determining such references as required full local knowledge. That the bulk of the work might not be increased, notes have been added very sparingly.

Mr. Griffiths has also prepared the index which is issued with the Register, while the introduction is contributed by the Rev. William Wolfe Capes, M.A., Canon of Hereford.

F. N. D.

CONTENTS.

	PAGE.
INTRODUCTION	i-lxxi
THE BISHOP'S INCOME lxi	
ITINERARY OF THOMAS DE CANTILUPE lxv	
THE OFFICIALS OF THE BISHOP lxix	
REGISTRUM THOME DE CANTILUPO	1
INDEX TO THE REGISTER	313

ILLUSTRATIONS.

THE SEAL OF BISHOP CANTILUPE	*Frontispiece*
ANCIENT WINDOW IN CREDENHILL CHURCH	*to face page* xlvii
THE CANTILUPE MONUMENT	,, ,, ,, lvi
FACSIMILE OF PART OF FOL. 34*b* OF THE REGISTER ...	*between pp.* 112 *and* 113

ERRATA.

Page xxv, line 8, *read* "bandied" *for* "banded".
,, xli, ,, 23, ,, "several" *for* "many".
,, xliii, ,, 16 ⎫
,, 49, ,, 6 ⎬ *read* "Much" *for* "Great".
,, 256, ,, 27 ⎭
,, lxv, ,, 8, *omit* "27 Sechtone".
,, ,, ,, 13, ,, "16 Mayfield".
,, lxvii, ,, 34, *read* "Ludlow" *for* "London".
,, 67, ,, 19, ,, "at" *for* "of".
,, 71, ,, 29, ,, "preceptum" *for* "perceptum".
,, 99, ,, 2, ,, "Wichford" *for* "Wichenford".
,, 116, ,, 20, ,, "1277" *for* "1276".
,, 120, ,, 20, ,, "Domini" *for* "Dominie".
,, 138, ,, 9, ,, "Reginald" *for* "William".
,, 141, ,, 30, *insert* "1276" *after* "April 25".
,, 142, ,, 18, ,, "1278" ,, "May 7".
,, 153, ,, 4, *omit* "and his seneschal".
,, 210, ,, 21 and 33, *transpose* "May 4" *and* "May 14".
,, 225, ,, 29, *read* "G[odefrido]" *for* "G[alfrido]".
,, 229, ,, 3, ,, "January 3" *for* "December 28".
,, 239, ,, 8, ,, "March 7" *for* "February 17".
,, 250, ,, 33, ,, "Micheldean" *for* "Great Dean".

INTRODUCTION.

The name of Cantilupe appears in two of the varying forms of the Battle Roll of Hastings, and the early home of the follower of the Conqueror has been thought to be a village of that name in la Manche,[1] apparently on no other grounds than the existence of a Château there, which was of some importance centuries later; the owners of this, however, had a different coat of arms from those of the same name in England. It is hard to speak with any confidence upon the subject, for the families who dwelt in the wolf's haunts[2] must have grown apace and wandered widely, since in France alone there are nearly thirty places which are known now by the name in slightly different forms.[3] It seems more probable, however, that the starting point of Duke William's follower was a village near Evreux in Eure, which also bore the name, in or near the lordship of Breteuil, in a district with whose ruling families some of his descendants had intimate relations. Several fiefs in the neighbourhood belonged to Cantilupes who lived in England somewhat later, before the choice had to be made between estates on either side of the Channel. It was there, as will be seen, that the future Saint retired for many months to find peace in a region where his mother Milicent must have been known as Countess of Evreux and daughter of Hugh de Gournay,[4] names associated with broad lands that had passed away from the English branches.

On his father's side, the family, which had taken root at Aston-Cantelow in Warwickshire, had been conspicuous for several generations, evil councillors of King John and his

1—Mem. de la Soc. des Ant. Norm. II 286.

2—But the name cannot be derived from *campus lupi* (Strange, *Life of T. Cant.*, p. 30), nor from *cantus=canton* (Le Boeuf and Aug. le Prevost), for the analogy of chante-coq, chante-raine, chante-pie, chante-grive, chante-caille, and others points to *cantare* as the root (v. Joret, *Revue Critique*, 1884).

3—Of these Chantelou is most common. There are also Chantelowe, Chantaloube, Canteloup, Canteleu, Chanteleux.

4—There is a strange story, written in the name of Dame Juliana Tregoz, the sister of the Bishop, telling how the widowed Queen, Blanche of Castille, married a noble chevalier, Sir Hugh de Gournay, "one of the most valiant in the world," and that at his death St. Louis "with the greatest lords in Parliament," to do him honour, went down into the mud which came halfway up their legs, and taking the body from the litter, carried it through the city of Rouen, where it was buried. (Dodsworth MSS. 64, etc., ap. A. T. Bannister, *Hist. Ewias Harold*, p. 105.)

son Henry, as Matthew Paris puts it,[1] and strong supporters of the Crown against the Barons. William, the second baron, was grand seneschal of the kingdom, and one of the co-regents during the King's absence in Gascony in 1242 and the following year, when his great influence is evidenced in the many references to him—nearly two hundred—in the official despatches sent thence to England at that time.[2] In his own and in his father's days the family estates had been largely increased by royal favour and—like the *felix Austria*—by alliances in marriage. The second baron bought the wardship of five great estates, marrying his wards into his own family. His successor married Eva Braose, who brought him Abergavenny as her dower. The list of his son's possessions recorded at his death was a very long one, and included estates in twelve different counties.[3] The brothers of the second baron also married heiresses; John held Snitterfield in Warwickshire by right of his wife, Margaret Cumin; John acquired Gresley in Nottinghamshire by union with Eustachia, whose son succeeded also to Ilkeston in Derbyshire. Another branch was settled at Deighton in Yorkshire. The family name therefore survived in various localities in England, though these are not so numerous as in France.[4]

Whatever may be thought of them as politicians, they were exemplary churchmen according to the standard of the age; one William enriched Studeley Priory where he was afterwards interred; others founded Beauvale at Gresley, and endowed with their grants the convents of Bruton[5] and Montacute.[6]

Thomas de Cantilupe[7] was born about 1218, not in the

1—*Hist.* 11, 533 (Rolls series).   2—Gascon Rolls.
3—*Inquis. post mortem*, 1st year Edw. I,
4—Besides Aston-Cantelow, the family name was attached to a Hempston (in Devonshire), and to a Chilton, near Yeovil, which was the domain of Sir R. Cantilupe in the 14th century (Drokensford Reg., p. 257, Somerset Record, Soc.). Cantlop, or Cantelope, in the hundred of Condover, was so-named before the Norman Conquest, and was afterwards in the possession of the Burnells. Another Cantelope, in Shropshire, belonged to Hugo de Wulonkelowe (Inquis. p. m. 101), and probably derived its name from a distinct source. The prebend of St. Paul's Cathedral, called Cantlers or Kentillers, from which Kentish Town is said to drive its name, has been thought to be connected with the family, but though a Roger de Cantilupe was Prebendary of St. Paul's in 1249 (Le Neve, III, 403) and another of the same surname was Dean later in the century, no evidence has been produced to warrant this assumption, yet later fancy has made Kentish Town the favourite residence of the Saint.
5—Cartulary of Bruton, p. 3 (Somerset Record Soc.).
6—Cart. of Montacute, p. 158.
7—By a curious mistake Dugdale (*Baronage*, I, 573) makes Thomas the Chancellor the uncle of Thomas of Hereford, and the brother of Walter, Bishop of Worcester. This has been repeated by Banks and in later books.

Castle of Hereford, as Antony Wood supposed,[1] but at his father's manor of Hamildene[2] in Buckinghamshire,[3] where a chapel was built in his memory by the Earl of Cornwall. He had four brothers; of these William, the third baron, was seneschal of Gascony, Hugh became archdeacon of Gloucester, and John and Nicholas were knights. Two of his sisters passed into noble families: Juliana marrying Robert de Tregoz, and Agnes becoming the wife of baron St. John. A third was betrothed, if not married to baron Robert Gregonet.

His mother died probably soon after his birth, for he was brought up by a noble matron of saintly character, and entrusted at the age of seven, with his brother Hugh, to the religious training of good teachers. While his father's time was taken up by affairs of state and attendance on the King, the boy was much left to the fostering care and guardianship of his uncle Walter, the high-minded Bishop of Worcester. We may estimate the nature of his influence upon his nephew's character, if we note the part which he took in the social history of his age as well as in the administration of his diocese. The heads of the family[4] had borne a sinister reputation in our annals as unscrupulous agents of the vilest and the most unstable of the preceding occupants of the throne, but Walter of Worcester (bishop 1236-1265) was a distinguished patriot as well as a sage and exemplary prelate. Staunch friend of Grosseteste, and resolute like him to control with a firm hand the spiritual interests of his diocese, he took a prominent part in the baronial movement against the misrule of the Court, and never faltered in his adherence to the popular cause. He said mass for Simon de Montfort on the battle field of Evesham,[5] having refused before to excommunicate him at the bidding of the Papal Legate. He was, says an annalist,[6] so high in moral virtues above the level of his contemporaries, that but for this one

---

1—Hist. I, 221 (ed. Gutch).

2—So reported several witnesses mentioned in the *Bolland. Acta Sanctorum*, Oct., p. 494; but Hambledon was in the possession of Gilbert de Clare during part of the reign of Henry III. It may have belonged to the dowry of Milicent which he restored to William de Cantilupe (Dugdale, *Baronage*, I, 731).

3—Not in Lincolnshire as Strange puts it (p. 35), a mistake for the Lincoln dioc. of the *Acta Sanct*.

4—Fulk and William the first baron.   5—*Ann. Mon.*, IV, 168.
6—Thomas Wykes. *Ann. Mon.*, IV, 180.

fault, he might with justice have been canonized as a saint, and he was taken away that he might not see the evil times that were to come. In ecclesiastical matters he was no hot-headed reformer, and deprecated even before the legate Otho the enforcement of the existing rule against pluralities, without regard to present interests, and to the examples given by himself, like other bishops, in their past careers.[1]

Of the nephew's early life scarcely anything is told us, except the boy's choice of a soldier's life as the career which he would like, and the uncle's prophecy that he would serve in the Church militant to the honour of God and of the martyred Thomas.[2] It is quite probable that he was at Oxford in 1237 as a student, as Wood affirms,[3] and he may have stayed some years there. It is certain that in 1242 a royal safe-conduct was granted to two sons of William de Cantilupe, "our beloved and loyal servant," to study at Paris or at Orleans,[4] and that the first of the two places was chosen for a long-continued residence by Thomas and Hugh.

The University of Paris, to which the young scholars went, had grown out of the Cathedral School, such as had existed from early days at Hereford, and in connexion with other Chapters of secular foundation. Two movements had been going on, and were almost completed, which were necessary for its development into the paramount centre of general study throughout Christendom. One consisted in its emancipation from the ecclesiastical trammels of the Bishop and the Scholasticus of the Cathedral, through which it became an independent corporation able to organise itself by Statute. The other was the gradual acceptance of the forms of Greek Philosophy, by which Aristotle was enthroned as "the Master of the Wise," and his influence was stamped, for the whole course of the Middle Ages, on the great scholastic systems. Early in the thirteenth century there was a panic at Paris, caused by pantheistic tenets conveyed through Arabian commentators; but confidence returned with more accurate translations of the Greek Philosopher due to the

1—Matthew Paris, *Hist.*, III, 418.   2— *Acta Sanct.*, p. 493.
3—Wood, *Hist.*, I, 221 (ed. Gutch), "In this year, if I am not mistaken, St. Thomas de Cantilupe came to the University to be initiated into Academic learning . . . our mother then was the common nursery of the chief nobility of England."
4—Gascon Rolls, I, 500.

fugitives from Constantinople; by the middle of the century the works lately forbidden became the authorized text-books in the lecture rooms of the Faculty of Arts. It was to study in this Faculty that the two brothers came to Paris; they were enrolled therefore under some Master who was a member in the one of the four Nations which was called the English, though it included all the students who were not drawn from any part of what now is France. Its name shews that many flocked thither from England, as do also the frequent references to Paris in the Registers of the English Bishops, when licences of non-residence were given to young incumbents and Archdeacons who desired to pass a few years at some seat of general study.

Four or five years must elapse till the Bachelors' degree was reached; before that each candidate must pass a kind of 'Responsions' by disputing (*respondere*) in Logic, and be able to produce evidence of attendance at the necessary Lectures. That done, he was qualified to 'determine,' that is, to maintain a thesis publicly in the Rue du Fouarre, and meet the arguments of rival students; this being apparently a common practice before it became a statutory obligation, thirty years or more after the Cantilupes were 'Artists.'[1] The subjects of the Lectures which they had to hear were of an austerely intellectual type, with little to appeal to the emotion or the fancy; the poets and orators of Rome were almost entirely excluded from the course; the Greek authors wholly so, for the language was known only to a solitary scholar here or there, more favoured or more enterprising than the rest. The range of study had indeed extended beyond the *Trivium* and the *Quadrivium*, which were taught, as elsewhere, in the Cathedral School at Hereford in the 12th century, when a Canon[2] invited the eminent scholar Giraldus Cambrensis to take up his abode there.

> *Floruit, et floret, et in hac specialiter urbe*
> *Artis septenæ predominatur honos.*
> *Hunc, ubi tot radiant artes, de jure teneris,*
> *Cum sis artis honos, artis amare locum.*

1—H. Rashdall, *Universities of Europe*, 1, 444
2—Simon de Fraxino, ap., *Anglia Sacra* II, 641.

But the Rhetoric of the *Trivium* then included more of the real literature of the Latin writers, and its influence is seen in the more graceful style of a John of Salisbury or Giraldus. The wider outlook of the next century was mainly in Philosophy, for the ban pronounced a while against much of Aristotle's works was removed when the Cantilupes were not long settled in their course of study; but for some time they were chiefly occupied with grammar and logic, with a sparing admixture of psychology. Only later in their terms could they attend the lectures in the ethics and the other treatises of the Greek Philosopher.

This one-sided training is reflected in the literary style. It cannot be said that the letters of Popes and Bishops included in this Register are models of graceful composition. The Lecturers for their part were careless of literary finish; their main object was to divide and sub-divide the theme, and to distinguish and define, that the whole might be mapped out with minute precision. They were hampered also by the scholars' natural desire to take it all down as from dictation, notwithstanding the directions which from time to time were ineffectually given. Books were few; scholars often were very poor, and anxious to make a library of note-books. But if the class had to squat upon the floor, like Arab children, as was said to be the good old custom,[1] they could not find it easy to write their notes at large.

There was one side of University life in which the Cantilupes were not likely to take part; they would not be found in the taverns of the suburbs, drinking 'good sweet wine,' and quarrelling with the vintner, like the students at the Bourg Saint-Marcel in 1229,[2] whose fray with the citizens and the police brought about a general secession to other seats of study, which ended after two years of dispersion in the enlargement of their academic privileges, and the discomfiture of their opponents. For the brothers came 'en grands seigneurs,' with a considerable following, under the charge of a Master of Arts, who was afterwards seneschal of Bishop Walter. Their life was exemplary and devout, as vouched for in later days by

---

1—H. Rashdall, *Univ.*, I, 438.　　　2—Matth. Paris, III, 166.

a member of the household,[1] with early masses and ample benefactions to the poor.

Canon Robert le Wyse of Gloucester, one of the witnesses who gave evidence after the Bishop's death, spoke of his 'inception' in Arts at Paris. If the term was used in its strict sense, it implied that two years after he 'determined' or became a Bachelor, he presented himself for examination, conducted a disputation in the 'Quodlibets,' and applied for the formal licence from the Chancellor by which he became qualified to begin (*incipere*) to teach in the Faculty of Arts. The whole course therefore would have lasted some six or seven years, ending with the inaugural disputation, and with the customary banquet to the Masters at his expense, which could not be dispensed with, and had to be followed by forty days of continuous disputation, and a residence of some years as lecturer, if this last was not formally excused.

Meantime some steps were taken in the ecclesiastical career. Benefices were bestowed upon him by his uncle as well as by other patrons. In Feb. 1244 a Papal dispensation allowed him to hold another benefice besides Wintringham which he already had, and this was followed by a further grant which enabled the two brothers, 'whose nobility, learning, and elegance of manners speak for them,' to enjoy more preferment.[2] By the practice of the age this would not carry with it any obligation of continued residence in England, or indeed of Holy Orders beyond the earlier stages, but the evidence of friends and admirers at a later date implies in his case a more than usual regard for the responsibilities incurred.

The First Council of Lyons in 1245 which he attended, like his brother, in the capacity of Papal Chaplain, must have supplied further materials to mature his judgment. Innocent IV, who summoned it, had been in humbler rank the partisan and seeming friend of Frederick II, but, by a change of attitude more complete that that of Becket, he now called the representatives of Christendom together to crush and to dethrone his rival. No large numbers answered to the call, for the Emperor's power was paramount over wide regions,

---

[1]—Hugo le Barber, *Acta Sanct.*, 496.   [2]—Papal *Regesta*, Sep. 1245.

and many were afraid or disinclined to stir against him. But under Papal encouragement jealousies and animosities found a ready voice; the partisans of Innocent clamoured down Thaddeus of Susa, the eloquent advocate of Frederick, and the Pope declared the Emperor deposed. Striking as was the scene when the prelates turned their torches downwards after the sentence of excommunication,[1] there were other proceedings which had more interest for the eyes and ears of the Englishmen who were present. A little company of delegates —with baron Cantilupe among them[2]—were there to read the summary of grievances which they were commissioned to lay before the Council. It was a long and bitter indictment of Papal exactions and misrule from which England had long suffered, but which had reached their climax lately in the conduct of the Papal agent Martin. Swarms of aliens intruded by *provisions* into the dignities and richest benefices of the Church; the neglect of charity and ministrations in the parishes burdened with such incumbents; the *non-obstante* clause which set aside all promises and pledges in favour of the applicant who could outbid competitors by interest or bribes; heavy contributions levied on churches and convents by compact between Pope and King; the endowments of pious founders diverted to objects wholly foreign to their wishes; the unexampled greediness and insolence of the Papal delegate —these were the grievances on which the Magnates and Commons of England were agreed, to the exposure of which Walter Cantilupe of Worcester must have listened with entire approval.[3] His nephews may have heard in earlier years Grosseteste and their uncle in their friendly intercourse deplore the prevalent abuses, but such impressions were likely to be weakened by years of study spent in Paris; now they would be revived and deepened by the weighty words which Innocent listened to in silence, postponing an answer which was never given. There was further talk of immunities to be granted to Crusaders, but the Crusade which the Head of the Church had most at heart was one against the crowned heretic at home, and on this were spent the energy and treasure called for repeatedly in the interest of the Holy Land.

1—Matth. Paris, IV, 456.   2—Matth. Paris, IV, 420.   3—Matth. Paris, IV, 527.

Whatever the English Chaplain may have felt on the matters brought before the Council; however they may have influenced his later judgment, little can have found utterance from him at the time, for marks of Papal favour followed shortly in several Bulls which sanctioned the possession of the benefices which he held together, in contravention of the requirements of the Canons.[1] He was allowed moreover by dispensation to pursue the study of the Civil Law, which had been prohibited at Paris in 1219 by Honorius III, as endangering the paramount importance of Theology in that great University. While banished from that centre, and also formally withheld in 1254 from clerical dignitaries and regulars, except by special favour, by letter of Innocent IV, it did not, however, lose its popularity elsewhere. Matthew Paris, a few years later, refers to the young scholars of the day, forsaking the liberal Arts and the study of Philosophy, and hurrying in crowds to the Lecture-Halls of the civilians, as the avenue to posts of dignity and profit.[2] Friar Bacon spoke with bitterness of the rewards by which the study was encouraged. "In the Church of God a civilian, though acquainted with Civil Law alone, and ignorant of Canon law, is more praised and promoted to ecclesiastical dignities than a Master in Theology. . . . Would to God I could see these quibbles and frauds of the jurists banished from the Church, and causes decided as they were forty years back, without all this rattle of legislation. . . . Then the study of Theology, of Canon Law, of Philosophy, would be exalted and perfected; then the princes and prelates would give benefices and riches to Professors in this high Faculty. . . . But civilians, and lawyers handling the Canon law like civilians now-a-days receive all the good things of the Church. . . . Thus the whole study of Philosophy goes to ruin, and with it the whole regimen of the Church; peace is driven from the earth, justice denied, and evils of all kinds ensue."[3]

The study however, which was forbidden at Paris, was freely allowed to nearly all at Orleans, which had ranked before chiefly as a School of Letters, but now became the main resort of all who did not care to travel so far as to

1—*Acta Sanct.*, 495. 2—Matth. Paris, VI, 293.
3—Rog. Bacon, *Opus Tertium*, p. 84, Rolls.

Bologna or to Padua. Not indeed that it had independent corporate rights, though Matthew Paris speaks of it as a *scholarium universitas* ;[1] it was subject in some respects to the authority of the Bishop and the Scholasticus of the Cathedral, till Clement V in 1306 removed the ecclesiastical restrictions, and conferred on it the constitutional right to organise itself by Statutes of its own, and elect its ten Proctors of the Student Nations.[2] Thither therefore went Cantilupe,[3] and made such progress in his legal studies that he was able at times to take the place of the Professor Guido, whose lectures he had attended; after his death it was reported by a Canon of Hereford that, on one of those occasions of which notice had been given, a member of the Class dreamed the night before that the Lecturer was seated in the Professor's chair with a mitre on his head.[4]

After acquiring the knowledge of Civil Law[5] at Orleans, which must have been a matter of some years, he returned to Paris, where his brother had remained in the Faculty of Theology meantime; he then began the study of Canon Law, as embodied in the *Decretum* of Gratian, who a century before had drawn up his great text-book of authorities on the questions with which the ecclesiastical courts could be concerned, putting therein the decrees of the Popes on the same level as the Canons of the General Councils. The development of the Roman law had served as a model for this code, and the studies at Orleans were therefore a fitting groundwork and preparation for those which were to follow. The two brothers did not now live together, but each had a separate household on an ample scale, with devotional exercises and abundant charities as before.

In the Lecture-Halls of the Professors of Canon law Thomas was sure to meet some of his fellow-countrymen of equal rank and means, for the Faculty specially attracted the young Archdeacons and other dignitaries, as well as the holders of rich benefices who had licences of non-residence from their

1—Matth. Paris, V. 250.   2—H. Rashdall, *Univ.*, II, 1. 142.

3—So John de Swinfield, Archdeacon of Salop, went to Orleans to study, and Peter de Cors had leave of absence to go there for the same purpose. Swinf., *Reg.*, 68a and 68b.

4—*Acta Sanct.*, p. 495.

5—Strange thinks it well to apologise for the Saint's legal studies. "Though a hard and knotty knowledge, yet he hoped to draw some honey out of the flints for his improvement" (p. 64).

Bishops, while they qualified themselves by study for the duties of the offices to which they were promoted. In the pages of the Register examples may be found;[1] and with their position thus assured there can be little doubt that the young ecclesiastics did not for the most part work too hard. The course was in a later age a long one, lasting six years before the degree of Bachelor could be taken, though it might be shortened if Civil Law had been already studied. For a licence three or four years more were needed; and this could not be dispensed with for a future lecturer in the subject. It was probably during this period of probation, and among these opportunities of intercourse with titled Englishmen, that we may place the complimentary visit of the French King to his lodgings of which Robert of Gloucester had heard some vague account.[2] The austere self-discipline of Louis IX may well have stirred the admiration of the student; it would certainly have been a congenial example at a later date.

During this period of his residence at Paris he could hardly fail to be deeply interested in the long dispute between the Dominican Friars and the University authorities, though it concerned especially the Theological faculty of which he was not yet a member. The Friars Preachers, intended by their founder to be champions of the Faith, had soon settled themselves, as a matter of course, in the great centre of general study at Paris. Received there with a ready welcome, and encouraged by Papal favour, they held aloof from all concerted action with the other Masters, and refused to submit to the authority of the Theological faculty whose privileges they enjoyed. The University, which excluded them from fellowship in consequence, was required to re-admit them by a Papal Bull, the *Quasi lignum*, and though it formally dissolved its corporate organization in order to escape control, the pressure was too strong, and the Mendicants finally prevailed.[3] The pertinacious self-assertion of the Order caused much heart-burning at Oxford and at Hereford, but these troubles were in later days; some indication of them may be found even in this Register,[4] and there are many more among the Chapter deeds.[5]

1—See pp. 8, 29, 45, etc. 2—*Acta Sanct.*, p. 496.
3—H. Rashdall, *Univ.*, I, 373. 4—See p. 232.
5—A compotus roll of 1273 mentions a sum of £16 13s. 4d. spent on a suit with the Friars Preachers at Rome.

What Cantilupe had learned at Paris and at Orleans he came, we are told, to teach at Oxford. It was a common practice in his age for men who loved a life of letters to pass from one University to another, and 'gladly learn and gladly teach' in various seats of learning. His contemporary Peckham, for example, went in early youth to Paris, was reader in Divinity at Oxford, returned to Paris, and was lecturer afterwards at Rome. Young students, attracted by a European reputation, sought their Professors wherever they could find them. So the earnest-minded crowded round the sages of old Greece; travelled from place to place to make themselves disciples of some famous teacher; and hung upon his lips to get more light, if might be, on the eternal problems of men's destiny and duty.

There are apparently no data as to the exact time at which Cantilupe transferred his residence to Oxford, but he must have been there some years before the highest office in the University was conferred upon him, one not likely to be given to a stranger little known. There was some excitement in men's minds there, which might remind him of what he had been familiar with at Paris. The University resented the renewed attempts of the Diocesan, the Bishop of Lincoln, to exercise authority from which it claimed to have been set free, and in 1256 a deputation of nine "Artists"—as Wood calls them— laid their grievances before the King. Matthew Paris, who had frequent access to the royal presence, warned him, as he tells us, to be careful of the critical condition of the Church,— "The University of Paris, foster-mother of so many holy prelates, is in no slight perturbation; if Oxford, the second school of the Church, or rather its mainstay, be at the same time disturbed in the same way, there is danger of total ruin to it." "Heaven forbid that," said Henry, "most of all in my days."[1] A compromise was accordingly arranged, with terms of peace. There was greater trouble still in 1258. Feuds of long standing between rival factions issued in a general fray between the Northerners, aided by the Welsh, and the Southerners, and in this a brother of the Welsh Prince was killed, and many were seriously wounded. In their fear of the King's displeasure they proposed to give large peace-

1—Matth. Paris, V, 618.

offerings to the members of the royal family. Henry replied that he valued the life of any of his subjects too highly for any price that could be paid. But the disturbances of the realm, and the warlike movements that ensued, diverted attention from Academic questions, though in the Lent following there was renewed offence, in the rescue of a criminal who with aid of scholars broke out of prison, and sought sanctuary, and abjured the kingdom. The affray at Oxford was a prelude to more serious strife, as is implied in the old rhyme[1]

Chronica si penses, cum pugnant Oxonienses,
Post paucos menses volat ira per Angliginenses.

A deed of conveyance of ground belonging to the Abbey of Oseney to the *Fratres de Penitentia* was attested in 1262 by Thomas de Cantilupe as Chancellor, but we are not told how long before or afterwards he held the office. The election to the post, which was tenable for two years, was made by certain regent Masters nominated by the Proctors, with confirmation by the Bishop of Lincoln, and it carried with it large and varied powers. The legal training of many years must have served him in good stead, for the Chancellor was *ex officio* a Justice of the peace, and before his court, or that of his delegates, all suits were brought in which members of the University were concerned; his powers in regard to these included imprisonment, excommunication, and banishment. Litigation was very frequent, and the number of advocates extremely large; *effrenata multitudo advocatorum* is the language of an ordinance of 1300.[2] The familiarity of Cantilupe with such procedure may in part account for the frequent occurrence of legal matter in his Register. The Chancellor had also a large administrative and financial competence which brought him into close relations with the townsfolk, not always to their satisfaction in regard to markets and assize. But of such grievances we find no mention. The classes concerned have left no materials for history; the admirers and the members of his household,[3] who reported at a later date, spoke only eulogies of the firmness of his administrative action, of the strict discipline with which he disarmed unruly students, and maintained impartial justice without regard to personal affronts. Of

1—Wood, *Hist.*, I, 258 (Gutch).   2—*Munimenta Acad.*, I. 77 (Rolls).
3—*Acta Sanct.*, p. 497.

the next year however (1263), when he was possibly in office still, so favourable an account could not be given. Peace was disturbed by threatening movements of the armed forces of the King and of the barons; the sympathies of the students were mostly with the latter—and with this perhaps the influence of Cantilupe may have been connected,—so the civil authorities thought it prudent to close their gates when Prince Edward was marching by, early in February, in fear of possible collision. Hot-headed youngsters, impatient of restraint, presently broke down a gate and forced their way outside, causing a riot for which the ring-leaders were arrested. The Chancellor applied in vain for their release; the townsmen, provoked by taunts or elated by success, renewed the strife; but the gownsmen gathering in force swept all before them, pillaged the shops of leading citizens, and broke open the casks of the Mayor who was a vintner.[1] A contemporary, who put English history into rhyming verse, was present at the scene, which he described in some detail, and as he was probably a Canon of Hereford,[2] and prominent in giving evidence of the saintly life of Cantilupe, a few of his lines may here be quoted as a specimen of the English people's language at that date.[3]

"And wounded ther was manion, ac the borgeis athe laste,
Hii begonne to fle vaste; hom thoghte longe er;
So that the clerkes adde the stretes sone iler;
The bowiare ssoppe hii breke, and the bowes nome echon;
Suththe the portereues house; hii sette afure anon
In the south half of the toune, and suththe the spicerie
Hii breke fram ende to other, and dude al to robberie;
Vor the mer was vinitor, hii breke the viniterie,
And alle othere in the town, and that was lute maistrie."

The mature scholar was soon called away to other work upon a different scene. King Henry had borne with impatience from the first the galling restrictions imposed upon his power by the Provisions of Oxford; a Pope had no scruple in declaring

---

1—Wood, *Hist.*, I, 264.

2—The Robert of Gloucester of the metrical history may be probably identified with the Canon of the same name, also styled le Wyse, who is often mentioned in this Register, and who gave evidence at the Commission of inquiry in 1307. The writer was at Oxford with Cantilupe, and shews intimate acquaintance with scenes at Hereford connected with Bishop Peter; the Canon also had familiar knowledge of the career at Oxford, where he seems to have been at the same time. The belief that the versifier was a monk rests on no evidence whatever.

3—Robert of Glouc., II, 743 (Rolls).

that his promise to observe them was not binding on his conscience. In face of his growing strength the barons were wavering and divided, and with the King's consent agreed to refer the constitutional question to the arbitration of Louis IX of France, in order to avert "the havoc and irreparable losses with which the whole land was threatened."[1] Cantilupe was chosen as one of the six advocates, who were to plead the barons' cause before the King of France.

At the conference of Amiens, where King Louis sat in state, Henry and his Queen were present, with notable supporters like Bishop Peter of Hereford, who after rough handling in his own Cathedral, and imprisonment at Eardisley, had fled to France for safety. Simon de Montfort had broken his thigh-bone on the way, and the Magnates of his party failed to appear, while for several days the representatives on both sides were busy with their pleadings. With what address or cogency they spoke we are not told, but their words mattered little; they served as prelude only to a foregone conclusion. The French monarch had too strong a sense of the divine rights of Kings, and of the weight of a Papal sentence, to hesitate in giving his award, which annulled the Provisions of Oxford, while re-affirming the authority of the "charters and laudable customs" of the kingdom (Jan. 24, 1264).[2] But those very charters seemed enough to vindicate the people's rights, which the Ordinances of Oxford did but confirm. The fence of words was soon followed by the clash of arms, and the barons triumphed on the battlefield of Lewes. While they governed in the King's name, the offices of State passed, as a matter of course, into the hands of men whom they could trust. From being Chancellor of Oxford Cantilupe rose to be Chancellor of the King, and received the Great Seal on Feb. 25, 1265.[3] He bore a name associated in the King's memory with many acts of loyal service, and for the sake of father and grandfather he willingly *(gratanter)* accepted, as he said, the choice which others made. "He folded the Patent

1—Rymer, *Fœdera*, July 20, 1261.

2—The monastic chroniclers indeed of Worcester, Tewkesbury, and Dunstable, who were all strongly on the baron's side, believed that Louis was influenced by the two Queens against his better judgment; thus one says *Rex Franciæ, ut dicebatur, ob favorem dictas provisiones quassavit omnino (Ann. Mon., IV, 448).* Another, *fraude mulieris serpentina deceptus et seductus, ibid.,* I, 177.

3—Madox, *Exchequer,* I, 70 (ed. 1769).

with his own hands, and had it sealed in his own presence," as the Scribe noted in the Patent Roll.[1] A grant of five hundred marks a year was made, to include the support of the Clerks of the Royal Chancery. The Roll of the household expenses of the Countess of Leicester contains an incidental notice at this time that illustrates the ruling influence which determined his appointment. On March 1st there is an entry of a complimentary gift of wine sent to the Chancellor at Salisbury, and a special messenger was despatched with letters to him in July.[2] The Earl of Leicester had attended at the funeral of William de Cantilupe at Studeley in 1251, and there seem to have been close relations between the families concerned.

There are few signs of the official activity of the new Chancellor; early in May he delivered the Great Seal to the Keeper of the Wardrobe to be kept till his return, we know not whence; a little later, when the royalists were already in the field, the King gave instructions—dictated of course by those in power—that Thomas de Cantilupe, if he should be still in London, should take action with others named to regulate the affairs of the Jewry, "without giving heed to Prince Edward or his officials."[3] Little further is recorded beyond the testimony of his admirers that he would accept no gifts from importunate suitors, and was ready to resign his office rather than set his seal to deeds unworthy of the King.[4] But as Henry was in fact a prisoner, and his control purely nominal, the risk could not have been great.

The battle of Evesham closed the period of civil strife, and on Aug. 18th the Great Seal passed into other hands by the King's unfettered choice. The ex-Chancellor received the King's pardon soon afterwards,[5] but went back to his books again, and probably without regret. Though Archdeacon of Stafford, and largely beneficed, the ripe scholar seemed to need yet more to qualify him for his ecclesiastical career. He returned therefore to Paris, at the age of forty-seven, to add the study of Theology to the courses in the three Faculties through which he had already passed. It was at this time

1—49 H. III, m. 18, March 29.
2—Botfield, *Rotulus Hospitii Com. Leic.*, p. 6.
3—Madox, *Exchequer*, p. 234.   4—*Acta Sanct.*, p. 497.
5—Patent Roll, 50 H. III, *Pardonatio Thome de Cantilupo quondam Cancellarii Regis.*

that he came into close relations with two future Archbishops of Canterbury, both of them eminent in the Lecture-Halls of Paris, from whom he received afterwards in England treatment of a very different kind, Robert Kilwardby, a Dominican, who was also his Confessor, and John Peckham, a Fransciscan Friar.

The course in Theology was commonly a long one. For four years expositions on the books of Scripture were attended, and for two more years lectures on the Sentences of Peter Lombard; after this an examination might be passed, and the licence for a degree having been obtained, the Bachelor could publicly expound some book of Scripture. Survivors of the Bishop testified that they had heard him deliver lectures of a cursory kind—that is, at some time when the regular lectures were not given, or in some less formal manner,—both on the Apocalypse and on the Canonical Epistles.[1] How much time this occupied is not definitely known, but it is recorded in an Episcopal Register that in 1268 a further dispensation for three years was granted him that he might study Theology while absent from his clerical duties in the diocese of Worcester, and an attorney was appointed to do suit in the Bishop's court for lands in Norton under Bredon.[2]

After some years he returned to Oxford and became a regent Master in the Faculty in which he had been studying at Paris *(rexit in Theologia)*. At the ceremony of conferring the degree Kilwardby, now Archbishop, delivered from his own personal knowledge a set eulogy, such as was customary after the *Vesperiæ*, or the formal disputation on the eve of the inception, declaring him to be pure and blameless, "unspotted from the world."[3]

For a year and four months he remained there to lecture, and during that period he was elected to the Chancellorship again, the duties of which office he relinquished in the year 1274, when another interest called him away from England.

A second time, after the lapse of nearly thirty years he was present as Papal Chaplain at a General Council held, as before, at Lyons, but under far happier conditions than

[1]—*Acta Sanct.*, p. 498.   [2]—Godfrey Giffard, *Reg*, fol. 7a.   [3]—*Acta Sanct.*, p. 542.

the First. The Chair of St. Peter was now filled by the noble-minded Gregory X., whose schemes of ambition centred in the rescue of the Holy Land, which was to follow on the union of a divided Christendom. Bishops and dignified ecclesiastics flocked in crowds from every quarter to take part in the reconciliation of the Greek and Roman Churches, and in the furtherance of ecclesiastical reforms. Among them came the mature scholar with personal experience enough of civil strife and a disorganized Church at home to welcome gladly the ideals of peace and union, with beneficent safeguards and corrections, which were laid before the Council. He may have met a great Archbishop who was also there, Eudes Rigaud of Rouen, who was well-known to have been indefatigable for years in the visitation of his diocese, as described in his journal in minute detail.[1] The memory of his resolute example was perhaps not lost on Cantilupe, who must have heard in early days of the artifices by which the monks of Tewkesbury evaded his uncle's questions when he came on his unwelcome visitations. At the Council beneficent reforms were in the air; but soon the guiding spirit of the movement passed away, and with him the bright visions of the Kingdom of God, and the hopes of enduring progress. But the frequent references to the Council in the pages of this volume shew that some practical steps were taken without delay to grapple with the abuses of Church Order, and that Cantilupe in the administration of his diocese was entirely loyal to the regulations framed at Lyons. The efficiency of the parochial system had been fatally enfeebled. Churches were given *in commendam;* their custody was entrusted to laymen, who might have no intention to proceed immediately, or even at all, to Holy Orders; patrons presented their children to rich benefices while they were still boys at school; foreigners, by provision from the Pope, claimed the enjoyment of the tithes of parishes in which they never lived. It was some check on these abuses when the Council decreed that no unqualified person should be admitted to the custody of any church for more than six months at a time; that those presented to a benefice who were in minor Orders should be bound to proceed in due course to the priesthood; and that residence should be enforced except after

[1]—*Registrum Visitationum Arch. Rothom.*, Th. Bonnin, 1852.

formal dispensation of the Ordinary. The mention of the Council in the entries of the Register[1] means commonly that these decrees would be enforced, and the numerous cases of acolytes and sub-deacons presented by the patrons—and those religious houses often—illustrate the laxity of recent usage. The regulations could not indeed be stringently enforced. Patrons were too powerful, public opinion was too weak, to make it possible to ignore claims confidently made.

Moved probably by the strong language lately heard at Lyons, Cantilupe returned no more to any scene of Academic study, but gave more time and thought to the benefices which he held. These, we know, were many, though we have no certain data to enable us to make out an exhaustive list, or ascertain how long they were in his charge, for some of the Episcopal Registers do not exist and entries of the institutions are in most cases missing. He was Archdeacon of Stafford and Canon of Lichfield, Precentor of York,[2] Prebendary of St. Paul's, London,[3] and also of Hereford; in addition to these offices he was incumbent of a number of parochial churches. Wintringham in the diocese of York he had held for thirty years;[4] Deighton, where the Yorkshire Cantilupes were settled afterwards, was given him by Dame Agatha Trussebut in 1247;[5] Hampton Episcopi in the diocese of Worcester was a gift almost certainly of his uncle Walter, like the churches of Rippel and Kempsey, which were also manors of the See; Dodderhill he may have owed to that Bishop's influence with the patrons, the Prior and Convent of Worcester. Another, Snitterfield in the same diocese, near Stratford-on-Avon, came to him probably from his uncle John, who possessed the manor by right of his wife, Margaret Cumin. Aston-Cantelow in the same county and diocese must have been in his father's gift, to whom the manor was confirmed by Henry III. Sherborne Decani,[6] (now Sherborne St. John's) in Hampshire, which he

---

1—See p. 36, etc.

2—To this Church he presented a cope, which was shown as his gift long afterwards; see York Minster Fabric Rolls, p. 229 (Surtees Soc.).

3—This has been supposed to be Cantlers prebend, but as to this no evidence exists; it appears to have been given not long before 1264. Papal *Regesta*, I, 417.

4—Papal *Regesta*, Feb., 1244. It was described as in Lincoln dioc.

5—Abp. Gray, *Reg.*, p. 99 (Surtees Soc.).

6—So called in the Sherborne charters (now at Queen's College, Oxford). One of these documents mentions the sale of some land of the Priory to him *(crofta que vocatur Shepmanspick)*. It was pleaded in later days that the Priory itself was under the protection of St. Thomas of Hereford (Act. 14 Edw. IV., 33).

visited several times during the period of his episcopate, was in the patronage of the St. John family, afterwards lords of Basing, into one branch of which his sister Agnes married. To this must be added the benefice of Bradwell,[1] in the diocese of London, which perhaps was given in pursuance of an indult granted by the Pope in 1245, and addressed to the Bishop of London.[2] He had doubtless canonical dispensations to hold all these together, and the public opinion of the age condoned the practice, excepting when the endowments were enjoyed by aliens abroad. Our informants, who were personal friends or members of his household, were careful to assure us that he was most exemplary in his regard for the responsibilities of the various charges which he held. He travelled frequently, they said, from one parish to another, and this implies perhaps long intervals between his terms of residence at Paris or at Oxford; he would have vicars who could preach well and do their duty; he shewed open-handed hospitality, and dispensed liberal alms-giving to the poor with thoughtful and delicate discrimination. The buildings on the glebes were substantially maintained, and the rights of the church upheld, even at the cost of occasional litigation.[3] He had ample means indeed for this, for his revenue from these appointments was estimated at a thousand marks, and he spent little on himself for his personal comfort.

Little is told us in detail of what he did besides during this short period of his pastoral activity. At Court he had been soon pardoned for allowing himself to be forced as Chancellor upon the King. He was made a member of the Council by the succeeding Monarch; in Feb., 1274, the Sheriff of Oxford was instructed to hand over to his keeping certain brawlers there who had been arrested for grave offences;[4] and he was named in company with Ralph de Hengham and others as a judge.[5] Meanwhile family affairs claimed some of his attention. He had lost in 1265 his uncle Walter, for whom he acted as executor.[6] His nephew George

---
1—*Acta Sanct.*, p. 542. 2—Papal *Regesta*, I, 223.
3—*Acta Sanct.*, p. 500. There is a memorandum of agreement to settle a dispute as to the tithes of salt between T. de C., Rector of St. Austin's, Doderhulle, and sundry parishioners (D. and C., Worcester, Doc. No. 285).
4—Close Rolls, Feb. 8, 1274.   4—Close Rolls, May, 1275.   6—See p. 134.

died in 1273, shortly after he came of age, and left no issue. The estates passed to his two sisters, of whom Milicent by a second marriage became the wife of Eudo la Zouche, ancestor of the Lords Zouche of Haringworth, who is named several times in our Register as patron of some family livings.[1] The other sister married Henry, Lord Hastings, ancestor of the Earls of Pembroke. Another uncle, Nicholas, had also died, leaving a son and heir who was brought into the King's Court on May 15, 1275, and delivered to the King by his uncle Thomas, as his marriage was at the disposal of the Crown. But he received him back again to be kept during the King's pleasure.[2]

Of the preferments which he now held the prebend at Hereford seems to have been the last acquired. We are told that in 1273 John le Breton, who was then Bishop, asked him as a favour to accept it at his hands, and further expressed the hope that he might be his successor.[3] The opportunity soon came for he died on May 12, 1275. On the 23rd William de Conflens,[4] Archdeacon of Hereford, and Luke de Bree (or Bray), Canon, brought the official tidings of his death, and licence was given to the Dean and Chapter to proceed to an election.[5] Cantilupe preached before the Chapter on the eve of the day fixed for that event. There was no agreement at the first; the choice was therefore left in the hands of a Committee specially appointed for the purpose *(compromissarii)*; these with one accord declared that they would have Thomas for their head. It is reported that there were several Canons who had the same Christian name, and that the question was asked eagerly, 'which Thomas'?[6] The compotus rolls of the Cathedral shew that there were two others of the Chapter who bore the same Christian name, but they do not appear afterwards as men of mark.[7] We are told indeed that

---

1—See p. 28.   2—Close Rolls, May 15, 1275.   3—*Acta Sanct.*, p. 500.

4—The entry in the Patent Roll calls him Walter de Confleys, but the Archdeacon's Christian name was William, and documents in the Archives at Hereford and Evreux made it clear that the usual form of the surname was Conflens. A Margaret de Conflens received a legacy by the will of John de Aquablanca.

5—Patent Rolls, May 23, 1275.   6—*Acta Sanct.*, p. 500.

7—Thomas Bruton and T. de St. Omer. The latter, however, became the Official of Archbishop Peckham, and taking his side against Cantilupe, was angry with a poor distraught woman who said that she had been cured at his tomb. insisting that it was due to the merits of Bishop Robert de Betune, for whom offerings were still made at Hereford—twelve shillings and fourpence in 1301 (Compotus Roll);—See *Acta Sanct.*, p. 622.

the name was then uncommon, perhaps suggested by that of Becket,[1] unlikely as it seems.

The Chapter appears to have been left unusually free to act, and their choice was accepted by both King and Pope. The Consecration took place on September 8th, but only the Bishops of London and Rochester were present with the Primate at the ceremony. The Registers of Bronescombe of Exeter and Godfrey Giffard of Worcester contain their letters of apology sent to Archbishop Kilwardby, but he did not conceal his annoyance[2] at the scant courtesy shewn by the prelates in the neighbouring Sees[3] to one whom he had himself delighted to honour at Oxford, and of whom he speaks in warm terms soon afterwards in his letter to Prince Llewelyn.[4]

Meanwhile the Bishop of Worcester had written to him in June to promise that, if he were allowed to collate to all the benefices which Cantilupe held of the Bishop's patronage, the same should be restored to him in case he should not be confirmed and consecrated.[5]

The Dean and Chapter held in trust for the See certain pontificals which were to be handed down from one to another of its Bishops.[6] These indeed were few at the time, for much had been plundered in the turbulent days when Peter de Aquablanca suffered. Those which remained are specified,[7] but Cantilupe added to their number,[8] as did also his successor.[9]

A like system prevailed with regard to the emblements and live and other stock on the Episcopal manors, according to an arrangement made by Bishop Ralph of Maidstone of which details are given us;[10] and this also was observed and enlarged by some of his successors.[11]

One of the first acts of the 'Elect of Hereford,' as he is styled, was to write to the Chapter to deplore the scandals caused by the two rival claimants to the office of Dean, who

---

1—Eyton, *Shropshire*, VII, 31. 2—Gervase, Cont., II, 286.
3—The Welsh bishops neither came nor cared to excuse their absence.
4—See p. 10. 5—Giffard, *Reg.*, June 17, 1275.
6—A mitre bought for Archbishop Peckham cost £173 4s. 1d., which was at least £2000 of present value. Peckh. *Reg.*, III, 957.
7—See p. 5. 8—Swinf. *Reg.*, f. 3a.
9—Orleton, *Reg.*, f. 12a. 10—See p. 38.
11—Compare with this the live stock bequeathed by Peter des Roches in 1238 to the See of Winchester. (Sandall, *Reg.*, p. 631. Hants Record Soc.)

disturbed the peace of the Cathedral and the City by the feuds between their partisans, and the excommunications which were scattered freely in their names;[1] while the corrective jurisdiction over the whole Deanery was, to his grief, entirely in abeyance.[2] The animosities in question began at a much earlier date, and to understand them fully we must go back to the times of Peter de Aquablanca, who ruled the diocese from 1240 to 1268. A Savoyard favourite of Henry III, he was long his trusted minister in affairs of state, employed in many confidential errands, and among others in the unscrupulous artifice, as it was regarded, by which the clergy and religious houses were pledged unwittingly to pay large sums to Pope and King; this caused the good hater, Matthew Paris, to say of him that his memory exhaled a sulphurous stench.[3] Not content with the widespread odium thus provoked, he engaged in a long quarrel with his Chapter, binding them with Papal sanctions to six months' residence on their prebends,[4] though himself for long periods absent from his diocese, and further disputing their rights of property and customary claims.[5] Meanwhile a swarm of kinsmen and fellow-countrymen had followed him to Hereford, and with his help were quartered in the dignities and benefices of the See. Here as elsewhere the rapid rise of the intruders was resented, for it must be owned that Englishmen at this time was fiercely intolerant of the foreigners amongst them. For their dislike of the Poitevin and Savoyard favourites of the King there was indeed good reason, as also of Italians who drew large sums by Papal provision from their churches; but we may judge of their narrowed sympathies when we find Spaniards spoken of as "hideous in their persons, contemptible in their dress, and detestable in their manners."[6]

At Hereford the presence of this intruded element caused much heart-burning, and at times unseemly strife even within

1—See p. 2.

2—As a territorial expression, the Deanery included eighteen parishes, with chapelries annexed, which were exempted from the direct jurisdiction of the Bishop. The Clergy presented by the patrons were instituted by the Dean; the churches were visited by him; the matrimonial and testamentary business passed through the hands of his officials; and he had also powers of coercive discipline in faith and morals which brought him into relation with all classes of the people. It was the suspension of these which Cantilupe so much regretted. Even as late as the eighteenth century apparitors went to and fro; offenders were summoned; and penitents in doleful guise were forced to confess their sins in Church before the congregation.

3—*Hist.* v. 510.
5—Document in the Archives of the D. & C.
4—Papal *Regesta*, I, 229.
6—Matthew Paris, V. 450.

the walls of the Cathedral. Peter de Langon, a Savoyard prebendary, was dragged out of his stall by Roger de Bosbury;[1] a financial agent of the Bishop, Bernard, Prior of Champagne, was murdered while he was hearing Mass near the altar in the chapel of St. Mary Magdalene, close to the Bishop's palace, and a chronicler at Tewkesbury writes of the black deed without a trace of pity, almost indeed with a vindictive triumph.[2] Finally the Bishop himself, when the troubles of the civil war were at their height, was besieged in the Cathedral and roughly handled by Thomas Turbeville, who "harlede him out of church," as Robert of Gloucester puts it.[3] He was carried thence into imprisonment in Eardisley Castle by Roger de Clifford, together with his countrymen whom he had made canons.[4]

Giles de Avenbury had headed probably the movement of resistance which culminated in embittered strife till Papal arbitrators arranged terms of peace. He signed a deed of compromise about Baysham Church in 1252 as Dean,[5] but a Papal letter speaks of his intention to resign in 1253, and an indult was granted to him to hold another benefice besides those which he had already.[6] In 1261 he was no longer Dean;[7] and in 1263 he held the Treasurership and four benefices, the total value of which barely reached forty marks on account of the frequent wars on the Welsh border.[8] Instead of voluntary resignation as proposed, Giles seems to have been forcibly deprived of his office,[9] but on what grounds does not appear. In the Obit notice of him on Oct. 20 it is said that he bore great labour and heavy charges in maintaining the rights and possessions of his church.[10] In any case he appealed sooner or later to the Ecclesiastical Courts, and in 1270 obtained from the Official of Canterbury a sentence in his favour. John de

1—Swinfield. *Reg.* 70a.
2—*Quidam Francigena, non religiosus sed irreligiosus, procurator Domini Episcopi Herefordensis, meritis suis exigentibus, morte miserabili, se in capella sua missam audiente, a quibusdam percutitur.*
3—II. 741.
4—*Flores Hist.* II. 480. *Ann Monast.*, I, 148, but Clifford had to pay dearly for the outrage, being fined 300 marks by Gregory X. (deed in Archives), and humiliated by the Bishop (*Acta Sanct.*, p. 509).
5—Charter in the Archives D. & C. Baysham stood for the parish of Sellack.
6—Papal *Regesta*, I. 293.   7—Charter in the Archives.   8—Papal *Regesta*, I. 392.
9—*De Decanatu suo spoliatus.* Gervase, II, 252 (Rolls).
10—Rawlinson, *Hereford*, App., p. 26.

Aquablanca, the Bishop's nephew, had been put into his place, after a short interval, by the votes, we may suppose, of the Savoyards and their friends in Chapter, under pressure from above, and John now appealed from Canterbury to Rome, betaking himself there in person, while the suit dragged on for years, till judgment was given in his favour. Meanwhile Cathedral and City were distracted by the quarrel; spiritual curses were banded to and fro; the coercive jurisdiction of the office was neglected to the grief of Cantilupe;[1] and Giles himself was unable to take possession of his place.[2]

John's uncle had left his sermons to him in his will, on condition of the payment of fifty pounds of Tours, but we may doubt if he cared much for such literature,[3] and in his visits to the Cardinals to expedite his suit ready money was more useful.

John le Breton, the successor of Peter in the See, had been canon himself, and under the influence of the party-spirit of the past, he seems to have looked with an unfriendly eye on the foreign influence imported. On some grounds only vaguely mentioned, as requirements of right and order, he deprived one of them, Peter de Langon, of his prebend, which he offered to Cantilupe in 1273. The acceptance of it was a questionable act on his part, shewing perhaps more social prejudice than judgment. Certainly it brought him much trouble and anxiety for the rest of his career. The ejected prebendary appealed to Rome, and as Cantilupe did not reinstate him when the prebend was vacated by himself, the suit which had been begun dragged on for sixteen years in the dilatory Papal Courts, costing the Bishop much expense and many letters to his proctors, in which he warned them to beware of the wiles of the Burgundians, and of canons of Hereford who might be on the spot.[4] Meantime he had bestowed the prebend on Henry de Woodstock, the Queen's Chancellor, who undertook to bear the charges of the lawsuit, and to give instructions to his agents,[5] but still the Bishop's reputation was at stake. At length the plaintiff was reinstated, and heavy damages awarded

[1]—See p. 115. [2]—See p. 32.
[3]—He had a library, however, which was to be sold at his death and the proceeds given to charity (Will in Archives of D. & C.).
[4]—See p. 13. [5]—See p. 18, but this relief did not last long.

him, long after Cantilupe and others concerned had passed away.

Besides John there were other members of the Aquablanca family of whom the Register makes mention, and commonly with some note of disfavour or of ill-repute. Emeric,[1] the Chancellor, claimed the patronage of All Saints' and St. Martin's in Hereford, as the representative of his brother John, ejecting the existing Vicar who pathetically appealed to his Diocesan for justice.[2] Their uncle had in earlier days possessed himself of the advowson of St. Peter's, to which he had no right; but after some time he formally renounced the claim.[3] A third brother, Aymon, also a canon, is mentioned in the will of John. Their nephew James[4] had been made Archdeacon of Salop while still a schoolboy and had held this office, with more preferment, while away for five years at his studies.[5] For some unnamed offence sentence of deprivation was passed upon him, and after many citations from the Bishop[6] he formally resigned his place. William de Conflens,[7] Archdeacon of Hereford, William de Gruyère,[8] Precentor of Lausanne, and Martin de Gaye,[9] who were canons, are known to have come from the same region, and there is no doubt that the Chapter was well packed with Bishop Peter's countrymen and partisans. To these may be added others of the beneficed clergy, like Peter and Pontius de Salins, (dits de Cors) of Cœur,[10] near Aquablanca, nephews of Dean John, who were repeatedly summoned by Cantilupe for non-residence and contumacy in non-appearance.[11] Cantorin, a physician of Bishop Peter, had been promised a benefice by the King,[12] and is found afterwards at Eastnor as Rector.[13] Gerard of Eugines, Rector of Colwall,[14] Peter de Vesino,[15] Martin de Chambéry,[16] Hugh

1—Emeric is said to have been a favourite Savoyard *prenomen*.
2—See p. 30.   3—Deed in Archives of D. & C.
4—Also called James de Vitri (*Acta Sanct.*, p. 510); he had been ordered to reside in Hereford and put vicars on the benefices which he held (Papal *Regesta*, 1, 229).
5—Papal *Regesta*, I, 338.   6—See p. 63, etc.
7—Conflans., now a faubourg of Albertville, stands on a rock which looks down on the meeting point of the Isère and the torrent of Arly. The name (from *Confluentes*) is found where Roman influence was early felt; elsewhere the old Gallic element has given the name of Condé to places at the junction of river courses.
8—Also called de Sarreta, and Treasurer of Lausanne, p. 136. He was a son of Count Rudolph III.   9—See p. 154.
10—Salins was near Moûtiers en Savoie; Cor or Cœur was near Aquablanca en Tarentaise.   11—See p. 126, etc.
12—Gascon Rolls, 4918.   13—See p. 6.   14—See p. 86.
15—Mugnier, les Savoyards en Angleterre, p. 195.   16—See p. 27.

de Tournon,[1] Geoffrey de Virieux,[2] and Vicini de Conflens,[3] belonged to the same neighbourhood.

The acceptance of the prebend of Preston by Cantilupe under such questionable conditions, and the troubles that ensued, could have left little doubt as to his sympathies when questions were at issue between Burgundians and others. His decision therefore was a foregone conclusion when disputes of the kind were referred to his decision; indeed he definitely says on one occasion that he will not willingly plant in his orchard an exotic or unfruitful tree.[4] Such a case occurred in 1276 when there was a contested claim to the prebend of Inkberrow between William Rufus and Humbert de Yanua,[5] who was the Chanter of the collegiate church of Aquabella, founded by Bishop Peter after the type of his own Cathedral Chapter. The question had been brought before the Papal Courts, but both parties in the suit resigned themselves unconditionally to the award of Cantilupe, which was promptly given in favour of the English claimant.[6]

The Bishop was soon made aware, if he did not already know, that the possessions of the See had suffered from aggressive neighbours. His predecessor, John le Breton, believed till lately to have been a notable lawyer in his day,[7] had shewn supine indifference to such wrongs, but the reins were now in stronger hands, and without delay the rights of the See were fearlessly asserted in the face of powerful opponents. The first of whom restitution was demanded was Llewelyn, Prince of Wales. Some districts of the border lands appurtenant to Montgomery, when Earl Roger held it, had been granted early in the thirteenth century to Bishop Giles de Braose by a son of Robert de Bollers. This was seized in the King's name in 1224, as part of the Honour of Montgomery, but was restored to Hugh Foliot on his appeal. It was again seized on the same grounds by the Constable of Montgomery in 1261-4.

1—See p. 126 The Château of Tournon had been given by Amedée IV, Count of Savoy, to his brother, Archbishop Boniface, who had also Eugines close by, at the junction of la Chaise and Arly.
2— See p. 136. Viriacum probably was Virieux near Culoz.
3—Called de Confleto in p. 184. cf *a ponte Confleti usque ad Loyam, Mugnier*, p. 220.
4—See p. 249.
5—Referred to also in Peckham *Reg.*, III, 1056.   6—See p. 84.
7—On the strength of a passage found in some copies of what was known as Matthew of Westminster, v. Britton (Nichols), Introduction, p. xix.

During the Civil War the surrounding district was occupied by Llewelyn, encouraged by the barons, and part of it was now reclaimed by Cantilupe, as belonging to the episcopal estates, no regard being paid by him to the repeated seizure of it in earlier days in the King's name. This included Chastroke, now called Castle Wright, Aston, and Muliton now Mellington.[1] Strong letters, one after another, demanded the unconditional surrender of these lands, under pain of the gravest spiritual censures.[2] The Archbishop of Canterbury was induced to write in the same spirit to urge restitution.[3] The critical condition of the Prince a little later, and his final overthrow decided the question of his claim, but it appears that the tenants of the disputed lands would not recognise the Bishop's title, and he wrote repeatedly to denounce the malcontents.[4]

In another suit Cantilupe resolutely braved the resentment of the great baron, whose support had given to Prince Edward the crowning victory of Evesham. Gilbert de Clare, Earl of Gloucester, had taken possession with his foresters of the episcopal Chase of Eastnor and Colwall above Ledbury, which had been given to the See by King Medruth with confirmation from Pope Innocent II.;[5] and this without protest apparently from John le Breton. His successor lost no time in insisting on his rights. The Earl was summoned to defend his trespass (Oct., 1275), but his great influence intimidated at first the local officers; many adjournments were allowed, which delayed the issue for two years. At length by the King's order the Earl's foresters were withdrawn; the Bishop, to assert his right, was allowed to hunt over the Chase; after which the Sheriff took possession of the woods. A writ was issued, in obedience to which the Justices came to hold an inquest; a jury viewed the lands and decided in the Bishop's favour in Jan., 1278. His servants many years afterwards had much to tell of the final scene in the long debate; how the Earl appeared in force with armed retainers, bidding the Bishop know that no sorry shaveling should take from him what he and his ancestors had long enjoyed in peace; then handing to the Justices what purported to be a royal writ to postpone the proceedings and dismiss the jury. The Bishop, it is said,

1—Eyton, *Shropshire*, XI, 155.   2—See pp. 9, 29, 31, etc.
3—See p. 10.   4—See p. 97.   5—Watkins, Cont. Duncomb's *Heref.*, p. 54.

retired to a wood hard by, from which he issued presently in full pontificals, with clergy at his side, and hurled anathemas at all who ventured to obstruct the course of justice. The Earl thereupon rode off, and the jury gave their verdict.[1] The Earl's foresters, insolent and menacing before, were overawed, and long afterwards some of them appeared as penitents before the Bishop, and sued for formal absolution.[2]

An entry in the Register[3] shews that the Bishop was prepared to put his champion in the field, to whom he paid an annual retaining fee to maintain his rights in duel. It was still the practice at the end of the thirteenth century even for religious dignitaries and convents to keep a professional duellist for time of need. Thus the Annals of Worcester mention two cases of the kind,[4] and in the Archives at Hereford the receipts are still preserved of the yearly payments of half a mark which were made (*pro feodo meo*) to Robert le Bret, *pugil* (1296), and to Robert de Melton Mowbray (1311) for services when needed by the Dean and Chapter.

In a third suit Cantilupe disputed the pretensions of a turbulent and litigious family on the Welsh borders of Shropshire. The Corbets were great barons who came over in the Conqueror's train from the Pays de Caux, and built a strong castle which commanded the valley of the Rea, naming it, like Earl Montgomery, after their Norman home.[5] There they were mighty hunters, and Peter Corbet in 1281 was specially commissioned by the King to destroy the wolves on his own land and in neighbouring counties.[6] Thomas Corbet, who had been succeeded by his son Peter in 1274, had been busy in lawsuits and disputes with his vassals, neighbours, kinsmen, and even with his son, and claimed peculiar rights over his Welsh lands which withdrew them from the sphere of common law. The family had suffered, like the See, from the aggressions of Llewelyn, but on the other side had encroached, as was urged by Cantilupe, upon the great manor of Lydbury, stretching over 18,000 acres, which was said to have been given it by a great landowner of early days, Egwin Shakbeard, after his cure at the shrine of St. Ethelbert. There it was urged in behalf of

[1]—*Acta Sanct.*, p. 511.
[2]—See p. 227.
[3]—See p. 104.
[4]—*Ann. Monast.*, IV, pp. 464, 467.
[5]—Eyton, *Shropshire*, XI, 194.
[6]—Rymer, Fœdera, May 14, 1281.

Cantilupe that much of a district called Longa Memida containing from five to seven miles of pasturage had been annexed.[1] At his instance therefore a writ was issued, and a perambulation of the land in dispute was arranged for March, 1278. A jury of belted knights was summoned, but several were challenged by Peter Corbet, and the rest refused to act without the due number of knights. At length, after remonstrances and threats of fines, a proper perambulation was made, and the boundaries fixed.[2]

Before Cantilupe's Consecration he wrote to the civic authorities of Hereford to beg them to respect the rights and privileges of the Cathedral and its clergy.[3] There had been much friction in the past; there were to be many quarrels in the future; and later pages of our Register illustrate in some detail the causes that led repeatedly to collision and disputes. The variety of conflicting jurisdictions accounted for much of the ill-feeling. The Church-land and the city-land: the King's men and the Bishop's men were marked off from each other by their different rights and obligations; there was distinct assize of bread and beer; the shopkeepers' privileges differed in each; the power of the Mayor stopped short at the precincts of the Close; and law-days were held in the Canons' Bake-house for the Bishop's Fee, or for that part of it inside the liberties which was called afterwards the Canons' Fee, within which the City Constable could make no arrest. Each prebend had indeed in some respects like independence, and claims for its own law-days and assize. Disturbers of the peace passed to a different police system when they crossed a street, to the grave risk of security and order. Some houses were partly in the Canons' fee and partly in the King's fee, and knavish occupants could transfer their furniture from one side to the other, and so balk the civic officers when they came to levy distraint upon their goods. Collision between such vested rights was unavoidable, and in Bishop Peter's time there was much hot dispute, after which a formal memorandum of agreement was drawn up, and enrolled by Royal mandate, November, 1262. Of this a copy was entered in our Register, called for doubtless by friction existing at the time.[4] Again the exclusive privileges of the

1—See p. 69, 'Longemimede.' *Acta Sanct.*, p. 512, 'Longa Memida.'
2—See p. 73.   3—See p. 6.   4—See p. 91.

Bishop's Fair were in Hereford, as were the like elsewhere, a constant source of irritation to the trading classes in the town. Given by special licence from the Crown for a fixed number of days, and extended afterwards by further grant, these monopolies of barter stopped all competition while they lasted; closed all the shops within the town; forced the country folks and traders from a distance to pay the Bishop's tolls, and buy and sell only for his profit. The custody of the city gates passed into his keeping, while his men displaced the municipal officials, and made the most of all their short-lived powers. The natural resentment of the townsfolk found expression at this time; the bailiffs refused to give up the keys of the gates as usual, in spite of the remonstrance of the Official of the Bishop, and called forth from him a stern rebuke,[1] which seems to have had effect, as we hear no more upon the subject.

The disputes with his lay neighbours could be settled, though with some delay, in the King's Courts at home. There was another of a different kind, which caused him far more anxiety, and of which he never saw the end. The hot-headed and litigious Bishop of St. Asaph, Anianus II.,[2] laid claim to the spiritual jurisdiction over several parishes in a district called Gordwr, on the Welsh border, which had belonged to the diocese of Hereford, thus repeating in another form the aggressions of Llewelyn. The question was brought before the Court of Rome, debated there, referred to Archbishop Peckham, and judges-delegate in England, against whose action Cantilupe, mistrusting their impartiality, appealed to Rome again, and it was left undecided at his death. The subject constantly recurs in his letters to his legal agents, and to friendly Cardinals and others, in connexion with the suit of Langon, and together they made large inroads on his peace of mind and purse.[3]

[1]—See p. 83.
[2]—The name of Anianus of Nannan recurs often in the annals of this period. He had been Prior of the Dominican house at Rhuddlan, was a militant Crusader with Edward I; after his return home he was embroiled with Llewelyn, whom he charged with wronging the Monasteries of his diocese. A number of the Welsh Cistercian Abbots formally defended Llewelyn from this charge (Haddan and Stubbs, *Councils*, I, 498), but a Charter of liberties was finally procured. In the Welsh war of 1282 the Cathedral of St. Asaph was burnt down, and Archbishop Peckham found it needful to rebuke him for leaving his flock, and to warn him not to excommunicate the English soldiers. By royal order he was forbidden to return, and Bishop Burnell took charge of his diocese meantime. In 1284 he was still in banishment notwitstanding repeated appeals from Peckham to the King.
[3]—The matter was afterwards referred to delegates in England, and a mixed jury of Welsh and English was assembled; their verdict was in favour of Hereford, and the boundary fixed on was the mid-stream of the Severn between two fords. Eyton, *Shropshire*, VII, 88.

It has been argued that the common practice of direct appeal to the Pope was beneficial to the suitors, and in the interests of justice, since it saved the expense of litigation in the courts of primary instance, and ensured the hearing of the cases by competent judges, while the official of a bishop might be biassed or ill-trained. The correspondence in our Register furnishes some evidence of weight on the other side. It illustrates in the first place the dilatory procedure of the Papal Curia that allowed cases to drag on for many years, as in both of those which have been lately mentioned. With the tardy action of the courts we must connect the notorious venality of high-placed officials there. A letter of Cantilupe to his proctors deals with the arrangements to be made for winning their support. Leading Cardinals are to be visited—the common euphemism for the presents to be offered—and the Bishop explains his views in some detail as to the way in which the sum of a hundred pounds which he provides is to be divided for the purpose. It is all that he can spare at present, and evidently not enough, though equivalent to at least fifteen hundred now. The Pope himself is named among the persons whose favour is to be bought, though the writer includes him with reluctance.[1] We must accept therefore with reserves the plea of justice ensured and expenses saved by such direct appeals. As in other respects a wise and benevolent despot could work the system to general advantage, but it might sadly fail in weaker hands. Of course it discredited the local authorities in all lands, weakened their influence, and disorganized the Church.

In connexion with these negotiations at the Papal Curia we read in all the contemporary documents of accredited financial agents, and to these references frequently occur in the pages of our Register. The Italian bankers seem in the thirteenth century to have completely displaced in the higher regions of finance both the Jews, who had a practical monopoly in earlier days, as well as the detested Caorsins from the South of France,[2] whom Grosseteste calls, "the traffickers and bankers of the Lord Pope."[3] They are spoken of as merchants, though we hear

---

1—See p. 274.
2—The name Caorsins was used afterwards without regard to Cahors or the South of France, and applied to foreign moneylenders of all kinds.
3—Matthew Paris, V, 404.

little of purely commercial dealings with them. The Crown indeed employed them at times to sell the wool, the chief English export, but they were more frequently used by it to collect the subsidies and tenths, and to advance the ready money needed for the service of the State. Their representatives accompanied the legates or Papal agents sent to England, and furnished the funds required for their exactions. They were also to be found in attendance on the Papal Curia, where they occupied a very privileged position. Preferment to high dignities in the Church caused often long delays, and always heavy charges,[1] pensions often to obliging Cardinals and others; to expedite the process the money-lenders' help was very needful; in the interest of high officials and of the Papal Treasury itself they were armed with a sort of international guarantee, in the form of the ecclesiastical censures and suspensions of defaulting debtors, by which the creditors were screened from loss. Thus letters Apostolic ran "If you find the money has not been paid you will excommunicate the Abbot and the convent, announcing it on Sundays and on feast days till satisfaction has been made to the merchants; if two months later they have not paid, you will suspend them from administration of spirituals and temporals." Some prelates groaned for years under the weight of burdens thus incurred. Archbishop Peckham, who as a mendicant friar had little to fall back on, was in dire fear that sentences of excommunication would be launched against him in default of payment of a debt of four thousand marks;[2] Walter Giffard of York pleaded to the Pope to be allowed to pay his debt off by instalments of a thousand marks;[3] he heard from a Cardinal that his pension of three hundred marks must be paid, or something grave would follow. Others, like Cantilupe, who had means to defray preliminary expenses, found advances very useful later on to pay proctors and advocates in the tedious lawsuits in which they were constantly involved, and to bribe Cardinals and even Popes to grant a favourable issue to their suits. Though we hear of individual names like Bardus of Poggibonzi,[4] and Lucas of Lucca,[5] they were really joint stock companies that were engaged. There was a curious fancy that, as in their corporate

1—A Bishop appointed by Papal provision was taxed at one third of his income.
2—*Reg. Ep.* Peckham, I, 50
3—W. Giffard, *Reg.*, p. 117.
4—See p. 12.
5—See p. 25.

status they had no souls to be stained with the guilt of usury, they were not liable to any penal sanctions. Few of the Italian towns are named in these relations with the Crown and Bishops; the great commercial communities of Genoa and Venice held aloof from them, while the names of the financing companies of Florence, Lucca, and Sienna constantly recur.

There was a dispute also with another neighbouring prelate, the Bishop of St. David's, who claimed the right to consecrate the church of Abbey Dore, as pertaining to his See, and was supported by baron Tregoz, a nephew of Cantilupe, who had pecuniary interests at stake. These, however, had no effect upon his uncle's judgment, nor was he deterred by the show of military force assembled; he resolutely proceeded on his way, under protection of his escort, and completed the ceremony at some personal risk. Finally after reference to the law-courts, the question was decided in his favour.[1]

The cases already mentioned are very far from exhausting the list of the disputes in which the Bishop was concerned, for which resort was had to the courts of law in his behalf, or proceedings of the kind were threatened. In the examples given he was defending the interests of his See, was in the position of a trustee bound to take action in behalf of others. But he was quite as tenacious of his rights, and as resolute to uphold them, when the risks or losses possible were of a more personal kind. He enforced his claim to have delivered to him the daughters of a deceased tenant, who were legally his wards;[2] he pressed at Rome his demand on the executors of Geoffrey de Coberleye;[3] he promptly threatened action against the Dean and Chapter of St. Paul's, whose seneschal had used violence at Barling to his bailiff;[4] **he** repeatedly threatened, summoned, excommunicated offenders who had trespassed on his woods, slighted his authority, or rescued the impounded cattle. Vigilant care indeed was needed to preserve the wild game in the Chase or woodlands. It appears from other Registers to have been a favourite sport—in which the clergy sometimes took their part—to invade the episcopal preserves, and vary the salt food on their tables in the winter months by more appetising fare. It reads strangely when we find in the Patent Rolls that the Bishop himself twice received

1—*Acta Sanct.*, p. 513.   2—See p. 65, 73.   3—See p. 106.   4—See p. 14.

the royal pardon for such trespass in the royal forests,[1] as indeed did Archbishop Peckham,[2] though it may have been in the case of Cantilupe some fault of the servants or foresters that was thus excused. Each reference to Courts of Law taken by itself is natural enough, shews no specially vindictive or litigious spirit. But what may surprise us is the frequency of their recurrence, and the large space in the Register which is filled with legal process. How shall we explain this feature? Had past neglect, and the weakness of his predecessor, made it needful to enforce the assertion of his rights? Was such resort to law but a more civilised form of the border warfare which had been going on for centuries on the Welsh frontier, expected therefore, almost required, by the public opinion of the age and place? Had the long years spent in the study of the Civil and the Canon law, with the experience of the Chancellorship at Oxford, influenced his judgment, and lessened the distaste, which might else be looked for in a Saint, for so much legal phraseology and practice? His admirers testified to the Commissioners of the placid calm and indifference to personal slights with which he treated at Oxford the petulance of wayward scholars,[3] but the acrimony with which he complained to the King that the quarters promised him at Powick had been given to the Earl of Gloucester[4] hardly agrees with such accounts, and embarrasses to some extent our judgment.[5]

Much of his time was taken up with the endeavour to enforce the canons of the Councils which were drawn up against the plurality of benefices in the Church, and the details fill many pages of this book. It had been forbidden by the Lateran Council in 1215, and the legate Otho had attempted to carry out the rule in England, but was met, as has been said already, with stout resistance from Walter Cantilupe of Worcester. It had been, however, re-enacted by the Second Council of Lyons, in connexion with the duty of the continuous residence of the incumbent on his charge. Our Bishop acted loyally on the instructions given, though the memory of his

1—Close Rolls April 28, 1279, and July 4, 1280.
2—He wrote a letter to the justices deprecating any interference with his recreation on his journey. *Reg. Ep.*, Peckh, III, 942.
3—*Acta Sanct.*, p. 497.   4—See p. 123.
5—Curiously enough another English Saint of the same century, St. Edmund, had also a litigious record.

own antecedents must have made it, for him as for others in like case, a most unpleasing task. He had, it is true, enjoyed the formal dispensations, for these were readily obtained by men of high rank or influence like himself. But it required some courage to insist—as indeed he rarely does—upon the moral aspects of the rule, on the personal oversight that was implied in a Rector's name and office. It was unfortunate moreover that one of the first to suffer from the enforcement of the rule was Hervey de Borham, Dean of St. Paul's,[1] whose name had been brought forward in competition with his own at the election,[2] and that several others belonged to the Burgundian, or intruded, element for which his sympathies were scant. He did not act hastily indeed; he had the offenders summoned time after time; waited patiently in court for the attendance which they seldom made; allowed excuses and adjournments which it was open to him to refuse. They did not take it seriously at first; were far away, or thought proceedings purely formal; did not at first present the pleas or dispensations which were valid; and so we have a tiresome iteration in the entries, which recite the same facts repeatedly without much seeming progress. At times a royal letter bars the way,[3] for the King will not have his clerks molested; or dignitaries, or wealthy ladies beg for a reprieve, which he was not unwilling to allow.[4] For very few were heartily in earnest in that movement of reform; most of the bishops were hampered by their antecedents, unlike Bishop Peckham, who as a friar had no past practice to clash with present theory; he indeed could denounce abuses which a King upheld, and refuse to confirm the election of a bishop who had been a pluralist himself.

John XXII. in the next century checked for a while these practices by the sweeping measures of his Constitution *Execrabilis*, but the whole system of dispensations procurable at Rome was a matter of favouritism and bribes, and there was warrant for the trenchant language of Prynne. "Notwithstanding all former canons, yet through the avarice, ambition, impiety of pluralists, dispensations and contrivances of Popes and Prelates for their own filthy lucre, they still increased more and more, and continued unredressed as a most

1—See p. 88. 3—See p. 169.
2—*Acta Sanct.*, p. 510. 4—See p. 135.

growing mischief and cancerous ulcer past all cure to the eternal infamy of those Popes, etc."[1]

The obligation of residence could not be easily enforced, especially by a Bishop who had ignored it for most of his adult life. A Constitution of Pope Boniface VIII.[2] had sanctioned dispensations in the case of the many minors—kinsmen often of the patrons—instituted to parochial cures, for whom clerical training, and even higher education with recourse to necessary books could hardly be provided except at a centre of general study. All the Bishops therefore granted licences to young Rectors and Archdeacons to go to Paris or to Oxford to pursue their studies, or have a pleasant time, if they were idle; and sometimes a tax was levied from them for the benefit of the fabric fund of the Cathedral. The licences were limited commonly at first to one or two years, but occasionally they spread over as many as seven. There was little security meantime that the purposes for which these were granted were fulfilled; the young incumbents failed frequently to appear for ordination at the stated times, and we hear therefore often of sequestrations for default.[3] Men of influence again and high-born ladies expected their nominees to attend them as their private chaplains, and their desires could not be always disregarded. The Crown had no scruple in using its ecclesiastical patronage for the payment of its servants, and angrily warned off the Bishop who was rash enough to summon the non-residents to their cures.[4] There were many others who gave trouble; aliens intruded by provision of a Pope, or by a Bishop like Peter de Aquablanca. It was difficult to learn if they had any special dispensation; they were often far away, and repeated citations were required to ascertain the facts; and hence the somewhat wearisome recurrence of such entries in the Register, and the scanty results of ineffectual attempts at discipline.

Among those who were cited on the ground of their non-residence the names of portionists frequently recur. The expression was a common one in those days; it has not quite disappeared from the diocese now. The prebends of the col-

---

1—*Intol. Usurp.*, &c., p. 232.

2—It is thus referred to in episcopal registers: *juxta formam Constitucionis D. Bonefacii, que incipit,—Cum ex eo.*

3—See p. 155.   4—Peckham, *Reg.* I, 252, and p. 169.

legiate churches of remote antiquity still here and there remained distinct, while the process of union had gone on elsewhere; the division of some manors among co-parceners—as the six who shared Acton Scott[1]—helped probably to preserve the old type unchanged, and may possibly have added to the number of such cases. In the diocese of York, as we see in the pages of the early Registers, the fusion of the several portions went on rapidly in the thirteenth century; in the diocese of Hereford they remained unchanged longer than elsewhere. Besides Pontesbury and Burford, which have their three portionists still, there was the same system at Bolde,[2] Bromyard,[3] Castle Holgate,[4] Condover,[5] Ledbury,[6] and Llanwarne[7]; there were six prebends even in the King's Chapel of Bridgnorth[8] representing the canonries existing in the earlier days in the wide-spread manor of Morville. The portionists of Pontesbury and Bromyard gave especial trouble to the Bishop; those of the latter were of the Aquablanca clan, and shared its self-assertion. Generally perhaps the portions were well-endowed, and many of them therefore passed into the hands of privileged aliens, who were non-resident, perhaps to the advantage of the peace and harmony of the divided parishes.

The Register does not throw full light on the conditions of the religious houses at this time. During the few years over which it spreads the Bishop did not find time to visit many; the formal reports on those which were visited by himself or by his delegates are not inserted; and we have only letters of general admonition to the monks. But these—like other evidence of the period—imply that the enthusiasm and high ideals of the conventual life were fading out of sight, and that the whole system was steadily declining. At Leominster Priory, of which we hear the most, the financial conditions were so bad that the King took it under his protection,[9] with the Abbey of Reading, of which it was a cell; this was itself three times sequestrated by the Crown to pay off its debts. There was much friction with the townsfolks who complained that they were not allowed to ring the bells

---

1—Eyton, *Shropshire*, XI, 380.   2—Ibid, I, 158.   3—See p. 126
4 At Castle Holdgate there were three prebendaries, a presbyteral, a diaconal, and a subdiaconal. Eyton, IV, 71.
5—Eyton, VI, 28.   6—See p. 254.   7—See p. 27.
8—*Rotuli hundred.*, II, p. 50. Five of the portions of Bridgnorth are entered with the names of their occupants in the *Taxatio Nic.*   9—See p. 37.

which they had bought themselves, or gain admission to the church in which they had established rights. As in many other cases the townspeople and the monks shared the use of the same building, but at Leominster there was no solid partition between the two portions, and to screen the conventual rooms from trespassers the monks often closed the outer doors at times when fugitives fled thither for sanctuary and priests needed the viaticum. It was believed also that the customary almsgiving had been curtailed and endowments misapplied. The Bishop wrote repeatedly and in strong language on these subjects, but found much obstinate resistance.[1] The chief change on which he had insisted was cancelled afterwards by Archbishop Peckham, who ordered that a chapel[2] should be built not far away for the needs which have been mentioned. At a later period of the Bishop's rule there was much scandal in connexion with the charges brought against the sub-prior of incontinence with a nun at Lingebroke and with various other women.[3] The Abbot of Reading resisted episcopal interference with the priory, claiming the exclusive right of placing and displacing the members of the cell. This led to somewhat bitter correspondence,[4] but Swinfield in 1285 allowed the claim after inspection of the early charters.[5]

At Wormesley the convent was found to be also deeply in debt. It was necessary to make injunctions that women should not be allowed at night within the walls, and that the rules of silence should be better kept. Some of the brethren were away in attendance on the inmates of great houses, and these perhaps should be recalled.[6] At Chirbury there had been notorious scandals from the free access of women and others to their buildings; canons of doubtful character should not be allowed to go out of doors except with companions who could be trusted. Discipline within the house was much relaxed; debts were dangerously large; alienations of property must be discontinued, and report made to the Bishop of the punishment inflicted on members of ill-repute.[7] Of Lingebroke, which he visited before the scandal above referred to was made known,

---
1—See p. 46.
2—This was in the Forbury, a name which recurs at Reading. The Chapel was dedicated to St. Thomas the Martyr and erected with the approval of Bishop Swinfield. Add Ch. MS., 19, 932. 3—See p. 265.
4—See p. 270, etc. 5—Swinf. Reg., f. 30a.
6—See p. 144. 7—See p. 147.

the Bishop speaks in more sympathetic tones, but implies that their Rule was not carefully observed; the restrictions on familiar intercourse and personal property had been relaxed, and more stringency of discipline was needed.[1] Of the intellectual condition of the inmates of the convents generally he writes with some contempt, regarding them as utterly ignorant in most respects, without independent judgment.[2]

In this, more than in most of the episcopal Registers of early days, little difference is made between the documents of personal and official interest. We have letters and entries therefore which have no connexion with the diocese, and among them many which concern the manor of Earley, near Reading. We learn from an entry in the Close Rolls of Feb. 3, 1276, that Cantilupe, being summoned frequently to London as a member of the King's Council, and having no convenient house where he could stay with his servants on the way, desired to have granted to him the custody of the lands and heirs of the deceased Henry de Earley, until they came of age. The manor was delivered to him by the King's steward on June 16, subject to a payment of sixteen marks yearly.[3] Next year, July 7, the custody of the lands of Philip de Arneleye was assigned him, and he paid a fine of two hundred pounds.[4] Further entries deal with the lands of Stephen de Kentisbury, who held of Philip de Earley in the Manor of North Petherton. This, however, had been assigned to the Hospitallers of Buckland, who were to pay henceforth to the Bishop the twenty-one pounds of yearly rent which had been fixed.[5] After the Bishop's death the officers of the Crown claimed from his estate the arrears of the sixteen marks for each year, without regard to the fine of two hundred pounds, regarding the two transactions as affecting different properties. It was ascertained, however, that it was one and the same manor in question, and that the name of Henry in the first deed was written in error for that of Philip, and Arneley for Earley.[6]

For some years the Bishop travelled to and fro to attend the meetings of the Royal Council, and in 1279 he with others

1—See p. 200.
2—*Penitus sunt ignari in pluribus*, p. 269.
3—Close Rolls. June 16.
4—See p. 166.
5—See p. 167.
6—See p. 178.

The Bishop's manors and houses.

represented the King during his absence in France.[1] He had also to be present at Provincial Synods, and there were frequent journeys through his diocese. Like other lords of many manors in that age he passed frequently from one to another of his large estates, reviewing the accounts and business transactions of his bailiffs, and with his numerous train consuming the produce of his lands. These journeys were possibly combined at times with formal visitations of the churches, when some amount of entertainment was expected from the resident Rectors, or the heads of religious houses, when they had the tithes, but there is little evidence of such visits in the Register.

Of the many manors included in the Episcopal estates a few were favourite residences on a larger scale. Such was Sugwas, with its timbered park and ample fisheries and close neighbourhood to Hereford, in the heart of which he seldom cared to stay. Bosbury, "where the Bishops held their state and lived in a fayre palace in the time of King Offa,"[2] was another of the best-loved manor houses, but since Bishop Scory dismantled the Court Hall in 1572 nothing but an old gateway survives. Whitbourne on the borders of Worcestershire, with its wide moat and Brinkestye wood to supply the fish and game needed for his table, tempted often to a longer sojourn, and from this many of the letters of the Register were written. In London there was the town house given by Bishop Ralph,[3] which he may have used, as Swinfield did,[4] but there is no evidence of this. Some of the documents are dated from Kensington,[5] where a manor had been given in early times to the Abbot and Convent of Abingdon, on the site of which Holland House was afterwards built. Others were written at Tottenham (Totenhalle),[6] where the Prior and Canons of Holy Trinity within Aldgate had the advowson, and perhaps a house in which he may have lodged. Earley, near Reading, which he practically leased by payment of a heavy fine, was a convenient resting place upon the road.[7] When he had occasion to go further southward he stayed awhile in or close to what had been his parish of Sherborne,[8] probably as the Prior's guest.

1—Patent Rolls, April 27.   2—S. Bentley, *Bosbury*, p. 18.
3—He bought of the Montalt family a house on Old Fish Street Hill, and left it for the use of his successors in the See (Stowe, *Survey*, p. 676).
4—Swinf. *Reg.*, f. 73b.   5—See pp. 24, 70, etc.   6—See p. 164.
7—See p. 113, etc.   8—See p. 34, etc.

We must infer indeed from the itinerary that in England, and later on in France, he accepted almost perforce the hospitality of the religious houses on his road, when he passed beyond the confines of his diocese. They were the recognised hostelries of the Middle Ages; when they sued for the appropriation of the parishes of which they were the patrons they insisted often on this burden, and a Constitution of Othobon enforced the obligation in such cases to provide convenient houses to entertain their guests.[1]

There is little evidence of continuous residence at Hereford, or of much use of the Hall, which then served more as a Court-house than a Palace.[2] These frequent movements to and fro and this variety of homes may explain the insertion of so many transcripts of much earlier charters. They were needed for reference at times when the originals could not be consulted, or were only to be found in different places. There was no Bishop's Registry in Hereford itself; some documents, we know, were deposited for safety in the Chapter House of the Cathedral,[3] like the thousands of private charters, quite unconnected with the ecclesiastical estates, which were stored there for safety during the thirteenth and fourteenth centuries, and still exist among the Archives. Others were placed—strange as it appears—behind the High Altar of St. Paul's in London,[4] and when the Bishop was leaving England, he wrote to the Dean and Chapter to beg that his representatives might have access to his deeds.[5] Some perhaps were left in the manor houses at Sugwas and elsewhere, and this may explain the loss of most of the originals, while many of the charters of the Dean and Chapter are preserved.

It has been noted that little regard is paid to chronological order in the arrangement of the various entries. Some appear to have been put in at hap-hazard; but the most marked irregularity is due to the insertion of the copies of letters and grants of earlier Kings and Bishops, or the records of proceedings in the Courts, for which search had been made in connexion with some passing need. Disputes with the town, for example, would lead to inquiry into the privileges granted and confirmed by various monarchs,[6] as also to the formal agreements made which were afterwards enrolled by royal order.[7]

1—Wilkins, *Conc.* II, p. 11.   2—It is called the *Curia Episcopi* in contemporary documents.
3—See p. 41.   4—See p. 182.   5—See p. 263.   6—See p. 93.   7—See p. 91.

Claims made by officers of the Crown for the arrears of subsidies or scutages from the Episcopal estates may account for the lengthy copies of financial statements connected with Peter de Aquablanca and John le Breton.[1] Any question raised as to the charitable distribution of the corn charged on the manor of Holme Lacy might cause the clerk to hunt up the original deed of the endowment of Bishop Peter, and write it out in full.[2] The transference of the sum due from the estate of the preceding prelate would require reference to the arrangement of Bishop Ralph, which pledged him and his successors to provide certain sums to be handed over at their death for emblement and farm-stock.[3] A new conveyance might call for the inspection of the record of an earlier lawsuit, as in the case of Cloppele and Ashe,[4] or land at Whitbourne.[5] A disputed charge of synodals might give occasion for a view of the ordinance of appropriation of Great Cowarne Church.[6] The last of these may be found in the Cartulary of Gloucester Abbey, but most of the rest would have been else unknown. Thanks to these passing needs we have in the Register much more varied entries and fuller information than could be expected in the few years which it seems to cover.

As there was no regular system of registration at this time, nor recognised official for the purpose, much variety may be naturally expected not only in the penmanship and style and grammar, but also in matters of more moment, so far as they were left to the discretion of the Bishop's clerks. Some features of difference indeed between this Register and others were due to the actual conditions of the See. Elsewhere mandates for institution were sent commonly to the Archdeacons, and Deans were instructed to install canons. But at Hereford the decanal office was practically in abeyance in consequence of rival claims to it; the Hebdomadary or a Dignitary therefore took its place; the Archdeacon of Hereford was a youth still in his studies, and the Archdeacon of Salop was in disgrace. Rural deans acted in their stead, and some of them had little cause to love their Bishop, who showered upon them orders to serve citations and excommunicate offenders till their office was no sinecure. On the other hand we hear nothing

1—See p. 35.   2—See p. 128.   3—See p. 38.
4—See p. 40.   5—See p. 43.   6—See p. 49.

of the gaol deliveries, elsewhere often mentioned, when criminous clerks were handed over by request to the charge of their Diocesan, to be kept in his official prison at his pleasure, and that sometimes for a long while. One such was lodged in durance for seventeen years on the charge of having stolen two dishes and a coverlet.[1] When such large numbers of all sorts and conditions had the tonsure, there must have been offenders in the diocese, and Cantilupe, with his strong sense of ecclesiastical rights, would certainly have claimed them.[2]. No mention again is made of the purgations by which such clerks were allowed to clear themselves by their own oaths, and those of friendly compurgators who were not cross-examined.

Nothing is said of the Visitations of the parish churches, for which it was by this time usual to make formal arrangements, at least once in three years, with due requirement of the customary procurations, and with much burdening at times of unwilling hosts, as when the Bishop's neighbour of Worcester stayed with one hundred and fifty horses at the Priory,[3] or Grandisson of Exeter went to visit Cornwall with a train of Dignitaries and a vast number of others (*in multitudine populosa*).[4] We may regret the silence on this matter because we lack the information we might else have as to the conditions of parochial life, and the vigilance of Episcopal supervision; such as we have elsewhere in notices of the shortcomings of the parish priests, the defective supply of service books and vestments, the enlargement of parish churches authoritatively enforced, the coadjutors appointed by the Bishop to relieve aged or disabled parsons, new ordinances to improve the financial conditions of the Vicars, else starved by the religious houses, the rights of the mother churches jealously guarded when private chapels were allowed for local magnates. It is hard to believe that much was done in this way by the Bishop when nothing was recorded, while so much space was given to proceedings against non-residents and pluralists unprovided with the purely formal dispensations such as he himself enjoyed in earlier years. The Register again does not supply details about

1—Wykh. *Reg.*, II, 444.

2—He had indeed a prison under his manor house at Ross in which some clerks were lodged, for two of them escaped, and the gaoler gave a bond of indemnity to Bishop Cantilupe and promised greater care. Swinf. *Reg.*, f. 25a. This should have been inserted in this Register.

3—*Ann. Mon.*, IV, 504.   4—Grand. *Reg.*, p. 320.

the diocesan synods, to which the clergy were all summoned to appear in person or by proxy, when their common interests were to be discussed or Episcopal regulations published.

As to the ceremonies of Confirmation this Register, like others, is quite silent, though the injunctions of some Bishops speak in peremptory terms, requiring parents to bring their young children to their Diocesan wherever they could find him, under pain of having to fast on bread and water every Friday till the duty was discharged.[1] But with prelates so much on the move it was not an easy task to find them. So Cantilupe, we are told, was careful on his journeys to wear some of his pontificals even as he rode along that when parents with little ones appeared upon the road he might without delay lay his hands upon them.[2] It was perhaps a somewhat rough and ready system.

The Ordination lists are given of course with much detail, even to the box of letters which is mentioned as the sole title of one of those ordained. The Orders were conferred in various places in the diocese or elsewhere, as at Leominster, Ledbury, Newent, and Tottenham, but never, it appears, in Hereford itself, which indeed he seldom visited and can hardly have resided in at all. He seems to have made no use of the Bishops with outlandish titles *in partibus infidelium*, whose services were found convenient by others who were constantly engaged in diplomacy or offices of state. The Cathedral Chapter, as a whole, he never treated as his council, though many of its members were in constant residence at this time; its collective judgment indeed he did not value highly, if we may trust certain disparaging remarks;[3] it was not yet purged of the Burgundian leaven; but some of the Canons were regularly employed by him as Officials, Treasurer, Commissaries, or Proctors. He did not air too publicly his mistrust of the foreign element, or let his agents in Rome be too outspoken.[4] Even John de Aquablanca, the litigious Dean, left a little in his will towards the outlay on the tomb of "the blessed Thomas."[5]

1—Wilkins, *Conc.*, II, pp. 132, 293.

2—*Acta Sanct.*, p. 509. *Portabat semper stolam ad collum suum subtus capam vel rodeundellum (chlamydis speciem).*

3—See p. 113.   4—See p. 234.

5—Document in the Archives of D. & C.

Cantilupe was vigorous in language, mighty in sequestrations and in excommunications, but few details are given of his corrective jurisdiction over the laity. Other Bishops left record of the penances imposed on deliberate offenders—the public fustigations in the churchyard, as of the fifty seven at Yeovil;[1] the doleful processions of bare-footed and half-clad culprits with the lighted candles;[2] the crusade enjoined for the abduction of two nuns;[3] but we do not learn how far Cantilupe was a terror to evil doers, clerical or lay, except when the rights or property of the Church were in any danger. But if we miss much that would throw light on the ecclesiastical or moral conditions of the times, we have ample details of the technicalities of litigation, congenial perhaps to the *doctor utriusque juris*, but hardly quite becoming to a Saint.

Towards the end of 1279 the Bishop made arrangements to leave England on some business not defined. His safe-conduct and letters of protection were procured;[4] his representatives were appointed to transact official business in his name;[5] his excuses were sent for non-appearance at ecclesiastical assemblies;[6] and he travelled southwards into Kent, as far at least as Ightham, from which letters are dated,[7] but then returned, giving up his intended journey, on which no light is thrown by any information which we have. Next year however events occurred, which resulted in a long absence from his See. A matrimonial suit between Petronilla Bebler and Richard de Bramford was brought before the Court of the Dean's delegate—called the sub-dean—at Hereford. Richard, against whom sentence was given, appealed to the Court of the Archbishop of Canterbury, ignoring the intermediate tribunal, that of the Bishop of the diocese. The sub-dean, disregarding the prohibition to proceed which was sent to him in due course, had Richard and his agent arrested, and flung in the mud the letter of the Official of Canterbury, who had fined him ten marks and insisted on his prompt obedience. Citations and excommunications followed; then a mandate to the Official at Hereford, and finally to the Bishop himself, under pain of suspension of his chapel and an interdict, if proceedings against the sub-dean were not taken. When two

1—Ralph of Shrewsb. *Reg.*, 602.   2—*Pal. Dun. Reg.*, 313.
3—Peckh. *Reg.* III, p. 916.   4—Patent Rolls, Aug. 28, 1279.
5—See pp. 219, 221.   6—See p. 224.   7—See p. 222.

years later disputed questions of jurisdiction between the Archbishop and the Suffragans were referred by Peckham to four experts, they decided that it was contrary to established usage for the Official at Canterbury to receive appeals from suitors in other dioceses before the matters had been brought before the Courts of their own Bishops in each case. This decision therefore negatived the claim which had been made to interfere at Hereford. At this stage Peckham himself, who had not long been consecrated, took no active part in the proceedings; the subject is not even mentioned in his Register, but it seems that Cantilupe, unwilling to suffer from the suspension of his chapel and the threatened interdict, resolved to leave England for a while, probably that he might have time to refer the matter in dispute to Rome. Indeed it seems that he must have taken the clergy of his diocese into his confidence, and obtained from them a contribution towards the expenses of his journey and appeal; there are several references in his correspondence to the funds expected from this source,[1] which was estimated at one hundred pounds, but they came in somewhat slowly, as he complains to his financial agents. The Papal chair was vacant from August, 1280, to March, 1281, and his retirement lasted longer than might have been expected.

Before he left he was allowed by royal licence to include in his will his custody of Earley, like his other lands and goods which did not pertain to his bishoprick.[2] He had the usual letters of protection granted him as going beyond seas;[3] he gave his instructions as before,[4] and this time for a long absence.

As Becket sought the cloistered calm of Pontigny to escape from his embittered relations with King Henry, so Cantilupe retired to Normandy when the dispute with the Official of Canterbury was at its height. The district which he visited must have seemed familiar to him from the associations of the past, close as it was to the village from which probably his family took its name, and to Breteuil which the first Earl of Hereford had owned, and to Gournay and Evreux, the names of which his mother bore, first as daughter then as wife.

1—See p. 252.
2—Patent Rolls. June 27, 1280.
3—Patent Rolls, April 10, 1280.
4—See pp. 245, 253.

xlviii   *Introduction.*

The Abbey of Lyre, in which he found a welcome, had special claims on his good will; its head was *ex officio* a Canon of his own Cathedral;[1] its financial agent lived in Castle Street in Hereford, from which centre he administered some of the conventual estates in England; a William of Chantelou—perhaps the Bishop's grand-father—had renounced his title to a fief in favour of the Abbey; two valuable benefices, Shinfield and Lydney had been transferred by it to his Chapter. In the midst of a gently undulating country the little Risle wanders through a fertile valley in which for two centuries already the monks of Lyre had made their home thanks to the pious liberality of William Fitz Osbern and Adelisia his wife. The shell of the Abbot's lodging and part of the stables are still standing, in which the village Curé and innkeeper are housed respectively; the fishponds too can still be seen; but beyond the sculptures of the high altar, which were carried at the Revolution to the village church hard by, nothing else remains of the buildings of a prosperous community of forty to fifty monks, multiplied indeed now tenfold by local fancy, and so well endowed that the inventory of its charters is spread over four large folio volumes.[2] From these it appears that it claimed to have in England forty-eight churches and eleven chapels, or at least some grant of tithes or pensions from them. A few years after his stay at Lyre it was popularly believed that a child had fallen into the Risle and was brought out dead, but was restored to life by the efficacy of the Bishop's prayers.[3] Here or in the neighbourhood he appears to have remained for at least a year. Some official entries in the Register are dated from other religious houses, such as the Abbey of Conches close by which had property in his own diocese,[4] and possibly Fontaine Sorêt,[5] where a Priory of Bec was settled. But these perhaps were only passing visits on his way to and fro.[6]

1—By a charter of 1269 the Abbot of Lyre was made a Canon of Hereford Cathedral, to which some advowsons had been transferred. The Abbot of Cormeilles enjoyed the same privilege. The Chapter of Chichester made the Abbot of Grestein a prebendary at the end of the 12th century; the Abbots of Athelney and Muchelney had prebends at Wells; and for a short time in the 12th century the Abbot of Bruton was *ex officio* a Canon of Coutances.   2—This is now in the Archives of Evreux.

3—*Acta Sanct.*, p. 514.   4—This was valued at £40 in the *Taxatio Nic.*
5—See p. 269.

6—In the course of these movements he may naturally have stayed at other places. In the Hospital at Lisieux certain pontificals are exhibited as having belonged to St. Thomas of England; at Argentan a comb is shewn which according to the local tradition was used by the same Saint when preparing to officiate in the Chapel. It is supposed that St. Thomas of Canterbury left them there, but there is no evidence that he visited those towns during his long stay at Pontigny and Vezelai and elsewhere; it is possible that St. Thomas of Hereford should have been named.

St. Thomas of Canterbury.   St. Thomas of Hereford.
ANCIENT WINDOW IN CREDENHILL CHURCH.

The stay in Normandy.

We find him also at Poissy close to Paris, where he might wish to look in upon old friends.[1] He stayed a while at Charenton to inspect the condition of some property which had been acquired there by Bishop Peter,[2] who had left it in his will to the collegiate church which he founded and endowed at Aquabella. A mysterious claim was put in for him afterwards by William de Cantilupe[3] on the ground that the estate had been bought with funds which belonged of right to the Church not to the private property of his predecessor. It is hard to see what evidence there could be of this, or why the claim should have been delayed so long if it were well grounded. There is no reference to any such flaw in the title in the letter which he wrote on the subject of the dilapidations on the property to Emeric the Chancellor,[4] who under his uncle's will was trustee for the estates of Aquabella.

During the whole of Cantilupe's stay in Normandy, which lasted from the summer of 1280 to the autumn of 1281, we find nothing in the Register to explain his motives, not a word about the disputed jurisdiction, or of any appeal to Rome on the subject. The entries in Wilkins' *Concilia* are silent as to the issue of the conflict. Peckham himself took no active part in it, though he vaguely refers in a later letter to the Bishop as "skulking in foreign parts," and trying to secure Papal orders against "so-called aggressions of the Court of Canterbury."[5] What really passed we cannot tell, but it appears that the Bishop on his way home waited on the Primate, and by his unassuming manners raised hopes in Peckham's mind of meek submissiveness in future dealings.[6]

Soon after his return there was fresh matter of dispute. On the death of Henry de Hawkley, Canon of Hereford and Lincoln, who had held benefices in various dioceses, the business of probate was claimed by the Court of Canterbury as belonging to its jurisdiction, and the Vicar of Ross, the Executor, was cited to appear before it. Robert le Wyse, the Bishop's Official, refused to recognise this claim; the Bishop himself was then required to have a citation served upon the Vicar,

1—See p. 255.   2—See p. 248.   3—See p. 296.   4—See p. 248.
5—Peckh. *Reg.*, I, 318.
6—*Ibid.* But it was said that they came into collision at Reading soon after Peckham's appointment.

and to deal with his recalcitrant Official. As he repeatedly refused, on the ground that notice of appeal to Rome had been already given, he was warned that he had fallen under sentence of excommunication. His letter of Jan. 7, 1282, in reply to the Archbishop, is respectful and dignified in tone; it is to be found, not in his own Register, but in that of Canterbury.[1] In an interview between them the Primate seems to have promised that if Cantilupe would submit to his ruling as to the matters at issue, he would practically refrain from any exercise of the powers which he claimed.[2] The Bishop, with whom it was a question of principle, not of personal dignity, naturally could not accept this offer; and on Jan. 15 he sent a clerk to the Archbishop with notice of appeal from the sentence of his Court; but at Lambeth in his presence on Feb. 7 Robert de Lacy, by mandate from the Primate, read the formal warning that, if he declined obedience, he was then and there under sentence of excommunication. The Dean and Chapter on their part put forth an appeal against the claim of jurisdiction in this case.[3] Peckham's correspondence on the subject betrays the worst features of his character, his domineering[4] and irritable temper and his free use of invectives. His letters to his Proctors at Rome, to a friendly Cardinal, and to the Bishop of London, whom he requests repeatedly on Feb. 17 and March 15 to excommunicate the offender in his name, abound in personal imputations against the man for whom he had felt singular affection as his benefactor and scholar at Paris. But now he can think only of his obdurate contumacy, of his spirit of Dathan and Abiram, of his malice as a wolf in sheep's clothing, of his deranged intellect, of his frivolous and blasphemous mendacities.[5] The bitterness of the feelings thus excited was out of all proportion to the real importance of the matter in dispute; it was further increased by the opposition of his Suffragans—among whom he believed that Cantilupe was a ringleader—to the enlargement of the jurisdiction of his Court. Twenty-one articles were drawn up by them to express their grievances,[6] which are set

---

1—Peckh. *Reg.*, I, 272.   2—Ibid., I, 383.   3—Deed in the Archives of D. & C.
4—He is described by Nic. Trivet as *gestu, incessu, et sermone glorioso et elato*.
5—*Non minus ex innata læsione cerebri quam ex pervicacia voluntatis—sub ovino vellere porrigens osculum.* Peckh. *Reg.*, I, 315-318. II, 393.
6—Peckh. *Reg.*, I, 325. These were also inserted at the end of this Register, but as they are to be found in Wilkins' *Concilia* they have been omitted.

The Bishop's death at Montefiascone.

forth in very technical language, but the main contention was that the Primacy—like the Papacy itself which of course they could not mention—was converting its Court into one of primary instance for the whole Province.[1] The objections of the Suffragans were replied to in a somewhat unyielding spirit, but he presently appointed four experts as commissioners to report upon past usages, and they in April advised that precedents were opposed to the claims of his officials.

Meanwhile the Bishop, without shewing to his friends any sign of impatience or resentment, had the notices of his appeal put up in public places, "not without the guilt of perjury," so Peckham wrote on March 31 to his proctors at Rome, adding that it was rumoured that the Bishop had started already on his journey to the Papal Court; and he warns them to be on the alert as his adversary was false and cunning.[2] They appear to have lost no time in representing that as under spiritual censure he ought not to be received. Two Cardinals were instructed to have inquiry made, and they reported that they could see no reason to exclude him from communion.[3] On his arrival therefore the Pope and Cardinals received him with due honour at Orvieto,[4] and members of the Papal household were present at the Mass which he celebrated soon afterwards. But the fatigues of the journey or malarial attacks aggravated internal disorders from which he had long suffered, and the malady with which he was struck down at Montefiascone had a fatal issue on Aug. 25.[5] With the Pope's sanction he received absolution from the Papal Penitentiary, and gave his last directions though he had made his will before he left his home. The funeral ceremonies were carried out in state at the Abbey of San Severo under Orvieto in the presence of several Cardinals, one of whom became Pope Nicolas IV;[6] but the flesh only was interred there, the bones from which it was removed being reserved for a resting place in his own Cathedral Church.

[1]—There were disputes as to jurisdiction somewhat earlier between Eudes Rigaud, Archbishop of Rouen, and his Suffragans, to decide which the former went to Rome. Questions at issue between Archbishop Warham and Bishop Foxe of Winchester, on rights of probate and administration, were settled by Henry VIII after reference to Rome.

[2]—Peckh. *Reg.*, I, 320.   [3]—*Acta Sanct.*, p. 522.

[4]—For the *urbs vetus* (Orvieto), which was a favourite residence of the Popes, Civita Vecchia was substituted in some earlier accounts.

[5]—"His crazy body worn out with former labours." Strange, p. 189.

[6]—*Acta Sanct.*, p. 525.

Of the remains which had been brought to England the bones were laid to rest awhile in front of the altar in the Lady Chapel at Hereford, while the heart, which had been bequeathed to Richard, Earl of Cornwall,[1] was taken to Ashridge, near Berkhamstead, where a monastery of the Order of Bonhommes had been founded already by the Earl, and a resting place was given to the relic in the Choir of the conventual Church.[2] It was said that Peckham forbade at first the interment in consecrated ground, till he was informed that absolution had been given him by the Pope's desire, and it appears that a letter to that effect from the Pope's Penitentiary was actually shewn to him at Leominster in December, 1282.[3] At a much later date Bishop Oldham of Exeter died excommunicate, and could not be interred duly till absolution came from Rome. Strange fancies came to the birth in after years that, as the bearers passed through the diocese of Canterbury with their precious freight, the blood poured from the dry bones, and that Peckham became childish in his later years as a punishment for his vindictive temper.[4] Several of the Bishops lost no time in shewing their sympathy for Cantilupe and their practical disregard of the Primate's censures. The very year of his death an indulgence of forty days was offered by Godfrey Giffard, of Worcester, to all who would pray devoutly for him at Hereford; this example was followed by the Bishop of London in 1285 and at Rochester in 1286. Archbishop Peckham indeed issued a notice of a like indulgence from Lugwardine in 1282, but its object was the improvement of the fabric of the Cathedral, and not a word was said of the late Bishop.[5] Five years later (1287) the remains were taken from the Lady Chapel and transferred to a place close to the altar of St. John the Baptist in the North Transept,[6] where a worthier monument had been erected

1—*Ann. Wigorn.*, 483 (Rolls).
2—The Earl is said by Holinshed to have brought over from Germany a box containing the Saviour's blood and to have deposited two-thirds of it in the Abbey which he founded at Ashridge, giving the rest to Hales. An early will describes a parson as "rector of the house of the blood of Jesus Christ at Assherugge." (Calendar of Wills, Court of Hustings, p. 574).
3—Document in the Archives of D. & C.
4—These stories however, were varied to apply to the Earl of Gloucester.
5—Copies of these indulgences are in the Archives.
6—Leland alone mentions the altar of St. John the Baptist, which was probably appropriated to the Parish of St. John, which had no church. For this altar alone the Treasurer was not required by the early *consuetudines* to provide the candles, for these were a charge on the parochial funds, to which the offerings at that altar doubtless went. At Rochester there was a like usage of an altar reserved for a special Parish. Godwin speaks of the monument as being in the North Transept, but when he wrote he knew nothing apparently of any further removal from that place.

by the care of his executors and the members of the Chapter.[1]

Mysterious tokens of approval from the spirit world accompanied the change and were vouched for by Bishop Swinfield who took a prominent part in the removal.[2] Then came an outburst of enthusiastic faith. The good news spread apace that a beneficent influence was potent there; the impotent, the sick, the fearful in dire peril called on his name and found a speedy help; pilgrims flocked from far and near to shew their thankfulness for mercies given, or beg for blessings yet in store. The monument was overlaid with precious gifts; votive offerings were hung up on every side; silver figures of the votaries themselves, or of the bodily members on which the cure was wrought; silver boats given by mariners who had been saved from raging storms; weapons that, but for like grace, had inflicted deadly wounds.[3] The royal family and great nobles visited the tomb, and the excitement spread for eighteen years with unabated force.[4]

When the concourse of the pilgrims to the tomb was at its height a curious dispute occurred which may serve to indicate the large number generally present. It was the custom—a purely English one according to the Bollandist writer—for those who hoped to profit in health by their visit and their prayers, to have themselves measured and to leave a wax taper of their own length at the tomb. These tapers were so numerous, beyond the number that could be actually used for lighting, that they were valued in the *Taxatio Nicholai*, about 1291, at twenty pounds, at least three hundred of present worth. Such surplus wax had been of old the perquisite of the Treasurer; now the Dean and Chapter claimed to share the profit, and after some debate terms were agreed on in 1289 to the effect that during the life time of Luke, the Treasurer, he should have two-thirds and the Chapter the

1—*Acta Sanct.*, 527. Strange is much confused in his account of this transaction, for which, he says, Edward III came over from Calais to be present (Life, p. 216).

2—He was awakened at Sugwas, where he slept, by tappings at his window which was far out of man's reach; and the heavy stone over the vault was easily removed by two domestic pages, though it required ten men to replace it.

3—For the list of the offerings see *Acta Sanct.*, p. 537.

4—It is curious that at this time, when the gifts of the devout came pouring into the Treasury of the Cathedral, a Canon, Alan de Creppinge, who was watching the interests of the Chapter at Rome and had to spend largely on its behalf, was threatened with excommunication if he did not repay the sum of sixty marks which he had borrowed for the Chapter from money-lenders of Pistoia. (Document in the Archives of the D. & C., dated 1290).

remainder.[1] He must have died soon after and disputes again arose with his successor John de Swinfield; in 1293 it was decided to refer the question to the arbitration of the Bishop.[2]

As early as April, 1290, Swinfield had addressed a letter to Pope Nicholas IV, urging the canonization of his predecessor. In 1292 the Bishops of Ely, Durham, and Bath and Wells made a like petition to Pope Celestine; Swinfield wrote again to the same effect in 1299. No answer appears to have been received. In 1305 the Magnates of England sent a weighty letter to Clement V, asking that the wonder-worker might be canonized;[3] this was signed by Edward I., who also wrote private letters on the subject to the Pope and to a Cardinal,[4] after special appeal had been made to him by the Bishop and the Chapter of Hereford.[5]

A commission of inquiry into the life and miracles of Cantilupe was then appointed, consisting of the Bishops of London and Mende with the Nuncio in England, William de Testa. These held their first meeting on July 13, 1307, in the Chapter House of St. Paul's. Their primary duty was to ascertain how far the anathemas of Peckham and his Official had been pushed; was Cantilupe really excommunicated by them? The language of the Primate in his letters seems to leave no doubt that the sentence had been issued;[6] but the Commissioners, after seeing the official documents of the Court of Canterbury, and learning what had passed at Orvieto and Monte Fiascone, decided that he was not actually excommunicate at his death. Either the sentence was conditional as pronounced, or the appeal to the Pope which had been already made, or Papal absolution at a later stage, deprived the sentence of its force. This preliminary question settled, the Commissioners—without the Nuncio—betook themselves to Hereford, where they stayed from August 30 to November 16, witnessing themselves the concourse of pilgrims and the profuse

---

1—Swinf. *Reg.*, 63b.　　　　　2—Deed in the Archives of the D. and C.

3—*Reg. Pal. Dunelm.* IV., pref., p. xxxi. The first name in the list is that of Gilbert de Clare, of the family which had robbed the See of its Chase.

4—Ibid., p. xxxii. Rymer, *Fœdera*, Nov. 2, 1305.

5—Anc. Kalend. and Inv. I. 33. *Littera Episcopi et Capituli Heref. directa Regi pro negotio canonizationis Beati Thome de Cantilupo.*

6—An entry in Peckham's *Register* states this definitely. *Subsequenter ipsum excommunicacionis sententia involutum et excommunicatum publice et solempniter denunciatum* (f. 159b).

abundance of the offerings, and examining in the Chapel of St. Catherine, which was between the Cathedral and the Palace, the witnesses who came before them to testify to the character of the Bishop and to the miracles that had been wrought.

The four months allowed by the Pope for the inquiry were nearly at an end when only seventeen of the marvels reported had been thoroughly investigated, and the evidence of one hundred and fifteen witnesses heard in their favour. Two hundred and four more had been officially described; as to these they could do no more than accept the sworn statements of Swinfield and others that they believed them to be genuine. The whole record of the proceedings was then sent to the Papal Court, and from the documentary evidence thus preserved the writer of the life in the *Acta Sanctorum*—said to be Father Suysken—drew up his detailed account of the career and miracles of the Bishop. As to the reported marvels it is not necessary to say much here;[1] they may be left to the examination of the curious in such matters. Of the sincerity of the witnesses there seems to be no doubt; but Swinfield's own evidence does not allow us to rate the value of his judgment in such questions very highly, and from others critical inquiry into the facts themselves, or insight into the mysteries of nervous maladies could hardly be expected.

After the report of the inquiry had been received no further steps were taken by Clement V, and Swinfield passed away without any sign that his hopes would be fulfilled.

The Commissioners had reported that the offerings at the tomb had been so bountiful that they had provided for the necessary outlay on two new *naves* (? bays) in the Cathedral, and on some part of the great Tower.[2] This seems at first to raise a difficulty, for the two bays most probably are those on the East side of the North Transept, and we cannot suppose that they were built after 1287, when the remains were transferred to the new tomb, at the time when, according to the evidence of Swinfield, the fame of the miracles began to spread.

1—They are examined in "the Hereford Miracles," by the Rev. A. T. Bannister (Transactions of Woolhope Club, 1905).

2—*Acta Sanct.*, p. 537, *Ecclesia de duabus navibus ampliata, et fabricatum in parte maximum campanile.*

Pilgrims with their offerings were then thronging round the tomb, making it impossible for building operations to be carried on. The style of the work also points to an earlier date, or at least to an enlargement designed probably when the whole transept was remodelled, though the work itself may have proceeded slowly. The position of Bishop Peter's monument proves almost certainly that the aisle was in course of completion before the tomb was erected, and before there could have been any thought of preparing the Transept to be the resting place of the Saint's relics.

But the indulgences offered by the Bishops in 1282 and following years, more perhaps in number than the few of which the evidences now exist, may throw some light upon the matter. The enlargement may have been going on for some time, and appeal made for outside help, of which indulgences of this kind were a common form. The devout who came to pray at Hereford did not come empty-handed, and their alms collected for some years might provide a fitting resting place for the monument which was now to be erected there. The Cathedral had then no fabric fund; the tithes of Shinfield had not yet been appropriated for the purpose; and the compotus rolls of this period assign only the equivalent of the stipend of one resident canon—of whom there were fifteen to twenty—to the *opus ecclesiæ*, or the maintenance of the buildings. Nothing more than the ordinary repairs of the scantiest kind could be undertaken without a special appeal for help from other quarters. This came in abundantly when the fame of the wonder-working powers spread abroad, and the commissioners may easily have misunderstood the information given them, and confused the earlier work, which was completed shortly before the excitement of the marvels spread abroad, with the much larger expenditure which followed. A fabric roll of 1291 survives, in which we see that sums amounting to four thousand pounds in present value were spent on the buildings in that year, nearly all of which was provided by the offerings at the tomb.[1] The years immediately before and after doubtless saw like lavish gifts and like expenditure. We have the receipts of London merchants who provided the *electrum* for the decoration of the monument, on which about a thousand pounds in

1—Archives of the D. & C.

THE CANTILUPE MONUMENT IN THE CATHEDRAL.

our currency were spent. The acknowledgments of the Goldsmith and the Sculptor shew that the work went on for years after the transference in 1287. Most, however, of the funds supplied were devoted to the enlargement and enrichment of the Central Tower, the date of which, therefore, is determined independently of its architectural features. The pride with which the inhabitants of Hereford contemplated the new work must have been turned into dismay when it was known that the foundations were utterly insecure to bear the added weight. Once more appeal was made to the sympathies of the outside world. On Nov. 20, 1320, the King issued a brief to authorize a general collection; Archbishop Walter urged that contributions were required also for the great expenses of the intended translation; Bishops offered indulgences as before; and the country was mapped out systematically for the collectors' rounds. One roll for the Deaneries of Norfolk is preserved,[1] in which the contributions of the several parishes are entered in detail. To make further provision for the future the Pope was asked to sanction the appropriation of Shinfield for the fabric fund,[2] the advowson having been already given to the Dean and Chapter.[3]

During these many years of thronging pilgrims and repeated expenditure upon the fabric, Pope followed Pope upon the throne, but nothing had been done to meet the wishes of the pious who complained that their patron was not enrolled among the Saints. Swinfield himself had passed away with his longings unfulfilled, and nothing to shew for his efforts and expenditure at Rome. Henry de Schorne, Archdeacon and Canon of Hereford, who had acted for the Chapter when the inquiry commenced, was at the Papal Court for two years at least, 1312 and 1313, to press the matter forward, and long afterwards he signed a deed in which he discharged the Chapter from all liabilities for money advanced by him and from claims for commons in Hereford, while he was acting as their

1—Archives of the D. & C.   2—Ibid.
3—It may be noticed that the description given above is not in harmony with what is found on page 76 of Dean Merewether's Statement (1842). But it should be observed that—of the documents mentioned as probably carried off by Silas Turner all are, and have always been, in the Chapter Archives; that Archbishop Peckham says nothing of indulgences for those who would work on the Cathedral, an obviously absurd condition; and that the translation referred to by Archbishop Walter was from the Transept to the Lady Chapel, not *vice versa*.

Proctor *in negotio canonizationis Sancti Thome de Cantilupo*.[1] At length, however, John XXII. despatched a Bishop to make more inquiries;[2] and the long looked-for Bull was issued on April 17, 1320, to sanction a title already given by the popular voice, and to order the observance of the festival on Oct. 2.

The King wrote[3] that he intended to be present at the ceremony of translation; but this for some reasons unexplained did not take place for many years, and though three historians mention the fact itself they tell us little of what passed,[4] save that the King was present at the ceremony, with many prelates and nobles, and a multitude of other people. Perhaps the large expenditure upon the buildings had delayed the translation and the erection of the Shrine which appears to have been set up in the Lady Chapel, where the relics were stored near their first resting place in the Cathedral.[5] Pilgrims indeed were now comparatively few,[6] and the offerings small;[7] but there the bones reposed[8] till the days of desecration and of pillage, when rude hands were laid on the riches of the Shrine and the relics flung aside as worthless trifles. Some indeed were gathered up with loving care, for there were many of the old faith—the so-called Recusants—in Hereford; tradition has preserved the names of the priests and others through whose hands they passed, and some account of the gifts which were made of them at various times, in the course of which an arm-bone was placed in a college of St. Omer, but disappeared at its suppression after its transference to Bruges; a shin bone, it is said, remained in the keeping of the Jesuit Fathers and is still preserved at Stonyhurst.[9]

It is not surprising, therefore, that no remains were found in the tomb when it was opened by Dean Merewether in 1846;

1—Archives of the D. & C.   2—Rymer, *Fœdera*, Aug. 7, 1320.
3—Rymer, Feb. 24, 1321.
4—Thomas Walsingham places it in 1350, as does William of Worcester; Henry de Knighton assigns it to 1348.
5—It is said that, when the Cathedral was restored in the last century, the old stones which formed the basement of the Shrine were found *in situ*, much worn by the pilgrims' knees. ("The Month," Jan. 1882).
6—In 1336 a Papal letter was sent to a Nuncio instructing him to reduce the tax which had been levied on the surplus of the wax tapers, which was now much smaller owing to the decrease of devotion (Papal *Reg*., II, 530).
7—A fabric roll of 1388 shows that the offerings at the Shrine were then twenty-six shillings and eight pence.
8—The *custos feretri* received twenty shillings as salary and the *custos reliquiarum* half a mark in the time of Edward IV. (Compotus Roll).
9—"The Month," Jan. 1882.

indeed the Priest of the neighbouring Chapel who was invited to be present at the time, knowing more of the history of the relics, seems to have expected that result. The monument itself was at that time brought forward a few feet from the wall on which one end before had rested.[1]

Some estimate of the character of Cantilupe, and of his relations to the times in which he lived, may naturally be now expected. His age was one of wonderful manysidedness and teeming life. The enthusiasm of charity in the movement of the Friars had fired countless hearts as it had not done since the early days of Christianity; an ardent thirst for knowledge sent its swarms of votaries to beg their way, if need were, to the great seats of general study, while riper students gave new form to the knowledge of the past in their comprehensive encyclopedias of learning. New theories of government were coming to the birth, with representative systems to replace the old feudal forms of Norman monarchy. Fore-gleams of science lighted up the cells of lonely thinkers, like Roger Bacon, that might with happier encouragement have anticipated the work of later times. The instinct of a larger humanism was discrediting the old conventual ideals, and Art was finding in its decorative forms the loveliest creations of the Architectural genius of the West. Meantime the instinct of justice combined with national prejudices to call out a passionate resistance to civil and ecclesiastical abuses. How far was Cantilupe typical of his age, and in what did his saintliness consist?

Some of the features which have been referred to were represented fully by the student in Arts and Theology, the trained Civilian and Canonist, by the friend of de Montfort, and the patriot jealous of aliens intruded in the offices of the Church. His large hearted and systematic charity was a main theme of his admirers' praises, as well as his persistency and courage in the defence of the rights for which he was trustee;

[1]—There is no evidence that the monument had ever been moved far from its present place in the North Transept. We read only of the translation of the relics, and of the Shrine in the Lady Chapel, which was probably destroyed when the relics were dispersed. If the heavy structure in stone had been transferred there with the Shrine, there could be no reason for a subsequent removal to the Transept, where the tomb must have been then known to be empty. There is no very early reference to the monument itself; the solid slab on which it rests has some carving on its upper face now covered, and had served before for other uses; the decorative treatment has no special appropriateness for a Bishop and a Saint; and the whole question presents difficulties which are not easily explained.

but they dwelt with equal fervour on qualities less winning to our eyes—the survivals of the ideals of the past. Not only did he grudge the body's simplest needs, and rise from table always, by his own admission, with a sense of unsatisfied desire;[1] not only did he excite the admiration of his servants by the filthy hair-shirt with its handful of lice that stirs our loathing;[2] but he shrank even from loving intercourse with his own sisters, repelling their advances with a sort of Manichean rigour, which became, it seemed, the Saint, but was quite unlovely in the man. His friends said much of his equanimity and patience, and there must have been something genial and winning to attract the sympathies and reverence of men like Swinfield, Robert le Wyse, and Ralph de Hengham, to say nothing of his household servants. But we may wonder to see the signs of what we should else call a litigious and unyielding temper, in which personal antipathies were carried far.[3] We may note with regret that he denounced all social intercourse with Jewish neighbours as the enemies of God and man, for whose expulsion from the kingdom he was urgent;[4] he even begged with tears that he might retire from the Council Chamber when it was once proposed to give a converted Jew authority to punish Christian rogues.[5]

His ideal of charity was doubtless not confined to almsgiving, nor his self-denial to mere asceticism, but prejudice and obstinacy had much to do with the litigation at Rome which drained his purse and tried his temper. Incorruptible as a judge himself, he yet stooped to bribes to gain his cause, and proposed to his representatives to move in crooked ways. It startles us to read that his confidential agent—not regarded as very scrupulous by his rivals—begged him to dictate only such a course of action as would be honourable and just.[6]

The last English Saint recognised by the undivided Western Church was still of the true medieval type, austere in his self-discipline, fearless in the assertion of the Church's seeming rights, but narrow in his sympathies, stern in his coercive moods, with more of the spirit of a Dominic than of a Francis, and therefore somewhat unattractive to our modern tastes.

1—*Acta Sanct.*, p 503.   2—*Acta Sanct.*, p. 504.
3—Note the attempt to claim property at Charenton bought by Bishop Peter with funds, as it was asserted, which had belonged to the See.
4—*Acta Sanct.*, 508.   5—Ibid, 507.   6—See p. 244.

THE BISHOP'S INCOME.

The official income of the bishopric of Hereford is not put at a high figure in contemporary documents. The *Taxatio Nicholai* of 1291 returns it at £449 1s. 5d. in temporals alone, including an item of £44 2s. 6$^1/_2$d., the value of property in the diocese of Worcester at Prestbury, Pulcomb, and Sevenhampton, and another of £10 for land at Eston in Wiltshire, but omitting the value of the house in London which was given to the See by Ralph of Maidstone. In another account of the same survey the lands in Worcestershire and Wiltshire are not included, and the whole exceeds £500 per annum.[1] Cantilupe had also by Papal grant the income of tithes in Ledbury and Bosbury appropriated to his table, on the ground of the meagre provision for a Bishop's wants.[2] It was called indeed by Swinfield the worst endowed Bishopric in England,[3] and its twenty-three manors[4] gave but a modest sustenance compared with the fifty of Winchester, some of which were large and rich. Lydbury North indeed covered a great extent of land but was returned at a low value, and this was due perhaps to its position on the Welsh border, where it was exposed to plundering forays. Though the actual value of this income was probably much larger than the taxable amount, Cantilupe was a poorer man as Bishop than as pluralist before, for he is said to have derived from his various preferments a sum as large as his episcopal income,[5] and though he spent freely on the buildings of his many parishes, and was munificent in charities, he had time to accumulate considerable savings. These he needed for the great expenses of the first year or two of office, though he may not have had, like Peckham and others who gained their Sees by Papal provision, to pay great sums to the Court of Rome. His predecessor died in debt, and money due for the cattle to stock the farms was not paid till September, 1278;[6] the charges on account of dilapidations were probably delayed if paid at all.

1—Willis, *Cathedrals*, p. 828, cf Swinfield *Reg.* f 78a.

2—p. 126. A similar grant was made to a preceding Bishop in 1243. (Papal *Regesta* I., 1243).

3—Household Rolls of Bp. Sw., p. xxviii.

4—The list in the *Taxatio Nic.*, p. 168, is Barton, Bishop's Castle, Bishop's Frome, Bosbury, Bromyard, Cloppele, Colwall, Cradley, Eastnor. Eaton, Grendon, Hampton, Hereford, Ledbury, Lydbury North, Ross, Ross Foreign, Shelwick, Sugwas, Tupsley, Upton, and Whitbourne.

5—*Acta Sanct.*, p. 499.   6—See p. 139.

A large fine was paid by him for the custody of the manor of Earley, as also for the purchase of the wardships in the Marmion estates, and these must have been drawn from private funds. But the costly litigation caused by his ill-advised acceptance of the prebend of Preston, and his unwillingness to reinstate Peter de Langon when he vacated it himself, together with the dispute as to jurisdiction with the Bishop of St. Asaph, brought vexation and embarassment that ended only with his life. Proctors and advocates had to be paid, and presents given to Cardinals and others who had to be conciliated; such expenses were a constant drain, and we find many indications of it in his letters. He borrowed a hundred pounds from William de Rotherfield, Dean of York,[1] in 1276, and gave powers to Nicholas the Penitentiary to contract a loan to that amount at Rome in 1278.[2] The executors of his brother Hugh lent him £102 6s. 6d. in 1279;[3] Peter of Chester, Canon of the Cathedral, found him a hundred marks;[4] with the consent of the Chapter he took two hundred marks from a reserve deposited in the treasury,[5] and he was indebted to John de Clare for eighty more.[6]

There are no signs indeed of extravagance or careless management; his letter to his Seneschal[7] implies a watchful scrutiny of his accounts and effective control of his financial agents. The sum spent on the livery of his servants, though equivalent to four hundred pounds,[8] compares favourably with that, nearly six times as much, which Bishop Drokensford paid for the same purpose.[9] But an episcopal household was necessarily large; bailiffs and farm-servants were numerous; repairs were costly in so many manor houses,[10] and the keep of the thirty or more horses needed to convey his retinue from one home to another could not be dispensed with.

It is difficult to ascertain the amount and sources of his private income. Of the very large landed estates of his family not much seems to have been ever in his hands, except for a time as a guardian and trustee. We read of a little messuage in Lincoln-

1—See p. 105. 4—Ibid. 7—See p. 108.
2—See p. 186. 5—See p. 219. 8—See p. 75.
3—See p. 213. 6—See p. 216. 9—Drokensf. *Reg.*. p. 102.
10—In 1356 the Bishop and Chapter passed a resolution that the houses belonging to the See and Chapter in Hereford and on the manors were excessive in number, expensive to repair, and should not be a burden on them. (Chapter Archives).

shire held under Edmund de Dynecourt;[1] property in the Manor of Barling was sold by him for sixty pounds in 1275,[2] but the bailiff had not settled his accounts in 1279.[3] Money was due to him in Ireland,[4] and he had estates in Somersetshire.[5] The mention of a bailiff in Charlecote (? in Warwickshire) points to landed interests there;[6] so also do the entries respecting Madresfield (near Worcester) and Bredenbury.[7] He had also the Manor of Berkham, which he sold to one of his pages, William de Nevyle, for £40 16s.;[8] the right of advowson of Alveston in the diocese of Worcester[9] is most easily explained by the possession of a manor there. His frequent visits to Tottenham (Totenhale)[10] may imply that he had a manor house in that neighbourhood, or he may have accepted hospitality from the Prior of Holy Trinity, but this is only matter of conjecture. On the whole from the very meagre references to him in the Hundred Rolls, or immediately after his death in the State Records, we may gather that his landed property was small. He had special licence to deal in his Will with the Manor of Earley,[11] and his interest in that passed to his sister Juliana.[12]

His Will unfortunately has not been preserved, but we have a list of the many legacies bequeathed by him, mostly in small sums, to his clerks and personal retainers.[13] These amounted to about four hundred and fifty marks, and were all paid in 1282. When the long suit about the prebend of Preston was brought to a close at Rome, sentence was pronounced that the executors of Cantilupe were to repay Langon £60 for every year in which the Bishop had detained the prebend. But Swinfield and de Montfort, the executors, showed that they had nothing left of his estate. They had laid out on his Obit what remained after payment of the legacies,[14] together with provision for his funeral and monument, and had secured discharge from the Court of Canterbury.[15]

1—Rot. Orig. 11th of Edw. I.
2—See p. 25.
3—See p. 164.
4—See p. 33.
5—See p. 262.
6—See p. 19, cf *Inquis. p. m.* p. 19.
7—See p. 71.
8—See p. 217.
9—Giffard *Reg.*, p. 44 (Worc. Hist. Soc.)
10—See pp. 67, 164, &c.
11—Patent Rolls, April 10, 1280.
12—Household Roll of Bp. Sw., p. cxxx.
13—Archives of the D. and C.
14—One hundred marks were expended on the obit, which was first celebrated Aug. 25, 1288. Swinf. *Reg.*, f. 45b.
15—Document in the Archives of the D. and C.

ITINERARY OF THOMAS DE CANTILUPE.

1275.

July 10.	Bradwell (Essex).
,, 16.	Windsor.
,, 18.	Windsor.
,, 29.	Sherborne Decani.
Aug. 10.	Prestbury.
,, 11.	Kempsey.
,, 15.	Dodderhill (Droitwich).
,, 27.	Sechtone.
Sept. 5.	Chartham.
,, 10.	Canterbury.
,, 11.	Chartham.
,, 12.	Boughton under Blean.
,, 16.	Mayfield.
,, 21 or 22.	Drayton.
,, 23.	Wokingham.
,, 26.	Sherborne Decani.
Oct. 4.	Sherborne Decani.

Oct. 9.	Windsor.
,, 16, 17, 18.	London.
,, 21.	London.
,, 26.	London.
Nov. 3.	London.
,, 4.	London.
,, 5.	Kensington.
,, 12.	Kensington.
,, 14.	London.
,, 16.	London.
,, 21.	London.
,, 25.	Sherborne Decani.
Dec. 1.	Sherborne Decani.
,, 18.	Prestbury.
,, 22.	Ledbury.
,, 27.	Hereford.

1276.

Jan. 4.	Prestbury.
,, 9.	Lambourn.
,, 15.	Winchester.
,, 20.	Winchester.
,, 27.	Sherborne Decani.
Feb. 19 and 20.	Hereford.
,, 23.	Sugwas.
Mar. 8.	Wenlock.
,, 27.	Ross.
Apr. 6.	Marcle.
,, 8.	Bosbury.
,, 14.	Prestbury.
,, 25.	Earley.
,, 30.	London.
May 7.	Westminster.
,, 11.	Kensington.
,, 12.	Westminster.
,, 15.	Kensington.
June 9.	Kensington.

June 21.	Bromyard.
,, 24.	Bishop's Castle.
,, 25.	Wigmore.
July 1.	Staunton.
,, 8.	Canterbury.
Aug. 11.	Leominster.
,, 13.	Whitbourne.
,, 24.	Sugwas.
Sept. 2.	Bicknor.
,, 20.	Gloucester.
,, 26.	Bosbury.
Oct. 6.	Colne St. Aylwin.
,, 14.	London.
,, 17.	London.
Nov. 1, 3.	Westminster.
,, 8, 11, 19.	Fulham.
,, 26.	Westminster.
Dec. 16, 17.	Earley.

1277.

Jan.	4.	Sandford juxta Oxford.	Sept.	18.	Leominster.
,,	7.	Bosbury.	,,	22.	Sugwas.
,,	11.	Leominster.	Oct.	2, 3.	Bishop's Castle.
,,	15.	Hereford.	,,	6.	Welbatch (Annscroft).
,,	17.	Preston.	,,	10.	Bishop's Castle and Pontesbury.
,,	18.	Bosbury.			
Mar.	17.	Bosbury.	,,	13.	Pontesbury.
,,	28.	Hereford.	,,	14.	Welbatch.
Apr.	6.	Sugwas.	,,	19.	Prestbury.
,,	13.	Earley.	,,	25, 26.	Bishop's Castle.
,,	22.	Kensington and Westminster.	,,	29.	Corsham.
			Nov.	8, 9.	Chetton.
May	11.	Earley.	,,	20.	Welbatch.
,,	30, 31.	Earley.	,,	30.	Bosbury.
July	7.	Worcester.	Dec.	4, 8.	Sugwas.
,,	10.	Whitbourne.	,,	8.	Hereford.
,,	14, 20, 22, 28.	Sugwas.	,,	15.	Prestbury.
Aug.	2, 7.	Sugwas.	,,	21.	Earley.
,,	28.	Prestbury.	,,	31.	London.

1278.

Jan.	25.	Denham.	July	4.	Leominster.
Feb.	11, 13, 18, 25.	Bosbury.	,,	6.	Bosbury.
Mar.	4.	Sugwas.	,,	15.	Earley.
,,	12.	Rock.	,,	22, 23.	Bedfont.
,,	16.	Welbatch.	Aug.	11.	Gloucester.
,,	21.	Clun.	,,	16.	Prestbury.
,,	28.	Knighton.	,,	22.	Newton.
,,	30.	Dilwyn.	Sept.	1.	Tichseye.
Apr.	1.	Eardisley.	,,	18.	Bosbury.
,,	8.	Ross.	,,	22.	Sugwas.
,,	13.	Newent.	,,	25.	Bromfield.
,,	25.	Earley.	,,	26, 27.	Bishop's Castle.
May	7, 8.	Bedfont.	Oct.	2.	Eaton juxta Leominster.
,,	18, 23, 24.	Tottenham.	,,	4, 5.	Sugwas.
,,	27.	Westminster.	,,	2.	Bosbury.
,,	31.	Tottenham.	,,	10.	Ledbury.
June	4.	London.	,,	28 or 29.	Tottenham.
,,	13.	Tottenham.	Nov.	8.	Tottenham.
July	2.	Bishop's Castle.	Dec.	17.	Whitbourne.

1279.

Feb. 13, 15. Sugwas.
,, 22, 23. Bosbury.
Mar. 14, 15, 16. Bosbury.
,, Newent.
Apr. 2. Prestbury.
,, 21. London.
,, 25. Tottenham and Westminster.
,, 26, 29. London.
May 1. Tottenham.
,, 4. London.
,, 7. Tottenham.
,, 14. Sherborne Decani.
,, 27. Ledbury.
June 2. Tottenham.
,, 27. Earley.
July 6. Earley.
,, 29. Hereford.
Aug. 4. Hasleye.

Aug. 13. London.
,, 17. Tottenham.
Sept. 1. London.
,, 5. Tottenham.
,, 6, 8. London.
,, 12. Sevenoaks.
,, 19. Ightham.
Oct. 7. Whaddon.
,, 19. Barnes.
,, 28, 28, 30. Earley.
Nov. 11. Earley.
,, 23. Calstone-Willington.
Dec. 1. Beckington.
,, 19. Colwall.
,, 20. Bishop's Frome.
,, 22. Lugwardine.
,, 25, 26. Hereford.
,, 28. Sugwas.

1280.

Jan. 3. Leominster.
,, 5. Eye.
,, 9. Bishop's Frome.
,, 13. Duntisborne.
,, 20, 23, 24. London.
,, 31. Earley.
Feb. 23. Flaxley.
Mar. 7. Lugwardine.
,, 31. Bosbury and Ledbury.
Apr. 4. Tenbury.
,, 15, 19. Whitbourne.
,, 30. Earley.

May 4, 14, 22. London.
,, 27. Earley.
June 23. Earley.
,, 28. London.
July 25. Charenton Bridge.
Aug. 12, 15, 29, 31. Charenton Bridge.
Sept. 2. Charenton Bridge.
,, 3. Poissy.
,, 15, 27. Lyre.
Oct. 9. Lyre.
Nov. 1. Lyre.

1281.

Feb. 11. Conches.
May 23, 26. Fontaine.
June 2. Fontaine.
,, 16. Brynun.
,, 21. Cumbisville.

July 1, 26. Fontaine.
Oct. 12. Bermondsey.
Dec. 10. Colwall.
,, 17. Staunton juxta London.
,, 21. Wenlock.

1282.

Jan. 1. Wigmore.
,, 13. Bosbury.

Mar. 7. London.
July 10. By Montefiascone.

THE OFFICIALS OF THE BISHOP.

ARCHDEACON OF HEREFORD.—William de Conflens, allowed to be non-resident for three years to study (p. 8); prebendary of Church Withington, and incumbent of Dixton; aft. Bishop of Gebanan.

ARCHDEACON OF SALOP.—(1) James de Aquablanca had the prebend de Castro (p. 242); was a portionist of Ledbury (ibid); resigned in 1280, being under sentence of deprivation (p. 63). [The entry of the collation of Richard de Swinfield to the office was afterwards cancelled.]

(2) Adam de Fileby (p. 253), canon of the Cathedral (p. 113); Canon of St. Martin's, London (p. 287); frequently Proctor for the Bishop; collated to the Deanery conditionally (p. 234); of doubtful relations to the Bishop (p. 244); died much in debt to the Chapter (Swinf. *Reg.* f. 60b.); cited by Archbishop Peckham.

OFFICIAL-PRINCIPAL.—(1) Luke de Bree (or Bray) (pp. 1, 116), canon (p. 112); appointed to exercise decanal jurisdiction (ibid); Treasurer of the Cathedral (p. 212); allowed to hold the Church of Bockleton with his dignity (Swinf. *Reg.*, f. 73b); benefited largely by the offerings of wax tapers at Cantilupe's tomb (*ibid.*, f. 63b).

(2) Roger de Sevenake (p. 63), portionist of Bromyard; Treasurer (Swinf. *Reg.*, f. 47a).

(3) Robert of Gloucester, appointed June 28, 1280, (p. 254); Chancellor of the Cathedral; Official to Bishop Swinfield; perhaps the poet-historian (p. xiv, n.).

VICAR-GENERAL (during the Bishop's absence from England).—
William de Montfort (p. 221) Precentor (p. 111).
Luke de Bree (p. 221), prebendary of Inkberrow (p. 122).

GUARDIANS OF THE TEMPORALITIES (during the Bishop's absence).—
William de Montfort (p. 222).
Walter de Redmarley, Canon (p. 222).

PENITENTIARY.—(1) Henry FitzWarin, appointed by the King. *Sede vacante* (p. 1); (2) Nicholas de Hereford (p. 34).

PROCTORS (1) in the Roman Courts.—
John de Barton (p. 210).
John de Beccles (pp. 105, 209).
John de Bitterley (p. 215); has the Church of Croft (p. 234).
William Brun (p. 273).
John de Clare (p. 15), Rector of Colwall (p. 195); one of the executors of Hugh de Cantilupe (p. 213); trusted agent of the Bishop (pp. 182, 262).
Adam de Fileby (p. 187).
Rector of Lindridge (Swinf. H.R., clxxiii).
William de Ludlow (p. 279).
Bardus of Poggibonzi (pp. 12, 213).
John Waleys or Walensis (p. 105).
Edmund de Warefelde (pp. 14, 15).

(2) In the Law Courts.—John de Kempsey (p. 16); Robert de Kempsey (p. 52); John de Hampton (p. 52).

(3) In all Causes.—Luke de Bree (p. 221); Roger de Sevenake (p. 221).

(4) In Episcopal Councils.—Robert of Gloucester (p. 224).

(5) In Ireland.—Thomas de Chaddeworth (p. 25).

ACCOUNTANT.—William de la Greve (p. 261).

ADVOCATES IN THE KING'S BENCH RECEIVING PENSIONS.—Hamo de la Barre, Alan de Walkyngham, William de Stowe, Adam de Arderne, John de Houghtone (p. 22).

ATTORNEY.—Maurice de Membury (p. 228).

AUDITORS OF ACCOUNTS.—John de Bradeham (p. 261); John de Clare (p. 261); Nicholas of Hereford (p. 261); Walter de Redmarley (p. 217), Canon (p. 17); Gerard of Ugina (p. 261).

CONSTABLE OF BISHOP'S CASTLE.—John de Salisbury (p. 171).

SENESCHAL.—John de Bradeham (pp. 3, 7).

SEQUESTRATOR.—Richard de Heyton (pp. 177, 194).

TREASURER (during the Bishop's absence).—Nicholas de Hereford, the Penitentiary (p. 252).

CLERKS.—Luke de Bree (p. 115); John de Clare (p. 15); John de Bradeham (p. 115); John de Kempsey (p. 117); John de Say (p. 117); Nicholas of Oxford (p. 117); Gilbert de Heywood (p. 116).

BAILIFFS.—John de Berkynge, b. of the Forest of Lydbury North (p. 20); William de Chilteham, b. of Whitbourne (p. 80), aft. of Ross (p. 108); John de Fairstede, b. of Barling (p. 164); Robert de Furches, b. of Whitbourne (p. 108); Nicholas de Hamptone, b. of Charlecote (p. 19); Gerard of Ugina, b. of Prestbury (p. 25); Richard, b. of Ross (p. 108); Walter, b. of Ledbury.

The b. of Hereford is referred to (p. 17), but like those of the other episcopal manors is not named.

CHAMBERLAINS, ETC.—Nicholas de Hodinet, Robert Deynte, *Acta Sanct.* (p. 534); Henry de Lacu (p. 76); Hamo le Dale (p. 170); Hugh le Barber, with Cantilupe at Paris and Oxford, *Acta Sanct.* (p. 533); Robert de Wytacre (do.); Richard de Kimberley, *in variis officiis*, *Acta Sanct.* (533).

CHAMPION *(pugil)*.—Thomas of Bridgnorth, whose salary was half a mark (p. 104).

CUSTOS OF WESTWOOD COPSES.—Madoc de Eyton (p. 146).

FORESTERS.—Russell and Witlock of Malvern (p. 159).

FOWLER.—Adam Harpyn (p. 26).

PARKER.—John le Blont of Ledbury (p. 43).

VALET.—William de Nevyle (p. 26).

WATCHMAN *(gayta)*.—William le Wayte, *Acta Sanct.* (p. 534).

The list is of course not complete. There were others on manorial estates of whom no mention occurs in the Register, and household servants of humbler rank are unnoticed. Of these at least a dozen received legacies under his will. (Notarial document in the Archives of the D. and C.)

fordensis; et idem Cancellarius habet penes se eadem acta, sigillo Domini consignata.

Oct. 5.—Walter, portionist of Pontesbury, appearing with the defence that he has the custody only of the Church of Stanton, at the pleasure of the Bishop of Salisbury, is required to produce evidence of this.

CONTRA WALTERUM, PORCIONARIUM DE PAUNTESBURY.—Acta coram nobis, Thoma, etc., in manerio de Sugwas, die Mercurii proximo post Festum Beati Michaelis, anno Domini M°CC°LXX° octavo, in negocio quo ex officio proceditur contra Walterum, porcionarium de Pontesbury; videlicet, cum idem Walterus multociens evocatus quod compareat coram nobis, etc., post varias contumacias contractas personaliter respondebat quod ecclesiam de Stauntone tenet ex causa custodie ad voluntatem Episcopi Saresbiriensis revocande. Idcirco nos, deliberacione habita, prefigimus eidem Waltero proximum diem juridicum post quindenam Pasche ad fidem nobis faciendam de dicta custodia, etc.

Oct. 5.—Engagement of Walter, portionist of Pontesbury, to proceed to Holy Orders at the next Ordination, and to produce evidence of his tenure of Stanton, under pain of the forfeiture of his portion.

LITTERA WALTERI PORCIONARII DE PAUNTESBURY POSITA IN HANAPERIO.—Noverint universi quod ego, Walterus, filius Reginaldi, porcionarius de Pauntesbury, bona fide promitto, et me presentibus obligo et astringo, quod in proximis Ordinibus celebrandis a Venerabili Patre, Domino Thoma, Dei gracia Herefordensi Episcopo, vel ab alio Curie Cantuariensis Suffraganeo, per litteras ipsius dimissorias, Domino concedente, ad Ordinem quem beneficii mei cura requirit me faciam promoveri. De custodia vero michi in ecclesia de Stauntone, Salesbiriensis diocesis, ad voluntatem Diocesani dumtaxat commissa, die juridico proximo post quindenam Pasche, dicto Domino Herefordensi, vel suis commissariis, in majori Ecclesia Herefordensi plenam fidem facere teneor, prout in actis judicialibus super hoc confectis, et sigillo dicti Domini Episcopi consignatis, plenius continetur. Si autem, quod absit, premissa fideliter non observavero, volo et concedo quod extunc porcione supradicta in ecclesia de Pontesbury ipso jure sim privatus. In cujus rei, etc.

Datum apud Sugwas, die Mercurii proximo post Festum Beati Michaelis, anno Domini M°CC°LXX° octavo.

Oct. 28 or 29.—The Bishop of Bath was empowered to decide as to the admission of Philip Burnell to the Church of Chetton.

COMMISSIO DE ECCLESIA DE CHETINTONE.—Memorandum quod iiij Kalendas vel v^{to} Novembris, anno gracie M°CC°LXX° octavo, apud Totenhale, commisit Dominus vices suas litteratorie Domino Episcopo Bathoniensi ad ordinandum de admissione Philippi Burnel, clerici, ad ecclesiam de Chetintone presentati, secundum quod viderit expedire. Et tantummodo ista vice.

Nov. 8.—Licence of non-residence to study granted for one year to William, Rector of Stanford.

STANFORDE.—Willelmus, Rector de Stanforde, habet licenciam studendi per unum annum a Festo Nativitatis Domini, et optinet litteram super hoc in forma communi. Data ipsius apud Totenhale, vj Idus Novembris, anno Domini predicto.

Nov. 8,—Licence of non-residence to the Rector of Kingsland[1] for one year, to be in attendance on Roger de Mortimer.

LENES.—Item dictis die, loco, et anno, concessit Dominus Rectori de Lenes quod possit, per unum annum continuum a Festo Nativitatis Domini proximo venturo, stare in obsequio Rogeri de Mortuo Mari.

Nov. 8.—Release of the sequestration at Stanford caused by the Rector's non-residence and his failure to appear at the Ordination. Notice given to Richard de Heyton.

ITEM STANFORDE.—Item supradictis die, loco, et anno, relaxavit Dominus sequestrum interpositum in fructibus Rectoris de Stanforde, suas litteras super hoc magistro Ricardo de Heytone dirigendo, eo quod in ecclesia non residet nec proximis Ordinibus suis affuit.

[1]—Kingeslene was a Rectory; Monkeslene belonging to the Abbey of Conches, and Erleslene to that of Lyre, had vicars only.

Feb. 15, 1279.—Custody of the Church of Pembridge committed to Emeric, the Chancellor. Mandate of induction.

Fol. 56.   PENEBRUGGE.—Item memorandum quod anno Domini M°CC° LXX° octavo, xv Kalendas Marcii apud Sugwas commisimus domino E[merico], Cancellario Herefordensi, custodiam ecclesie de Penebrugge, pro nostro libito revocandam. Et quod mandavimus tempore memorato domino L[uce de Bree], Thesaurario Herefordensi, quod ipsum dominum E[mericum] in corporalem possessionem dicte ecclesie induceret.

Feb. 15.—The Chancellor, under distraint ordered by the Crown, engaged to appear before the Barons of the Exchequer in the interest of the Bishop, the Dean, and himself, concerning various scutages claimed as in arrear from the time of Bishop Peter.

CANCELLARIUS HEREFORDENSIS.—Item predictis die et loco, dictus dominus Cancellarius, per nos ad mandatum Domini Regis districtus, nobis fideliter repromisit quod in quindena Pasche erit coram Baronibus de Scaccario, responsurus pro nobis et Decano Herefordensi, et pro seipso, de diversis scutagiis que Dominus Rex exigit, et que a retro sunt de tempore bone memorie Episcopi Petri.

Feb. 13.—Sequestration was released, at the instance of the Earl of Cornwall, on a moiety of the fruits of William de Monkton, Rector of Dorsington. Notice sent to Richard de Heyton.

DORSINTONE.—Memorandum quod Idibus Februarii, apud Sugwas, anno predicto, relaxavit Dominus, ad instanciam Comitis Cornubie, medietatem fructuum domini Willelmi de Moneketone, Rectoris ecclesie de Dorsingtone. Et littera illius relaxacionis directa fuit magistro R. de Heytone.

Feb. 22.—Mandate to the Official to see that John de Clare, on whom the Church of Colwall had been conferred from Michaelmas last, bears the expense of the clerical stipends and other charges, and receives the income, except the corn in the barns.

RELAXACIO SEQUESTRI DE COLEWELLE.—Thomas, etc., Officiali suo salutem, etc. Quia volumus quod dominus J[ohannes] de Clare, cui ecclesiam de Colewelle contulimus a Festo Sancti

Michaelis preterito, stipendia sacerdotum et clericorum ecclesie deserviencium, cum aliis oneribus ecclesiam tangentibus antedictam, agnoscat; volumus et mandamus quod oblaciones et alias obvenciones omnes que a dicto Festo hucusque ad dictam ecclesiam obvenerunt, faciatis dicto J[ohanni] plenius assignari, de nostro dono et gracia speciali; blado existente in horreis dumtaxat excepto. Datum apud Bosebury, viij Kalendas Marcii, anno Consecracionis nostre quarto.

Feb. 23.—The Bishop conferred the Church of Whitbourne on Walter de la Burcote, and wrote to the Dean of Frome to induct him.

COLLACIO ECCLESIE DE WYTEBURNE.—Item memorandum quod apud Bosebury, vij Kalendas Marcii, anno Domini M°CC°LXX° octavo, contulit Dominus ore tenus domino Waltero de la Burkote ecclesiam de Wyteburne, intuitu caritatis. Et tunc scripsit Decano de Froma quod ipsum W[alterum] inducat, etc.

Feb. 23.—Collation of John de Clare to the Church of Colwall, and mandate of induction sent to the Dean of Frome.

COLLACIO ECCLESIE DE COLEWELLE.—Item eo tempore contulit Dominus ecclesiam de Colewelle domino J[ohanni] de Clare, caritativo intuitu. Et tunc Decano de Froma extitit demandatum quod eum induceret, etc.

Promise, at the instance of the Abbot of Wigmore, that William de Bray, presented by the Abbot and Convent, shall be admitted to the Church of Hopton Wafers, if his legitimacy be established before Easter, or if before Trinity and he be then ordained. If he do not come before the following Eastertide the Bishop will either accept a nominee of the Abbot and Convent, or nominate another to be presented by them, as they may prefer.

WILLELMUS DE BRAY.—Memorandum quod Dominus noster, ad instanciam Domini Abbatis de Wygemor, Willelmo de Bray, clerico, graciam hanc promisit; videlicet quod, si idem W[illelmus] citra Pascha fuerit legitimatus, licet citra idem tempus non fuerit in Sacro Ordine constitutus, ipsum ad presentacionem Abbatis et Conventus de Wygemor ad ecclesiam de Hoptone Waffre admittet; quod si infra idem tempus non veniat, dum tamen venerit citra

Festum Trinitatis, et fuerit legitimatus, et in Sabbato ejusdem Festi Sacro Ordine ordinatus, ipsi eandem ecclesiam, de nostra speciali gracia conferemus; quod si infra idem Festum non veniat, dum tamen veniat citra Quatuor Tempora proximo sequencia, dictus Abbas eligat de duobus alterutrum, vel quod nominandum a nobis Abbas et Conventus presentent ad ecclesiam memoratam, vel quod nominando ab eodem Abbate eandem ecclesiam conferamus.

Mar. 14.—Appeal to the Courts of Canterbury and of Rome against the partiality or irregular proceedings of the Archdeacon of Carmarthen and the Prior of Wombridge, judges-delegate in the suit with the Bishop of St. Asaph. This was read to the witnesses in Latin, and then explained in French before dinner in the hall of Bosbury.

PROVOCACIO.—Timentes ne Archidiaconus de Karmardyn et Prior de Wembrugge, judices a Sede Apostolica delegati in causa appellacionis inter nos et Episcopum Assavensem, nimis faventes contra nos, non citatos legitime, non monitos, nec confessos, processum ullam faciant, aut aliquam censuram ecclesiasticam in nos ferant, Sedem Apostolicam et tuicionem Sedis Cantuariensis, aut Judices Principales si commissarii eorum premissa attemptaverint, provocamus et appellamus in hiis scriptis.

TESTES IPSIUS PROVOCACIONIS.—Isti interfuerunt huic appellacioni,—Cancellarius Herefordensis, Thomas, vicarius de Bosebury, Hugo, capellanus de eadam, Ricardus de Bodeham, clericus, Robertus de Boneshulle, clericus, magister Robertus de Gloucestria, magister Gilbertus de Heywode, Willelmus de Faukeburne, capellanus, Johannes de Kemeseye, clericus, et Bartholomeus de Suntyngge, clericus.

MEMORANDUM.—Prescriptam provocacionem fecit dictus Dominus Herefordensis apud Bosebury, in aula sua, ante prandium, et legit eam primo Latine; deinde Gallice eam exposuit coram predictis, die Martis proximo post Festum Beati Gregorii, anno Domini M°CC°LXXviij°·

Mar. 16.—Commission to the Official to act for the Bishop in regard to the Archdeacon of Salop and Peter Eymer.

COMMISSIO.—Thomas, etc., Officiali suo salutem, etc. In causa quam ex officio nostro movemus Archidiacono[1] Salopsire, necnon et

[1] So in MS.

P[etro] Eymer, Canonico Herefordensi super contumacia, etc., vobis committimus vices nostras. Datum apud Bosebury, xvij Kalendas Aprilis, anno predicto.

Mar. 16.—Commission to Alan de Creppinge, Canon of Hereford, to hear the suit between the Priors of Chirbury and Alberbury and the Rector of Worthen of the one part, and John, Rector of Welshpool, on the other part.

COMMISSIO.—Thomas, etc., magistro A[lano] de Creppinge, Canonico Herefordensi, salutem, etc. In causa seu negocio que vel quod inter religiosos viros de Chyrebury et Abberbury ecclesiarum Priores et . . . , Rectorem ecclesie de Worthyn,[1] ex parte una, et Johannem, Rectorem ecclesie de Pola, vertitur seu verti speratur ex altera, committimus vices nostras. Datum apud Bosebury, xvij Kalendas Aprilis, anno predicto.

Apr. 2.—Memorandum that all the documents relating to Peter Eymer were handed to the Official.

MEMORANDUM.—Memorandum quod die Pasche, anno Consecracionis nostre quarto, apud Prestebury magistro L., Officiali nostro, omnia instrumenta contra Petrum Eymer habita, que in cofferis nostris fuerant tunc inventa, unacum prescripta commissione tradita extiterunt.

Apr. 22.—Writ to the Bishop to distrain on John de Aquablanca, and to appear with him and Emeric, the Chancellor, to answer for certain scutages due in the time of Bishop Peter. The writ was sent for execution to the Official, for sequestration without delay.

Edwardus, Dei gracia Rex Anglie, etc., Venerabili in Christo Patri, T[home], eadem gracia Episcopo Herefordensi, salutem. Mandamus quod distringatis Johannem de Aqua Blanka, unum executorum testamenti Petri de Aqua Blanka, quondam Episcopi Herefordensis, per beneficia sua ecclesiastica que habet in Episcopatu vestro, quod eum habeatis coram Baronibus de Scaccario nostro apud Westmonasterium, a die Sancti Michaelis in xv dies, ad respondendum nobis, una vobiscum et unacum Emerico de Aqua Blanka, executore predicti testamenti, cui eundem diem dedimus,

---

1—Portions of Chirbury, Alberbury and Worthen had been claimed by the Bishop of St. Asaph as belonging to his Diocese.

de diversis debitis et scutagiis que nobis debentur de tempore predicti Petri. Et vos ipsi tunc sitis ibidem, et habeatis ibi hoc breve. Teste R. de Nortwode, apud Westmonasterium, xxij die Aprilis, anno regni nostri vij.

Breve Regis cujus istud transcriptum existit, x Kalendas Maii, anno predicto, Officialis Herefordensis execucioni demandandum, fuit transmissum; ita quod ipsum breve, Domino Episcopo Herefordensi seu suo certo attornato tradendum, postquam fuerit plenarie executum, traderet modis omnibus tempestive, ne primus dies placiti aliqualiter impediatur. Et quod, collectis fructibus J[ohannis] de Aqua Blanka in autumpno, ipsos teneat sub arto sequestro, sub pena execucionis; et quod Episcopum certificet super hiis in premissis; hoc fuit missum per Senescallum.

Oct. 29, 1278.—Another writ to the Bishop to distrain on Emeric and John de Aquablanca.

Edwardus, etc., Thome, etc., salutem. Quum Emericus de Aqua Blanca et Johannes de Aqua Blanca, executores testamenti Petri de Aqua Blanca, etc., clerici sunt, vobis mandamus quod distringas, etc.; ita quod eos habeatis coram Baronibus de Scaccario, etc., a die Pasche in xv dies, ad respondendum, etc. Teste Johanne de Chabeham, apud Westmonasterium, xxix die Octobris, anno regni nostri sexto.

Omnia bona tam Johannis de Aqua Blanca quam Emerici sunt sequestrata.

Jan. 21, 1279.—Writ to distrain on Thomas le Breton and John de Ross, executors of Bishop John, and bring them before the Treasurer and Barons of the Exchequer, to answer for a debt of £41 10s. due from his estate to the Crown.

Edwardus, etc., Thome, etc. Quia Thomas le Bretone, frater Johannis le Bretone, et Johannes de Ros, executores testamenti predicti Johannis le Bretone, quondam Episcopi Herefordensis, clerici sunt, et non habent laicum feodum, etc.; ita quod eos habeatis coram predictis Baronibus apud Westmonasterium, in crastino Clausi Pasche, ad respondendum fratri Joseph de Chauncy, Priori Hospitalis Sancti Johannis Jerusalem in Anglia, Thesaurario nostro, unacum vobis et aliis executoribus testamenti predicti, quibus eundem diem dedimus, de xljli. xs. quos predictus defunctus ei debet, ut idem Prior dicit, sicut racionabiliter monstrare petit quod inde respondere debet. Et habeas ibi tunc hoc breve. Teste R. de Nortwode apud Westmonasterium, xxj die Januarii, anno regni nostri septimo.

Fol. 57. *The Bishop writes to the Nuns of Lyngebroke to express his pleasure at the zeal and loving union of which he found evidence at his Visitation of their Convent; he exhorts them to observe their vows and the rule of their Order; to limit themselves strictly to the fitting uses of chapter-house, dormitory, refectory, infirmary, and cloister; to go beyond the Convent buildings only in case of urgent need or solemn processions. The work-rooms should be visited only by those who have duties there, and not even by them unaccompanied. Private property must not be allowed in any form, even when friends and relatives send presents for dress. Women of marriageable age must not be received as boarders. Care should be taken in the choice of domestic servants, and Confessors must be men of exemplary character.*

LITTERA MONIALIBUS DE LYNGEBROKE TRANSMISSA.—Thomas, etc., caris filiabus in Christo, Priorisse et sanctimonialibus in Cenobio de Lyngebroke Deo servientibus, per temporalia sic transire ut pertingatis eterna. Regnum celorum, mansionibus multis (teste Veritate) distinctum, de hoc seculo nequam ad diversos tramites penitencie salientes, atque extra mundi contagia per varias virtutum semitas gradientes de penitencia, quasi de torculari, sibi exprimit et colligit meliores, mansionum celestium tabernacula multiplicatis premiorum stipendiis ingressuros. Inter quos Ordinem vestrum, a viro vite et literature mirabilis, Augustino, cooperante Sancto Spiritu institutum, tanto majori sanctimonia muniendum esse perspicimus quanto vos, que in eo vivitis et estis professe, propter sexus fragilitatem lacius estis exposite insidiis hostis antiqui. Profecto non incidetis in eas si perfectam[1] obedienciam, veram paupertatem et castimonie puritatem, sine quibus in religione salus esse non potest, necnon et quasdam salutares observancias, quas ad conversacionis vestre decorem infra subicimus, cum bone consciencie testimonio alacri studio peragatis, a malo et specie mali qualibet abstinentes. Vos igitur Deo date que, abnegantes vos ipsas et renunciantes seculo, Christi servicio vos perpetuo mancipastis, omni custodia vos servare debetis, et portas sensum obserare, ne umquam introitus pateat maligno spiritui ex quo vobis aut aliis, in pravorum desideriorum ardore, vel saltem levi cogitacione, detur

1—In MS. profectam.

occasio delinquendi. Eapropter in Cenobio vestro certa sunt loca que vos exire non convenit; ut possitis Domino cordis et corporis innocenciam conservare. Introire debetis oratorium; in quo provideatis vobis prudenter orando ne, in temptacionem aliquam incidentes, prolabamini in delictum. Accedatis ad capitulum, in quo juste puniatis cotidiana commissa. Intretis dormitorium et refectorium horis aptis, in quibus corpus ad sustentacionem, ne deficiat, recreetis; temperancia tamen semper assistat, ne ex refeccionis superfluitate caro recalcitret, et eam deserat fortitudo in temptacionibus dum quiescit. Ad infirmariam vero ille ex vobis quarum debilitas vel infirmitas id exposcit, secundum doctrinam Apostoli, pro solacio et infirmitatis remedio optinendis accedant. Maneatis ceteris horis in claustro; in quo, ut premittitur, corporeos sensus vestros claudatis, intelligentes inter vos et mundum chaos magnum esse firmatum; solumque Deum mentis oculis contemplantes, aliquid de eterne vite dulcedine pregustetis. Et predicta loca personis secularibus, et religiosis quibuscumque aliis a vobis, vacua debent esse, ne ex frequenti conversacione, vel saltem aliqua exterorum, quies vestra vel contemplacio perturbetur; immo (quod deterius est) cum bonum et malum sint immediata contraria, ex quo abstinetis a bono, cogitacione facili vanitatibus secularibus inhiatis. Ad dicta tamen loca memorate persone ex necessaria seu justa causa, non frequenter, accedant, set raro ut vobis vel vestrum alicui eloquantur; et tunc nulla vestrum, nisi confitendi causa, sola conveniat ad loquendum, set cum socia probate religionis et fame, que omnium eorum que inibi dicuntur et fiunt valeat esse testis. Ad officinas autem ille ex vobis quibus ex officiis certis id competit possunt accedere, cum bona teste ut premittitur, et non sole. Loca vero cetera a premissis vobis reputetis penitus interdicta, nisi quod infra septa vestri Cenobii processionum sollempnia debitis temporibus faciatis; et amodo processionis causa vel alia vestrum Cenobium nullatenus exeatis, nisi evidens necessitas aut utilitas hoc manifeste suadeat; et tunc que exit exeat cum Superioris licencia, et bonam habeat comitem testem secum. Sane zelus bone religionis et caritatis unitas, quos in nostra Visitacione apud vos vigere reperimus, letificant nos in Christo; obsecrantes ipsum pro vobis quatinus in vocacione qua estis vocate digne coram Domino ambuletis, cum omni humilitate, paciencia, mansuetudine, benignitate, modestia; pacis vinculo, caritatis unitate, et spe retribucionis voluntarie paupertatis invicem supportantes, et carnis opera, que sunt fornicacio, inmundicia, inpudicia, inimicicia, contenciones, emulaciones, ire, rixe, dissensiones, secte, invidie, ebrietates, commessaciones, sancte professionis et sacrarum observanciarum transgressiones, et hiis similia fugientes, carnem vestram cum viciis et concupicienciis crucifigatis. Aliqua vero inter vos reprehensione digna vobis scribimus corrigenda; videlicet quod nulla vestrum pro se vestienda aut calcianda possessionem aut redditum in manu sua teneat, eciam cum licencia Priorisse, quamvis hujusmodi possessio vel redditus, pro eo quod bona vestri Cenobii ad id non sufficiunt, vestrum alicui a parentibus vel amicis datus existat; set vestre Priorisse integraliter restituatur, ut exinde illis quibus illa liberalitas fuit facta secundum suas indigencias subministret; alioquin in proprietatem et secularem sollicitudinem donatarie tales facile possent incidere, votum suum temere violando. Preterea quod nulla secularis domicella nubilis etatis inter vos aliquatenus commoretur, quantumcumque amicorum vestrorum aut potentium instancia super hoc sollicitet vestram quietem; et vobis fit hec inhibicio propter multa incomoda que ex hoc vobis acciderent, ut superius est expressum. Obsequiales vestros castos habeatis et mundos, ne eorum conversacio vobis prebeat malum exemplum. Nulla ex vobis ultra annum maneat professa. Item deinceps eligatis vobis confessores de commorantibus in nostra diocesi; videlicet de fratribus Minoribus Conventus Herefordie, aut aliis religiosis vel secularibus viris competentis litterature, boneque conversacionis et vite, in dicta diocesi, ut consuevistis. Aliquos ad ministrandum vobis sacramentum penitencie, preterquam de nostra speciali licencia,[1] . . . Dictas vero correcciones faciatis amodo firmiter observari, sicut evitare vultis canonicam ulcionem. Hanc quidem nostram epistolam per vestros penitenciarios pluries in anno, in lingua Gallica vel Anglica, quam melius noveritis, procuretis vobis exponi, secundum ejus doctrinam viventes. In hujus mortalitatis festivo decursu vestri laboris fructum in eterna beatitudine capiatis! Angelus magni consilii in hiis vobis semper assistat! Datum[2] . . . .

Mar. 15.—*Collation of Nicholas of Oxford, deacon, presented by the Abbot and Convent of Wigmore to the Vicarage of Hughley. Mandate of induction sent to the Dean of Stottesdon.*

Fol. 57b. COLLACIO VICARII DE HUGEFELDE.—Memorandum quod Idibus Marcii apud Bosebury, anno Domini M°CC°LXX° octavo, contulit

1—Some words are lost, as a scrap has been torn away.   2.—No date or place is given.

domino Nicholao de Oxonia, diacono, vicariam ecclesie de Hugefeld, ad presentacionem dominorum Abbatis et Conventus de Wygemore, verorum patronorum ipsius, intuitu caritatis. Et eisdem die, loco, et anno Decano de Stottesdone litteratorie extitit demandatum quod dictum Nicholaum poneret, etc. Dictus autem Nicholaus tunc litteram institucionis non habuit.

Mar. 20.—Roger de Thonglonde, presented by Roger de Bradley, is instituted by letter to the chapelry of Thonglonde. Mandate of induction sent to the Dean of Wenlock.

INSTITUCIO RECTORIS DE THONGLONDE.—Item memorandum quod xiij Kalendas Aprilis, anno prescripto, fuit dominus Rogerus de Thonglonde,[1] capellanus, in ecclesia de Thonglonde litteratorie institutus, ad presentacionem domini Rogeri de Bradeleye, veri ipsius patroni. Et tunc in ea corporaliter fuit inductus per Decanum de Wenloke, prout habuit in mandatis.

Dec. 13, 1277.—Bull of Pope Nicholas III. directing inquiry to be made respecting alleged dispensations for plurality of benefices granted by preceding Popes to Geoffrey de Aspale, Chancellor of the Queen, which were lost during disturbances in London.

BULLA MAGISTRI G[ALFRIDI] DE HASPALE.—Nicholaus Episcopus, Servus servorum Dei, Venerabili fratri, Thome, Episcopo Herefordensi, et dilectis filiis Priori Predicatorum ac Ministro Minorum Fratrum Ordinum, Provincialibus Anglie, salutem, etc. Quia nobis dilectus filius, magister Galfridus de Aspale,[2] clericus, Cancellarius karissime in Christo Filie nostre, Alianore, Regine Anglie illustris, peticione monstravit quod felicis recordacionis Innocencius Quartus cum eodem magistro quod, preter duo beneficia Ecclesiastica curam animarum habencia que tunc optinebat, primo, et postmodum pie memorie Alexander Quartus, predecessores nostri, Romani Pontifices, quod beneficia Ecclesiastica, similem curam habencia, eciam si eorum aliqua personatus vel dignitates existerent, quorum proventus certum annuum valorem attingerent, si ei canonice offerentur, libere percipere ac licite retinere valeret, per suas sub certa forma litteras dispensarunt. Verum quia dicte littere, que in quadam domo Civitatis Londoniarum reposite, ac tempore generalis tur-

1.—Thonglonde (Thungelonde in the Taxatio, Thonglonde in the None) was a chapelry of Munslow, then in the Deanery of Wenlock.
2.—The King prohibited the Bishop of Chichester, July 1, 1281, from requiring residence on his benefice of Geoffrey de Aspale, "our beloved clerk." Rymer, Fœdera.

bacionis Regni Anglie casualiter amisse fuisse dicuntur, idem magister dubitat ne super hujusmodi beneficiorum retencione possit sibi obstaculum interponi. Quare nobis humiliter supplicavit ut providere sibi super hoc, de benignitate Sedis Apostolice, curaremus. Nos itaque industriam vestram ad hoc ex nostro officio eligentes, discrecioni vestre per Apostolica scripta mandamus quatinus, vocatis qui fuerint evocandi, de tenoribus litterarum ipsarum et earum amissione, per vos ipsos et non per alios, diligencius inquiratis si de tenoribus et amissione hujusmodi ac litteras ipsas vicio falsitatis carere legitime vobis constiterit; super quibus consciencias vestras volumus onerare. Tenores ipsos in auctentica faciatis redigi documenta, eandem vim et auctoritatem cum originalibus habitura. Datum Rome apud Sanctum Petrum, Idibus Decembris, Pontificatus nostri anno primo.

Apr. 21, 1279.—Authority given to the Bishop of Lausanne to collate Richard de Swinfield to the prebend held by Martin de Gaye, in the event of his death before Michaelmas.

EPISCOPO LAUSANENSI.—Domino Lausanensi Episcopo[1] salutem, etc. Quoniam intelleximus quod magister Martinus de Gayo, Canonicus Herefordensis, in vestris partibus graviter infirmatur, adeo quod de ejus convalescencia non speratur, nolentes Ecclesie Herefordensi cui presumus nostro posse aliquod prejudicium iminere, vestre Paternitatis caritati, de cujus bonitate confidimus, potestatem concedimus per presentes, ut prebendam prefati magistri Martini, cum eam vacare contigerit, magistro Ricardo de Suynefeud, viro moribus et sciencia multipliciter insignito, nostro nomine conferatis, presentibus usque ad Festum Beati Michaelis futurum proximo valituris. Quid autem feceritis in premissis nos reddatis, si placet, per vestras litteras cerciores. Datum Londoniis, xi Kalendas Maii, anno Domini M°CC°LXX° nono.

Mar. 9.—Letters dimissory from the Bishop of Worcester for Richard de Acton to be ordained deacon by the Bishop of Hereford.

DIMISSORIE RICARDI DE ACTONE.—G[odefridus], permissione divina Episcopus Wygorniensis, dilecto filio Ricardo de Actone, subdiacono, nostre diocesis, salutem, etc. Ut a Venerabili Patre,

---

1—William de Chaumpvent, Dean ot St. Martin-le-Grand in London, was made Bishop of Lausanne in 1274. (Patent Rolls).

Domino Herefordensi Episcopo, ad Ordinem diaconatus licite valeas promoveri, etc. Datum apud Hertlebury, vij Idus Marcii, Consecracionis nostre anno undecimo.

May 7.—Memorandum that a letter patent respecting the transfer of the wardship and marriage of the heir of [Robert] of Earley was entrusted to Maurice de Membury.

MAURICIUS DE MEMBYRY.—Memorandum quod septimo die Maii, apud Totenhale, tradita fuit Mauricio de Membury, iter arripienti versus partes suas, littera Domini Regis patens de vendicione et concessione custodie et maritagii terre et heredis de Arleye.

Apr. 25.—Sale of the rights of wardship and marriage of the heir of Robert de Walissnede to his widow Alice.

CONCESSIO CUJUSDAM MARITAGII.—Omnibus Christi fidelibus, etc., Thomas, etc., salutem, etc. Noverit universitas vestra nos vendidisse et concessisse Alicie, que fuit uxor Roberti de Walissnede, pro quadam pecunie summa, maritagium Roberti, filii et heredis predicti Roberti, simul cum custodia omnium terrarum et tenementorum que prefatus Robertus de nobis tenuit in villa de Walissnede, usque ad legitimam etatem predicti Roberti, cum omnibus pertinenciis et excahetis ad dictam custodiam pertinentibus. Et si de ipso Roberto antequam ad plenam etatem perveniat humanitus contigerit, volumus et concedimus pro nobis et successoribus nostris, quod predicta Alicia vel ejus assignati habeant custodiam predictam, et maritagium Helye, fratris predicti Roberti, usque ad legitimam etatem ejusdem; habendum et tenendum, etc. In cujus rei, etc. Datum apud Westmonasterium, die Sancti Marci Evangeliste, Pontificatus nostri anno quarto.

Apr. 26.—Mandate to the Official to induct William de Bray, or his Proctor, to the Church of Hopton Wafers.

HOPETONE WAFRE. VIDEATUR SUPER HOC IN ij° FOLIO PRECEDENTI.—Thomas, etc., Officiali suo salutem, etc. Mandamus vobis quatinus Willelmum de Bray, clericum, per magistrum Rogerum de Ludelawe vel alium Procuratorem suum in corporalem possessionem ecclesie de Hopton Wafre, ad presentacionem religiosorum virorum Abbatis et Conventus de Wygemore, patronorum verorum ipsius, nomine custodie inducatis, et defendatis inductum ; ipsum Willelmum et suos de fructibus ecclesie memorate libere administrare amodo permittentes. Valeatis. Datum Londoniis, vj Kalendas Maii, Consecracionis nostre anno quarto.

Apr. 29.— Institution of Hugh de Chalbenore to the Church of Kington, on the presentation of the Abbot and Convent of Tyrone after composition between them and the Earl of Hereford. Mandate of induction.

KYNGTONE.—Thomas, etc., Hugoni de Chalbenore, diacono, salutem, etc. Ad ecclesiam de Kyngtone, ad presentacionem religiosorum virorum, Abbatis et Conventus de Tyron,[1] habita composicione inter eos et Dominum Comitem Herefordie et Essexie in Curia Domini Regis, te caritative admittimus, et rectorem canonice instituimus in eadem, secundum formam Constitucionis, etc. In cujus rei, etc. Datum apud Londonias, iij Kalendas Maii, anno Domini M°CC°LXX° nono.

PRO EADEM.—Officiali suo salutem, etc. Quoniam Hugonem de Chalbenore, diaconum, ad ecclesiam de Kyngtone admisimus, etc., vobis mandamus quatinus dictum H[ugonem] in corporalem possessionem, etc. Datum ut proximo supra.

Nov. 1248.— Letter of Pope Innocent IV. denouncing excommunication on any who laid violent hands on the Abbot and monks of Flaxley (also called Dene) or extorted tithes from them, and providing for the absolution of various classes of offenders.

LITTERA PROTECCIONIS DOMUS DE FLAXLEYA.—Innocencius Episcopus, Servus servorum Dei, Venerabilibus Fratribus, Cantuariensi Episcopo et Suffraganeis ejus, et dilectis filiis, Abbatibus, Prioribus, Decanis, Archidiaconis, et aliis ecclesiarum Prelatis in Cantuariensi Provincia constitutis, salutem, etc. Non absque dolore cordis et plurima turbacione didicimus quod ita in plerisque partibus ecclesiastica censura dissolvitur et canonice sentencie severitas enervatur, ut viri religiosi, et hii maxime qui per Sedis Apostolice privilegia majori donati sunt libertate, passim a malefactoribus suis injurias sustinent et rapinas, dum vix invenitur qui congrua illis proteccione subveniat, et pro fovenda pauperum in-

---

1—At the date of the Taxatio of Pope Nicholas IV Kington paid a pension to Titley, a cell of the Abbey of Tyrone, which had the advowson. It passed soon after to St Mary of Llanthony, which was allowed to appropriate it on the condition of the payment of half a mark for the choristers of Hereford Cathedral. (Charter in the Archives of D. & C.)

nocencia se murum defensionis opponat; specialiter cum dilecti filii, Abbas et fratres de Dena, Cisterciensis Ordinis, tam de frequentibus injuriis quam de ipso cotidiano defectu justicie conquerentes, universitatem vestram litteris petierunt excitari, ut ita videlicet eis in tribulacionibus suis contra malefactores suos prompta debeatis magnanimitate consurgere, quod ab angustiis quas sustinent et pressuris vestro possint presidio respirare. Ideoque universitati vestre per Apostolica scripta mandamus atque precipimus quatinus illos qui possessiones vel res, seu domos predictorum fratrum vel hominum suorum irreverenter invaserint, aut ea injuste detinuerint que predictis fratribus ex testamento decedencium relinquantur, seu in fratres ipsos, contra Apostolice Sedis indulta, sentenciam excommunicacionis aut interdicti presumpserint promulgare, vel decimas laborum seu nutrimentorum ipsorum, spretis Apostolice Sedis privilegiis. extorquere; monicione premissa, si laici fuerint, puplice candelis accensis excommunicacionis sentencia percellatis; si vero clerici vel canonici regulares seu monachi fuerint, eos appellacione remota ab officio et beneficio suspendatis, donec predictis fratribus plenarie satisfaciant; et tam laici quam clerici seculares, qui pro violenta manuum injeccione anathematis vinculo fuerint innodati, cum diocesani Episcopi litteris ad Sedem Apostolicam venientes, ab eodem vinculo mereantur absolvi. De monachis vero et canonicis id servetur, ut, si ejusdem claustri fratres manus in se injecerint violentas, per Abbatem proprium; si vero unius claustri frater in fratrem alterius claustri presumpserit violenciam exercere, per injuriam passi et inferentis Abbates absolucionis beneficium assequatur, eciam si eorum aliqui priusquam habitum perciperent regularem tale aliquid commiserint propter quod ipso actu excommunicacionis sentenciam incurrissent, nisi excessus eorum esset difficilis et enormis, utpote ad mutilacionem membri vel sanguinis effusionem processum au[t] [manu] violenta in Episcopum vel Abbatem injecta . . . . . .[1] cum processus hiis similes sine scandalo nequeant preteriri. Si vero in clericos seculares manus injecerint pro vitando periculo, mittantur ad Sedem Apostolicam absolvendi, villas autem in quibus bona fratrum predictorum vel hominum suorum per violenciam detenta fuerint, quamdiu ibi sunt, interdicti sentencie supponatis. Datum Anagnie, . . .[1] Novembris, Pontificatus nostri anno sexto.

1—There are here omissions in the MS.

Apr. 29.—Institution of John of Bristol, subdeacon, to the Church of Stoke Lacy, on the presentation of the Abbot and Convent of St. Peter's, Gloucester. Mandate of induction. The Chancellor and Adam de Fileby, as guardians of the portionists of Bromyard, objected that he ought to be presented to them first, but withdrew their protest.

Fol. 58b. STOKE LACY.—Thomas, etc., domino Johanni de Bristollia, subdiacono, salutem, etc. Ad ecclesiam de Stoke Lacy, ad presentacionem religiosorum virorum, dominorum Abbatis et Conventus Sancti Petri Gloucestrie, verorum patronorum ipsius, te caritative admittimus, et rectorem canonice instituimus in eadem. In cujus rei, etc. Datum Londoniis, iij Kalendas Maii, anno Domini, etc., LXX° nono. Eisdem die, loco, et anno, mandatum fuit Officiali, etc. Et memorandum quod E[mericus], Cancellarius Herefordensis, et magister Adam de Fileby, custodes porcionariorum de Bromyarde, primo se admissioni dicti domini J[ohannis] opposuerunt, asserentes presentatum sibi primo, racione dicte custodie, presentari debere, et deinde per ipsos Episcopo; set postmodum de hac assercione destiterunt omnino.

Apr. 25.—Two letters, under the seals of Master Ardicio and Friar John of Darlington, chief collectors of the tenth, were handed to the Seneschal, one of which, duly witnessed, was to be given to the collectors in the diocese of Worcester, to the effect that they should make no demand on the Bishop for his manor of Prestbury; the second to the collectors in the diocese of Hereford, that they should tax the See for the last two years of Bishop John.

MEMORANDUM DE LITTERIS PRO DECIMA.—Item memorandum quod vij Kalendas Maii, apud Totenhale, tradite fuerunt due littere, ambe sigillis magistri Ardichionis[1] et fratris J[ohannis] de Derlintone,[2] principalium collectorum decime, consignate, magistro J. de Bradeham; ita quod unam adjunctis testibus faceret tradi collectoribus dicte decime in Wygorniensi diocesi deputatis, que illos inhibebat ne decimam deinceps exigerent ab Episcopo Herefordensi pro manerio suo de Prestbury in Episcopatu Wygorniensi existente; et quod aliam traderet collectoribus dyocesis Herefordensis pro ipso Episcopatu taxando de ultimo biennio quo Episcopus Johannes fuit superstes.

1—Afterwards named as Ardicio de Comite, *primicerius* of Milan; he was a Papal Chaplain, and afterwards Bishop of Modena, and often mentioned in Papal Reg. I.
2—John of Darlington, a Friar Preacher, was made Archbishop of Dublin by Papal provision, the elect of the chapter being rejected, as holding more benefices than his dispensations warranted. Papal Reg. ii 457.

Memorandum that the sequestration on the Church of Ludlow is released till August.

RELAXACIO SEQUESTRI.—Memorandum quod sequestrum ecclesie de Ludelawe est relaxatum usque ad Festum Beatri Petri ad vincula.

May 4.—Licence of non-residence to study for one year from Michaelmas granted to Thomas Cantoke, Rector of the Church of Ballingham. Similar licence granted to the Rector of Beckbury.

LICENCIA STUDENDI.—Thomas, etc., domino Thome Cantoke, Rectori ecclesie Sancti Dubricii, salutem, etc. Tuis precibus inclinati ut scolasticis disciplinis a Festo Beati Michaelis, anno gracie M°CC° septuagesimo nono, vacare possis per annum continuum, etc., tibi damus licenciam per presentes. In cujus rei, etc. Datum in crastino Invencionis Sancte Crucis, anno superius annotato. Hujusmodi licenciam habet Rector de Bekkebury.

May 4.—John de Beccles, deputed by Adam de Fileby, is instructed to watch over the Bishop's interests in the actions at Rome moved by Peter de Langon and the Bishop of St. Asaph, and to report the proceedings in full, as also his own terms. He is also to deal promptly with the petitions drawn up by Adam against John de Aquablanca and Emeric, Chancellor of Hereford.

JOHANNI DE BEKKLES.—Thomas, etc., dilecto sibi in Christo clerico, Johanni de Bekles salutem, etc. Ex relatu magistri Ade de Fileby, Canonici Herefordensis, accepimus quod causam nostram quam habemus contra Petrum de Langone in Romana Curia super prebenda de Prestone plene instructam, vobis idem magister commiserit defendendam. Quocirca vestram prudenciam, de qua multum confidimus, attente rogamus quatinus ipsam causam usque ad Festum Beati Michaelis, secundum informacionem vobis traditam ab eodem magistro, ac omnia alia negocia nos qualitercumque ibidem tangencia, defendere ac promovere sollicite studeatis, opemque et operam Procuratoribus nostris in audiencia ad resistendum et contradicendum quibuscumque impetracionibus adversariorum nostrorum, et maxime Episcopi Assavensis et suorum fautorum, quorum maliciam plurimum formidamus contra nos impendere, toto nisu; et pro labore vestro vobis satisfaciemus secundum arbitrium magistri Ade prefati, vel in Anglia cum ad eam veneritis, vel in Curia prelibata. Et quid de premissis egeritis, necnon et de omnibus aliis emergentibus in Curia que videritis nobis scribenda, nobis per vestras litteras sepius faciatis constare. Describatis eciam nobis quamcito poteritis, si possitis usque ad annum intendere nostris negociis in Curia, et pro quanto. Insuper peticiones quas predictus magister Adam formari fecit contra Johannem de Aqua Blanca et Emericum, Cancellarium Herefordensem, ante recessum suum, ac tradidit magistro E[dmundo] de Warefelde, Procuratori nostro, faciatis cum ea celeritate qua poterit expediri, et ipsas peticiones invenietis penes Johannem, substitutum ipsius magistri E[dmundi]. Datum Londoniis, iiij die Maii, anno Domini M°CC° septuagesimo nono.

May 1.—Mandate to the Official to release the sequestration on the Church of Newland.

RELAXACIO SEQUESTRI NOVE TERRE.—Officiali suo graciam, etc. Sequestrum interpositum in fructibus ecclesie Nove Terre, nos et officium nostrum ex quibuscumque causis tangentibus, relaxetis; sustinentes Rectorem ipsius in dictis fructibus liberam administracionem habere. Datum apud Totenhale, primo die Maii, anno Domini M°CC° septuagesimo nono.

May 14.—Appointment of Edmund de Warefield and John de Barton as Proctors in the Roman Court.

PROCURATORIUM E[DMUNDI] DE WAREFELD ET J[OHANNIS] DE BERTONE.—Omnibus presentem litteram audituris notum existat quod nos, Thomas, Herefordensis Episcopus, ad impetrandum pro nobis litteras gracie et communis justicie; necnon ad contradicendum hujusmodi litteris contra nos per nostros adversarios impetrandis pariter, et ad consenciendum in Judices et in loca; dilectos nobis in Christo, magistrum Edmundum de Warefelde et Johannem de Bartone, nostros in Romana Curia sub alternacione facimus Procuratores; ratum habituri, etc. In cujus rei, etc. Datum Londoniis, iiij die Maii, anno predicto.

May 4.—Mandate to the Hebdomadary to induct Richard de Swinfield to the prebend which Martin de Gaye had vacated by death.

COLLACIO PREBENDE QUE FUIT M[ARTINI] DE GAYO.—Thomas, etc., domino . . . Ebdomodario in eadem, salutem, etc. Cum prebendam quam nuper tenuit magister Martinus de Gayo in Ecclesia nostra predicta, que vacavit per mortem ipsius magistri, magistro Ricardo de Swynefeld contulerimus intuitu caritatis, vobis mandamus quod eundem magistrum Ricardum, vel suum Procuratorem nomine ipsius, in dictam prebendam, cum omnibus suis pertinenciis, inducatis, stallum in Choro et locum in Capitulo, prout moris est, assignantes eidem. Valeatis. Datum apud Shyreburne, ij Idus Maii, Consecracionis nostre anno quarto.

May 27.—Sir Malcolm, Canon of Wells, was inducted to the Church of Chetton on the presentation of Hugh Burnell. Letters of institution to be given at the next interview with the Bishop.

MALCOLONUS.—vj Kalendas Junii, anno Domini M°CC°LXX° nono, apud Ledebury, fuit dominus Malcolonus, Canonicus Wellensis, inductus in corporalem possessionem ecclesie de Chetintone, ad presentacionem domini Hugonis Burnel, militis, veri patroni; et tunc dominus decrevit quod in proximo colloquio suo adinvicem idem dominus M[alcolonus] institueretur litteratorie in ecclesiam antedictam.

June 27.—A writ, ordering postponement in the collection of scutage, was given to W. de Redmarley, to be handed to the Sheriff of Hereford in case he should distrain for the same. The writ was not transcribed.

PRO RESPECTU SCUTAGII.—Memorandum quod die Martis proximo post Nativitatem Beati Johannis Baptiste, apud Arleye, traditum fuit domino W. de Rudmerleye quoddam breve Domini Regis, Vicecomiti Herefordie per ipsum tradendum, de respectu scutagii habendo. Tamen ipsum breve dicto Vicecomiti non deberet tradi nisi ipse faceret districcionem pro scutagio memorato; cujus brevis transcriptum tunc nullatenus habebatur.

June 27.—A writ from the Justices in Eyre coming for pleas of the Forest into Gloucestershire, on account of trespass in the Forest of Dean, was deposited in the Bishop's coffer. No copy was made.

PRO TRANSGRESSIONE FACTA IN FORESTA DE DENE.—Item dicto die habebatur in coffero Domini quoddam breve regium Justiciariis Domini Regis de foresta proximo Itineraturis in Comitatu Gloucestrie tradendum, pro transgressione facta in foresta de Dene; cujus similiter non habebatur transcriptum.

Aug. 4.—Luke de Bree, the treasurer, is commissioned to audit the accounts of the executors of Richard of Hereford, with coercive powers.

CONTRA EXECUTORES R[ICARDI] DE HEREFORDE.—Thomas, etc., magistro Luce [de Bre], Thesaurario Herefordensi, salutem, etc. Ad exigendum et audiendum compotum seu racionem administracionis executorum domini Ricardi, dicti de Hereforde, defuncti, et in eventum ejusdem compoti bene seu male redditi ad absolvendum seu puniendum executores prefatos, vobis committimus vices nostras, cum cohercionis canonice potestate. Datum apud Haseleye, iiij die Augusti, anno Consecracionis nostre quarto.

July 30.— Licence of non-residence to study granted for one year to Symon, Rector of Bitterley and of Rushbury.

LICENCIA RECTORIS DE BUTERLE STUDIENDI.—Item memorandum quod dominus Symon, de Buterleye et Russebury ecclesiarum Rector, habet licenciam standi in scolis per unum annum integrum, a Festo Sancti Michaelis, anno Domini M°CC°LXX° nono, in forma communi. Et fuit data ipsius littere iij Kalendas Augusti, anno Consecracionis nostre quarto.

July 29.—The Prior and Canons of Wormsley are allowed to appropriate the Church of Lyonshall, of which they had the advowson, because of their piety, hospitality, and charity; the rights of the See and the Cathedral Church being reserved.

APPROPRIACIO ECCLESIE DE LENHALES ECCLESIE DE WORMLEYA.—Thomas, etc., viris religiosis, Priori Sancti Leonardi de Wormeleye ac Canonicis loci ejusdem, salutem, etc. Si officii nostri debitum id requirat ut ad opera pietatis et elemosinarum largicionem pauperibus faciendam fideles quoslibet invitemus, quanto magis tenemur nos ipsi efficaciter facere supradicta, super quibus faciendis alios informamus ; hinc est quod, cum adeo manifeste paupertatis onere sitis oppressi quod necessitates plurimas paciamini et defectus, considerata sanctitate religionis vestre

---

1—"To the Justices in Eyre for pleas of the Forest in the County of Gloucester. Order not to aggrieve Thomas, Bishop of Hereford, for trespassing in the Forest of Dean in taking two wild boars and a wild swine without the King's licence, as the King has pardoned him." Close Rolls, April 28, 1279.

probate, ex eo quod hospitalitatem sectantes pauperes ac debiles devote suscipitis, et eisdem impenditis solacia caritatis, Deo ac ecclesie vestre predicte, vobis et successoribus vestris, ecclesiam de Lenhale, nostre diocesis, cujus estis veri patroni, in usus proprios possidendam inperpetuum donamus, conferimus, et assignamus, et insuper auctoritate pontificali tenore presencium confirmamus; salvis nobis et successoribus nostris, ac Ecclesie Herefordensi, que ab antiquo percipere consuevimus in eadem, cum aliis omnibus oneribus ad que ecclesia predicta tenetur; reservata eciam nobis ordinacione vicarie in ecclesia memorata. In cujus rei, etc. Datum Herefordie, iiij Kalendas Augusti, anno Domini M°CC°LXX° nono.

July 6.—Memorandum of a debt of £102 6s. 6d. to William Daubeny and John de Clare, executors of Hugh de Cantilupe, Archdeacon of Gloucester, to be repaid at Christmas, 1280; also of a debt of one hundred marks to Peter of Chester to be repaid at Boston fair on July 8, 1280. The copies of the acknowledgments are strung on a file attached to the Register.

MEMORANDUM DE DUABUS OBLIGACIONIBUS DOMINI.—Memorandum quod Dominus tenetur domino Willelmo de Albaniaco et Johanni de Clare, et aliis executoribus testamenti bone memorie Hugonis de Cantilupo[1], quondam Archidiaconi Gloucestrie, in centum duabus libris, sex solidis, et sex denariis sterlingorum, eisdem, seu eorundem uni, vel suo certo nuncio, ad Novum Templum Londoniarum, ad Nativitatem Domini M°CC° octogesimo, sine dilacione ulteriori solvendis. Item Dominus tenetur domino Petro de Cestria[2] in centum marcis sterlingorum ipsi vel suo certo nuncio, solvendis in nundinis Sancti Botulfi, ad quindenam Nativitatis Sancti Johannis Baptiste, anno Domini M°CC° octogesimo. Et ad hec duo predicta debita, ut predictum est, solvenda dominus se per duas litteras obligavit. Et ipsarum litterarum data fuit apud Arleye, in Octabis Apostolorum Petri et Pauli; quarum quoque transcripta cuidam filacio istud registrum sequenti attachiata fuerunt.

Master Bardus of Poggibonzi is thanked for his services as Proctor in the suit with Peter de Langon, which would otherwise have been in a critical state. John de Bitterley is sent, not to take his place, but to push matters on. Money will be remitted speedily.

BARDO DE PODIO BONISII.—Thomas, etc., dilecto Procuratori suo in Romana Curia, necnon et amico speciali, magistro Bardo

1—Hugh de Cantilupe, the brother of the Bishop, and fellow student at Paris.
2—Peter de Cestria is entered as prebendary of Huntington in the Taxatio of 1291.

de Podio Bonisii, salutem, etc. Cura vestra sollicita laborum et diligencia circumspecta, que in nostris et nostrorum negociis [h]actenus impendistis, nos forcius obligant et inducunt ut vobis, unacum competenti remuneracione laboris, teneamur ad gracias speciales. Quippe satis experimento didicimus quod causa quam nos et nostri contra P[etrum] de Langone hactenus habuimus et habemus in casu caduco[1], iminente nostrorum negligencia, pluries exstitisset, nisi vestro fuisset laudabili presidio relevata. Nec tedeat vos quod per magistrum Johannem de Buterleye, presencium portitorem, denarios vobis non transmittimus, quia de hiis in proximo recipiendis competens remedium faciemus apponi. Dictum autem magistrum Johannem ad vos et ceteros amicos nostros in Curia mittimus, non ut vestrum procuratorium in aliquo revocemus, set ut vos et alios amicos nostros qui in variis negociis fueritis implicati stimulare possit et excitare ad nostrum negocium viriliter expediendum; priori vestro procuratorio in suis viribus remanente.

Matthew, Cardinal of St. Mary's in Porticu, is assured that the action taken with regard to the Bishop of St. Asaph and John de Aquablanca is due to zeal for the interests of the Church, not to personal antipathies.

DOMINO MATHEO RUFO, CARDINALI.—Venerabili in Christo Patri et Domino, Domino Matheo,[2] Dei gracia Sancte Marie in Porticu Diacono Cardinali, Thomas, etc., seipsum ad vota devotum, cum debitis reverencia, obediencia, et honore. Tanto calliditatis studio sese prosecuntur adinvicem litigantes, ut alter in alterius prejudicium, modo varia, modo non vera, sepius suggerendo, modo injuriosa insontibus impingendo, calcato justicie cultu, alter faciat quicquid possit. Hinc est, Pater reverende, quod, cum Venerabilis Pater Dominus [Anianus], Assavensis Episcopus, et Johannes de Aqua Blanca, qui se dicit Decanum Herefordensem, pro quo vestras litteras nuper recepi, meos se fecerint adversarios, non admiror si queque vobis suggerant, eciam tacita veritate, quibus estimari[n]t sua negocia prosperari. Ego tamen vester ab antiquo, de dominacione vestra et prudencia circumspecta sic confido ut adversancium dictis in mei prejudicium et fame mee lesionem fidem vobis adhibere non placeat, donec vobis legitime constiterit me erga eos, vel eorum alterum, quod absit, injuriam commisisse. Qualiter autem dictum Decanatum contuli, formam seu modum collacionis, si vobis

1—In MS. *caduci.*   2—Matthew de Ursinis, v. Papal Reg. I. 451.

placuerit, lator presencium vestre amicicie poterit intimare; aliique nuncii, quos in brevi ad Curiam propono transmittere, Domino concedente, unacum eo de quo alias vobis scripsi per Matheum, puerum vestrum, tocius facti et juris vobis expriment veritatem, per quam luculenter apparebit quod nec odium nec invidia nec accepcio persone cujusque, set zelus et amor Ecclesie mee, et jurium ejusdem conservacio, me ad prefatum collacionem induxit.

Aug. 13.—Authority given to John de Bitterley to act as Proctor in the Court of Rome, not to be used except in case of urgent need.

PROCURATORIUM J[OHANNIS] DE BUTERLEYE.—Universis Christi fidelibus, etc., Thomas, etc., salutem, etc. Ad impetrandum tam litteras gracie quam communis justicie, necnon ad contradicendum, etc., dilectum nobis in Christo magistrum Johannem de Buterleye in Romana Curia nostrum facimus Procuratorem, etc. Datum Londoniis, Idibus Augusti, anno gracie M°CC°LXX° nono. Et injunctum est dicto magistro J[ohanni] quod suo procuratorio non utatur alio procuratorio revocando, nisi aliqua necessitate urgente.

June 25.—Writ to Walter Hopton directing him to hold inquiry at Abergavenny as to whether the corn and stock at the Castle, worth £77 4s. 4½d., were handed over to Peter de Montfort in 1260 in the name of Bishop John.

LITTERA REGIS DE BERKEVENY.—Edwardus, Dei gracia, etc., dilecto et fideli suo Waltero de Hoptone salutem. Sciatis quod assignavimus vos ad inquirendum, unacum hiis quos vobis duxerimus associatos, per sacramentum proborum et legalium [hominum] de Berkeveny et de visneto ejusdem, etc., qui nulla affinitate attingant executores testamenti Johannis Britonis, quondam Episcopi Herefordensis, et magistrum Thomam de Cantilupo, nunc Episcopum loci illius, vel Petrum de Monte Forti, filium et heredem Petri de Monte Forti; et si predictus Johannes liberavit, xj die Aprilis, anno regni Domini Henrici Regis, patris nostri, xliiij, predicto Petro, patri predicti Petri, blada et instaurum in Castro et in manerio de Berkeveny, precii lxxvij libr. iiij s. et iiij d. et ob., ut predicti executores et magister Thomas dicunt; vel si dictus Johannes prefata blada et instaurum eidem Petro non liberavit; et si idem Petrus blada illa et instaurum non habuit, aut recepit per predictum Johannem aut per alium, nec eciam ad manus suas aliquo alio modo devenerunt, ut predictus Petrus, filius et heres ejusdem Petri dicit; quia tam idem Petrus quam prefati executores et magister Thomas, inter quos placitum est inde coram Baronibus de Scaccario nostro, posuerunt se inde in inquisicionem predictam; et ideo vobis mandamus quod ad certos diem et locum, quos ad hoc provideritis, inquisicionem illam capiatis. Mandavimus enim Constabulario nostro Castri predicti de Berkeveny quod, ad certos diem et locum, quos ei scire facietis, predictam inquisicionem coram vobis venire faciat. Et inquisicionem predictam distincte et aperte factam habeatis coram prefatis Baronibus apud Westmonasterium, a die Sancti Michaelis in xv dies, sub sigillo tuo et sigillis eorum per quos facta fuerit; et hoc breve. In cujus rei, etc. Teste R. de Northwode apud Westmonasterium, xxv die Junii, anno regni nostri septimo.

The above, with the letter to the Constable of Abergavenny, was sent to John de Clare, together with a letter to the Bishop's Seneschal to urge that the inquiry should be held at a time when he could be present, and before March 18, that the return might be made before Parliament met.

MEMORANDUM.—Prescripta littera, et eciam littera directa Constabulario de Berkeveny unde supra fit mencio, misse fuerunt de Totenhale domino J[ohanni] de Clare per R. de Castro, die Jovis proximo post Assumpcionem Beate Marie, unacum littera Domini Senescallo suo super hiis mittenda, ut simul per dictum dominum J[ohannem] dicto Senescallo transmitterentur. In dicta autem littera Senescallo continebatur quod instaret erga dominum Walterum de Hoptone, quod dicta inquisicio caperetur per ipsum diebus et locis quibus ipse Senescallus posset interesse, et hoc citra Festum Sancti Edwardi, ita quod posset per dominum Walterum de Rudmerle, vel Willelmum Grys, in parliamento post Festum Sancti Michaelis Londoniis, ad Scaccarium retornari.

Sept. 1.—Acknowledgment of a debt of eighty marks to be repaid to John de Clare at Christmas.

MEMORANDUM DE OBLIGACIONE DOMINI ERGA J[OHANNEM] DE CLARE.—Memorandum quod Dominus, per suas litteras obligatorias, Johanni de Clare, Rectori de Colewelle, tenetur in quater viginti marcis bonorum sterlingorum eidem Johanni, vel suo certo Procuratori, dictas litteras restituenti apud Novum Templum Londoniarum ad Natale Domini, anno ejusdem M°CC°LXX° nono, sine ulteriori dilacione solvendis. Et dicte littere obligatorie date erant Londoniis, Kalendis Septembris, anno Domini supradicto.

Sept. 1.—Alan de Creppinge is allowed to hold the farm of the Church of Blaisdon for three years on condition that one mark be given yearly to the poor of the parish.

DE ECCLESIA DE BLECHEDONE.—Item eisdem die, loco, et anno, concessit Dominus magistro Alano de Creppynge per litteram suam quod ecclesiam de Blechedone possit tenere ad firmam a Festo Sancti Michaelis, anno Domini M°CC°LXX° nono, per tres annos continue subsequentes ; proviso quod ecclesie bene deserviatur, etc., et quod, quolibet anno dum duraverit dicta firma, j marca per visum Officialis et presbiteri loci parochianis pauperibus erogetur.

Sept. 8.—Instructions to Walter de Redmarley and other auditors of the accouuts of the See to pay fifty marks to Roger de Kirkton on production of the Bishop's letter.

MEMORANDUM DE J LITTERA LIBERATA ROGERO DE KYRKETONE.— Thomas, etc., domino Waltero de Rudmarleye, et aliis auditoribus generalis compoti Episcopatus Herefordensis, salutem, etc. Liberate super compotum prefatum dilecto nobis in Christo, Rogero de Kyrketone, vel suo certo nuncio presentes litteras deferenti, quinquaginta marcas ; et qui vestrum ipsam pecuniam liberaverit retineat istas litteras pro warento. Valeatis. Datum Londoniis, octavo die Septembris, Consecracionis nostre anno quarto.

Sept. 8.—Mandate to Richard de Kimberley to give William de Nevile possession of the manor of Berkham, and hand over to him the enclosed bond, on receipt of the £11 16.

PRO WILLELMO DE NEVILE.—Thomas, etc., Ricardo de Kyneburleye salutem. Quia Willelmus de Nevile fecit nos securos de xj li. xvj. s., in Festo Omnium Sanctorum proximo futuro nobis apud Arleye solvendis, tibi mandamus quod manerium de Berkham, cum omnibus suis pertinenciis, et integre cum fructibus hujus anni, liberes nomine nostro eidem, scilicet a tempore compoti Prepositi redditi de manerio memorato. Mittimus eciam tibi litteram dicti

Willelmi obligatoriam de pecunia memorata; quam eidem restituas cum tibi solverit eandem pecuniam. Valeas. Datum Londoniis, octavo die Septembris, Consecracionis nostri anno quarto.

Sept. 6.—Letter to the Prior of Leominster, asking for hospitality for his valet, William de Nevile, during the Bishop's absence.

PRO EODEM W[ILLELMO] DE NEVILE.—Thomas, etc., domino Stephano, Priori Leominstrie, salutem, etc. Quoniam valletus noster, Willelmus de Nevile, negociari habet in partibus Herefordie, quem nolumus in alicujus servicio commorari dum a partibus illis aberimus quin in nostro reditu ad nostrum servicium sit paratus, vestram amiciciam requirimus et rogamus quatinus, quociens dictus Willelmus ad vos vel vestrum Prioratum contigerit declinare, eum exhibeatis, si placet, nostris precibus et amore; tantum facientes in hac parte, si placet, ut nos vobis pro eo teneamur ad grates et gracias speciales. Bene valeatis. Datum Londoniis, vj die Septembris, anno Consecracionis nostre quarto.

Sept. 8.—Bond of William de Nevile for the payment of £11 16s. on All Saints' Day. He names two sureties, and in case of default will submit unreservedly to the Bishop's ruling and to distraint by the Sheriff or others.

OBLIGACIO DICTI W[ILLELMI DE NEVILE].—Universis Christi fidelibus, etc., Willelmus de Nevile salutem in Domino. Noveritis me teneri Venerabili Patri in Christo, Domino Thome, Dei gracia Herefordensi Episcopo, domino meo, in undecim libris et sexdecim solidis bonorum et legalium sterlingorum ex causa mutui; quam quidem peccuniam dicto Domino Episcopo ad Arleye in Festo Omnium Sanctorum, anno Domini M°CC°LXX° nono, vel eciam suo certo nuncio restituenti hoc scriptum, persolvam fideliter, ulteriore dilacione rejecta; dampna et expensas que et quas dictus Dominus Episcopus, vel ejus nuncius, in hac parte fecerit et incurrerit, occasione predicte pecunie sibi dicto termino plenarie non solute, plene refundam eidem; super quibus credetur simplici dicto suo, absque juramento et alia probacione. Ad que omnia et singula supradicta firmiter et fideliter observanda obligo me et omnia bona mea habita et habenda, et maxime ea que in manerio meo de Berkham poterunt inveniri; subiciens me in hiis omnibus et singulis cohercioni et districcioni Vicecomitis Baroke [seu] eciam alterius

Judicis ecclesiastici vel secularis, quem idem Dominus Episcopus, aut nuncius suus, elegerit in hac parte, ut me ad simplicem denunciacionem per dictum Dominum Episcopum, aut ejus nuncium, sibi factam, per quamcunque censuram seu districcionem possit compellere ad plenariam solucionem tam dictorum dampnorum, et eciam expensarum, quam debiti principalis. Renuncio eciam in hiis omnibus et singulis, omni juris auxilio tam canonici quam civilis, Constitucioni de duabus dietis[1] edite in Concilio Generali, privilegio crucesingnatis indulto et eciam indulgendo, et maxime excepcioni[2] non numerate peccunie, ac omnibus litteris Apostolicis impetratis et impetrandis, Regie prohibicioni, et omnibus aliis que contra hoc scriptum aliqualiter poterunt obici vel apponi. Et ad majorem securitatem inveni fidejussores dominos Willelmum de Albiniaco et Johannem de Clare, qui se in hac parte, si necesse fuerit, debitores constituunt principales. In quorum omnium testimonium tam sigillum meum quam dictorum fidejussorum sigilla presenti scripto sunt appensa. Datum Londoniis, viij die Septembris, anno Domini supradicto.

Sept. 12.—Commission of sundry Visitations to the Official during the Bishop's absence in foreign parts.

MEMORANDUM DE VISITACIONIBUS TRADITIS DOMINO OFFICIALI.— Memorandum quod xij die Septembris, anno Domini M°CC°LXX° nono, apud Sevenhoke, Domino itinerante[3] versus partes transmarinas, tradite fuerunt magistro R[ogero], Officiali Herefordensi, Visitaciones ecclesiarum monialium de Lyngebroke, de Stoke Edith, de Aura, de Lydeneye, de Todeham, et de Wolastone. Et Officialis repromisit dictas Visitaciones cum earum abstractis Cancellario Domini in suo reditu restituere.

Sept. 5.—The Bishop pledges himself to hold the Chapter harmless as regards the two hundred marks deposited in their keeping by the Collectors of the Tenth for the Holy Land, of which he has now the sole charge.

OBLIGACIO DOMINI DE CC MARCIS ERGA CAPITULUM HEREFORDENSE DE DECIMA.—Noverint universi quod, cum venerabiles et discreti viri, frater Johannes de Derlintone, Dublinensis Electus

---

1—*Const. de duabus dietis :* ne quis ultra duas dietas extra suam diocesim per litteras Apostolicas ad judicium traki possit; 4th Lateran Council. ch. 37; Mansi xxii, 1023.
2—*Excepcioni,* legal plea.
3—The intended journey seems to have been relinquished, but no reasons are given.

et magister Ardicio, primicerius[1] Mediolanensis, collectores decime in subsidium Terre Sancte in regno Anglie a Sede Apostolica deputati, ducentas marcas sterlingorum penes nos, Thomam, Dei gracia Episcopum Herefordensem, et Ecclesie nostre Cathedralis Capitulum, de pecunia decime supradicte in civitate et diocesi Herefordensi collecta, nuper ad nostrum rogatum deposuissent, prout in littera super hoc confecta, sigillo nostro et Capituli nostri signata, plenius continetur; nos, predictus Thomas Episcopus, indempnitati Capituli nostri predicti provideri in quantum possumus affectantes, dictam pecunie summam in nostro deposito a dicto Capitulo nobis totaliter traditam esse fatemur, casumque fortuitum, et specialiter vis majoris, incendii, rapine, et furti predicti depositi, in nos de plano et expresse suscipimus; eidemque Capitulo nostro, bona fide et per legitimam stipulacionem, corporali prestito sacramento, plenam securitatem et omnimodam indempnitatem, quoad Sacrosanctam Sedem Apostolicam collectoresque supradictos, et quoscunque alios occasione predicti depositi, firmiter promittimus per presentes. Et ad hec omnia fideliter observanda obligamus nos, etc., predicto Capitulo nostro, quousque a dicto deposito per nos plenarie fuerit liberatum; obligamus insuper nos modo supradicto ad omnia dampna, sumptus, et expensas, que, quos, et quas dictum Capitulum incurret vel sustinuerit occasione predicti depositi, super quibus omnibus credetur simplici verbo Procuratoris dicti Capituli, sine alterius onere probacionis vel eciam juramenti. Renunciamus autem in hiis omni juris auxilio, etc. Datum apud Totenhale juxta Londonias, quinto die Septembris, anno Domini M°CC°LXX° nono.[2]

Sept. 5.—*Joint bond of the Bishop and Chapter for the repayment of the two hundred marks.*

OBLIGACIO DOMINI ET CAPITULI DE DICTIS CC MARCIS RECEPTIS IN DEPOSITO.—Universis, etc., Thomas, etc., et Capitulum Herefordense salutem, etc. Noverit vestra universitas quod nos, et uterque nostrum, voluntarie nos optulimus ad recipiendum, et recepimus, depositum ducentarum marcarum sterlingorum de pecunia decime a collectoribus ejusdem decime in civitate et diocesi Herefordensi specialiter deputatis; obligantes efficaciter nos, et nostrum alterum, in solidum, et omnia bona nostra, ad restitucionem seu

---

1—*Primicerius*, archpresbyter, a military term for the head of the leading file of the Roman legion.

2—This and the two following entries appear to have been cancelled. One is not printed, as being practically a repetition of the above.

solucionem dicti depositi plenarie faciendam Venerabili Patri in Christo, Domino Johanni, Dei gracia Electo Dublinensi, et magistro Ardicioni, Primicerio Mediolanensi, Domini Pape Capellano, collectoribus decime Terre Sancte in regno Anglie a Sede Apostolica constitutis, vel eorum alteri, aut alicui alii Sedis Apostolice ad hoc nuncio sufficienti, quandocunque depositum petitum fuerit, cum omnibus expensis et dampnis que occurrent exinde ; suscipientes eciam in nos periculum et casum vis majoris, etc. ; renunciantes insuper, etc. . . . Super premissis vero omnibus et singulis supponimus nos jurisdiccioni et potestati dictorum principalium collectorum et cujuslibet alterius nuncii sufficientis Sedis Apostolice ad hujusmodi depositum, cum expensis et dampnis, repetendum et efficaciter optinendum. In cujus, etc. Datum quinto die Septembris, anno supradicto.

Sept. 19.—Appointment of the Treasurer and Roger de Sevenake, Canon of Hereford, as his Proctors in all causes.

PROCURATORIUM MAGISTRORUM L[UCE] DE BRE ET R[OGERI] DE SEVENAKE IN OMNIBUS CAUSIS.—Pateat universis quod nos, Thomas, etc., in omnibus causis et negociis nos et Ecclesiam nostram Herefordensem qualitercumque tangentibus, dilectos nobis in Christo magistros Lucam, Thesaurarium, et Rogerum de Sevenake, Canonicum Herefordensis Ecclesie, nostros conjunctim et divisim facimus Procuratores, etc. Et pro eisdem et eorum altero, etc., judicatum solvi promittimus, sub ypotheca rerum nostrarum. Datum apud Eyhtham, xiij Kalendas Octobris, anno Domini supradicto.

Sept. 19.—Appointment of the Treasurer and the Precentor as his Vicars-General, with commission to procure the assistance of a Bishop for purely Episcopal functions.

COMMISSIO DOMINORUM PRECENTORIS ET THESAURARII.—Thomas, etc., magistris Willelmo de Monte Forti, Precentori, et Luce [de Bre], Thesaurario Ecclesie Herefordensis, salutem, etc. Ad faciendum et expediendum omnia, tam ad legem diocesanam quam jurisdiccionem pertinencia, que ad nos spectant racione Episcopalis dignitatis in Herefordensi civitate et diocesi, ita quod ea que de premissis per diocesanos solos Episcopos exercentur fieri procuretis per aliquem Episcopum Catholicum graciam Sedis Apostolice optinentem, vobis vices nostras ac immediatam et plenariam conferimus potestatem, cum canonica cohercione; constituentes vos sub alternacione nostros Vicarios in premissis; dantesque vobis, et vestrum alteri, specialem potestatem providendi de personis ydoneis dignitatibus, officiis, et aliis quibuscunque beneficiis ecclesiasticis ubicunque existentibus, et ad ordinacionem nostram conferendo seu presentando canonice devolutis. Volumus tamen quod exercicium premissorum resideat penes occupantem omnino. Datum apud Eyhtham, xiij Kalendas Octobris, anno Domini supradicto.

Sept. 19.—Commission of the Treasurer and Roger de Sevenake to represent the Bishop as his Proctors in all ecclesiastical assemblies.

Fol. 61b.

PROCURATORIUM MAGISTRORUM L[UCE] DE BRE ET R[OGERI] DE SEVENAKE AD COMPARENDUM IN CONGREGACIONIBUS, SYNNODIS, ETC.—Pateat universis quod nos, Thomas, etc., magistros Lucam, Thesaurarium, et Rogerum de Sevenake, Canonicum Herefordensis Ecclesie, ad comparendum pro nobis in omnibus Congregacionibus,[1] Sinnodis, et Conciliis Domini Archiepiscopi Cantuariensis et Suffraganeorum suorum, nostros conjunctim et divisim facimus Procuratores; dantes eisdem, et eorum alteri, specialem potestatem consenciendi et contradicendi, prout expedire viderint, vice nostra; ratum habituri, etc. Datum apud Eyhtham, xiij Kalendas Octobris, anno Domini M°CC°LXX° nono.

Sept. 19.—Mandate to the bailiffs and others to obey William de Montfort and Walter de Redmarley as guardians of the temporalities of the See.

DE CUSTODIA TEMPORALITATIS.—Thomas, etc., omnibus ballivis suis et ceteris fidelibus suis, libere tenentibus et aliis, salutem, etc. Cum custodiam omnium temporalium bonorum et negociorum nostrorum, ubicunque consistant, commiserimus magistro Willelmo de Monte Forti, Precentori, et domino Waltero de Rudmarleye, Canonico Herefordensis Ecclesie, et eos sub alternacione in premissis custodes immediatos et principales sub nobis fecerimus, vobis precipimus firmiter injungendo quatinus eisdem custodibus, et eorum alteri, in omnibus premissis et premissa contingentibus, sitis respondentes, intendentes, et obedientes totaliter tanquam nobis. Datum apud Eyhtham, xiij Kalendas Octobris, anno Consecracionis nostre quinto.

1—*Procuratorium ejusdem pro pannis recipiendis.* These words were here added on the margin, but do not refer to the text.

Sept. 19.—Special licence to Luke de Bree to profit by the farms of any churches which may be canonically in his keeping.

LITTERA MAGISTRI LUCE DE BRE DE FIRMIS RECIPIENDIS.—Thomas, etc., magistro L[uce de Bre], Thesaurario Herefordensi, salutem, etc. Ad recipiendum firmas ecclesiarum sitarum in nostra diocesi quas vobis canonice tradi contigerit, vobis damus licenciam licenciam specialem, ut de eisdem firmis vestrum comodum faciatis, dum tamen eedem ecclesie debitis non fraudenter obsequiis, etc. Datum apud Eyhtham, xiij Kalendas Octobris, anno Domini M°CC°LXX° nono.

Sept. 19.—Letters dimissory granted to Thomas of Bridgnorth for all Holy Orders.

LITTERA DIMISSORIA J[OHANNIS] DE BRUGES.—Thomas, etc., Johanni de Bruges, clerico, salutem, etc. Ut a quocunque Episcopo Catholico, graciam Sedis Apostolice optinente et tibi volente imponere manus sanctas, ad omnes Sacros Ordines licite valeas promoveri, tibi licenciam liberam concedimus, etc. Datum apud Eyhtham, xiij Kalendas Octobris, anno Domini supradicto.

Oct. 7.—The Bishop sends to Matthew, the Cardinal, a frontal which had been suggested by his own page as an acceptable present, with its superfrontal, and regrets that the work-women have been so long about it. A duplicate of the letter is sent by other hands,

DOMINO MATHEO LE ROUS, CARDINALI.—Venerabili in Christo Patri, Domino Matheo, Dei gracia Sancte Marie in Porticu Diacono Cardinali, suus Thomas, humilis sacerdos Herefordensis Ecclesie, paratam ad sua beneplacita voluntatem, cum omnimodis reverencia et honore. Quemadmodum Matheus, domicellus vester, inter cetera ornamenta congruencia vestre capelle, michi ex parte vestra frontale, tanquam magis oportunum, duxerat nominare; ita frontale et superfrontale, qualia in littera mea responsiva descripsi, utinam Paternitati vestre placencia, per Durancium et socios suos, cives et mercatores Florencie, vobis transmitto; nec moleste feratis, si placet, si dicta ornamenta tardius ad vos venerint quam exprimat littera memorata, quia, licet fecerim operatrices eorum ut accelerarent in operando quam plurimum excitari, vix tamen secundo die Octobris eadem ornamenta poterant extrahi de manibus earundem completa. Ceterum si qua volueritis in Anglia que per me vestrum poterunt expediri, michi vestro in omnibus obedituro precipiatis secure. Hanc litteram duplicatam vobis transmitto per portitores diversos, ut ad vos veniat saltem alterutra, si unam illarum casu fortuito ad vos contigerit non venire. Conservet Paternitatem vestram Altissimus et prosperis semper florere faciat incrementis. Datum apud Waddone, Nonis Octobris, anno Domini M°CC°LXX° nono.

Oct. 11.—The Archbishop is informed that Robert of Gloucester will act as the Bishop's Proctor in Episcopal Councils.

PROCURATORIUM MAGISTRI R[OBERTI] DE GLOUCESTRIA IN CONGREGACIONIBUS EPISCOPORUM.—Venerabili in Christo Patri, J[ohanni], Dei gracia Cantuariensi Archiepiscopo, tocius Anglie Primati, Thomas, etc., salutem, etc. Ad tractandum vice nostra una vobiscum et Consuffraganeis nostris, in vestris Conciliis seu Congregacionibus, super negociis que per vos et per dictos Venerabiles Patres inibi tractari contigerit; necnon ad mancipandum officium, quatenus ad nos spectat tractatus hujusmodi, dilectum nobis in Christo magistrum Robertum de Gloucestria nostrum facimus Procuratorem; dantes eidem potestatem consenciendi, etc. Conservet vos Deus per tempora diuturna. Datum v Idus Octobris, anno Domini M°CC°LXX° nono.

Oct. 11.—The Bishop expresses regret that from ill health he cannot take part with the Primate and his Suffragans in their deliberations as to the maintenance of the rights of the Church.

EXCUSACIO DOMINI DE NON VENIENDO AD QUANDAM CONGREGACIONEM.—Venerabili in Christo Patri, Domino J[ohanni], Dei gracia Cantuariensi Archiepiscopo, tocius Anglie Primati, Thomas, etc., salutem, etc. Adversa valitudine prepediti quominus ad presens venire Londonias et tractatui vestro ac Consuffraganeorum nostrorum super reformacione ecclesiastice libertatis ibidem habendo, ut dicitur, valeamus adesse, vestram Paternitatem obsecramus attente quatinus excusatam hanc nostram absenciam habeatis; pro certo tenentes quod vobis assisteremus alacriter in premissis si infirmitas nostrum non tardaret accessum. Annuat Altissimus ecclesiastica negocia sub manibus vestris prosperari. Datum ut proximo supra.

Oct. 30.—Dispensation to Richard de Bedstone to receive Holy Orders, notwithstanding his illegitimate birth.

DISPENSACIO CUM RICARDO DE BEDESTONE, ACOLITO.—Thomas, etc., Ricardo de Bedestone, acolito, salutem, etc. Cum per legitimam inquisicionem nobis constiterit te paterne incontinencie imitatorem non esse, etc.; tecum auctoritate Apostolica, quam penes te deponimus conservandam, super natalium defectu, etc., misericorditer dispensamus, etc. Datum apud Arleye, iij Kalendas Novembris, anno Domini M°CC°LXX° nono.

October 28.—Collation of Ralph de Hengham to the prebend and canonry resigned by Peter Eymer.

COLLACIO PREBENDE DE MORTONE FACTA DOMINO RADULFO DE HENGHAM.—Thomas, etc., domino Radulfo de Hengham[1] salutem, etc. Prebendam et canonicatum de Mortone in Ecclesia Herefordensi, vacantem per resignacionem magistri Ade de Fileby, Procuratoris magistri Petri Eymer, canonici ejusdem prebende, specialem ad resignandum potestatem habentis, tibi conferimus intuitu caritatis. Datum apud Arleye, v Kalendas Novembris, anno Domini M°CC°LXX° nono. Et in crastino mandabatur [Ebdomodario] in Ecclesia Herefordensi quod dictum dominum Radulfum, etc., in dictam prebendam induceret, eidem stallum in choro, etc.

Oct. 29.—Request that the Bishop of Worcester will have Ralph de Hengham inducted into the Church of Morton, with the chapelry of Waddon, which are annexed to his prebend.

LITTERA MISSA DOMINO WYGORNIENSI, PER QUAM DICTUS DOMINUS R[ADULFUS] POSSESSIONEM ECCLESIE DE MORTONE, ANNEXE PREBENDE PREDICTE, [OBTINUIT].—Venerabili in Christo Patri, Domino G[alfrido], Dei gracia Wygorniensi Episcopo, suus Thomas, Ejusdem permissione humilis Sacerdos Herefordensis Ecclesie, salutem, etc. Cum quandam prebendam in nostra Ecclesia Herefordensi, vacantem, cui ecclesia parochialis de Mortone, cum capella de Waddone, vestre diocesis, existit annexa, domino Radulfo de Hengham, clerico, contulerimus intuitu caritatis, vestram Paternitatem affectuose rogamus quatinus eundem dominum Radulfum

---

[1]—Ralph de Hengham had acted as Justice in the suit between the Earl of Gloucester and the Bishop, and lived to bear witness on his behalf before the Papal Commission in 1307.

in possessione dicte parochialis ecclesie, cum suis pertinenciis, plenarie faciatis induci, si placet. Paternitatem vestram nobis conservet Altissimus, et prosperis semper florere faciat incrementis. Datum apud Arleye, iiij Kalendas Novembris, anno Domini M°CC°LXX° nono.

Nov. 11.—Institution of Richard de Tedestile to the Church of Newton, on the presentation of Johanna de Newton.

INSTITUCIO DE NEUTONE.—Thomas, etc., domino Ricardo de Tedestile, presbitero, salutem, etc. Ad ecclesiam de Neutone, nostre diocesis, ad presentacionem Johanne de Neutone, domine de eadem, vere patrone ipsius, te caritative admittimus, et Rectorem canonice instituimus in eadem. Datum apud Arleye, juxta Radinge, in crastino Sancti Martini, anno Domini M°CC°LXX° nono.

Mandate of induction to Newton.

EXECUCIO IPSIUS.—Officiali suo salutem, etc. Mandamus vobis quod dominum Ricardum de Tedestile, presbiterum, ponatis in corporalem possessionem ecclesie de Neutone, etc.

Nov. 23.— The Bishop regrets that he cannot comply with a request of the Archbishop, as he has already conferred the prebend vacated by the death of Henry de Hawkley.

ARCHIEPISCOPO PRO PREBENDA QUE FUIT H. DE HAUEKELE.— Domino J[ohanni], Dei gracia Cantuariensi Archiepiscopo, etc., Thomas, etc., salutem, etc. Sciat vestra Paternitas reverenda quod die Sancte Cecilie, Virginis ac Martiris, immo verius in noctis principio subsequentis, litteras vestras recepimus, de morte magistri H[enrici] de Hauekele[1] mencionem quamquam lugubrem facientes; ante quarum recepcionem, ob certos rumores quos de morte ejus habuimus, suam prebendam, quam in Herefordensi Ecclesia tenuit, tam voce tenus quam litteratorie, intuitu caritatis, contulimus, novit Deus; et propterea non moleste feratis, si placet, quod hac vice non implevimus quod mandastis, pro certo scientes quod, si ante collacionem ad nos vestre Dominacionis littere pervenissent, mandatum corditer fecissemus. Quamcito quoque comode poterimus,

---

1—The question of jurisdiction as to the probate of the estate of Henry de Hawkley caused the grave dispute between Archbishop Peckham and Cantilupe, and the appeal to Rome.

vobiscum collacionem faciemus affectatam, Domino concedente. Vestram sanctam Paternitatem conservet Omnipotens, etc. Datum apud Calestone, die Beati Clementis.

Dec. 20.—Institution of . . . de Corve to the Vicarage of Holy Trinity at Wenlock.

VICARIA SANCTE TRINITATIS DE WENLOKE.—Memorandum quod xiij Kalendas Januarii, anno Domini M°CC°LXX° nono, apud Fromam Episcopi, fuit dominus . . . [1] de Corve, presbiter, institutus in vicaria ecclesie Sancte Trinitatis de Wenloke. Et mandatum fuit, etc.

Dec. 22.—Dispensation for Holy Orders to Ralph of Wigmore, notwithstanding his illegitimate birth.

DISPENSACIO CUM RADULFO DE WYGEMORE, CLERICO.—In forma suprascripta dispensavit Dominus cum Radulfo de Wygemore, clerico, super defectu natalium; videlicet apud Lugwarthyn, xj Kalendas Januarii, anno Domini M°CC°LXX° nono.

Dec. 19.—Submission of three foresters of the Earl of Gloucester, who came to be absolved from the sentence of excommunication incurred by them for molesting the Bishop when he took possession of the Chase of Malvern.

DE FORESTARIIS MALVERNIE.—Memorandum quod die Martis proximo ante Natale Domini, anno Ejusdem M°CC°LXX° nono, venerunt Robertus Wytlok, Johannes le Rede, de Blechingeleye, et Rogerus de Boltisham, forestarii Domini G[ilberti de Clare], Comitis Gloucestrie, in foresta Malvernie, ad Dominum Thomam, Dei gracia Herefordensem Episcopum, apud Colewelle, timentes se ligari excommunicacionis sentencia quam idem Dominus Episcopus fecerat promulgari in omnes illos qui ipsum maliciose impediverunt, seu impediri aliqualiter procurarunt, quin chacie sue Malvernie libertate et ipsius libera seysina gauderet, et maxime primo die quo ipsius chacie cepit seysinam; et humiliter petierunt munus absolucionis ab Episcopo memorato in forma juris ipsis impendi. Qui quidem Episcopus eos a sentencia antedicta absolvit in forma subscripta, videlicet quod nunquam ab eo die Episcopum Herefordensem quin pacifice et plenarie suam in ipsa chacia optineat

1—Name omitted.

libertatem impedient, seu procurabunt aliquatenus impediri; ad que fideliter observanda sacramentum corporale omnes et singuli prestiterunt, ordinacioni dicti Domini Episcopi, quantum ad penitenciam suscipiendam et faciendam pro commisso hujusmodi, quandocunque idem Dominus Episcopus voluerit, et eos super hoc premuniverit, se totaliter submittentes.

Dec. 28.—The Preceptor of the Hospitallers at Buckland is notified that Maurice de Membury is the Bishop's attorney to receive the rents of North Petherton. Letters patent appointing Maurice seneschal at Earley.

DE FIRMA DE NORTPERETONE RECIPIENDA.—Thomas, etc., venerabili viro, Preceptori Hospitalis Sancti Johannis Jerosolemitani de Boclaunde, salutem, etc. Noveritis nos fecisse dilectum nobis in Christo Mauricium de Membury, attornatum nostrum ad recipiendum a vobis firmam nostram de Nortperetone, dum in manu nostra fuerit ipsa firma; et ad faciendum quitanciam de receptis. In cujus rei, etc. Datum apud Sugwas, v Kalendas Januarii, anno Domini M°CC°LXX° nono.

DE CUSTODIA ET SENESCALCIA TERRARUM QUE FUERUNT PHILIPPI DE ARLE.—Et ipsis die, loco, et anno, constituit Dominus Mauricium de Membury antedictum custodem et senescallum terrarum que fuerunt Philippi de Arleye, usque ad legitimam etatem heredum dicti Philippi; quorum custodia et maritagium habuit Dominus ex tradicione Domini Regis. Et super hoc habuit dictus M[auricius] litteras Domini patentes.

Jan. 9, 1280,—Appointment of the Prior of Wormesley as coadjutor of the Prior of Chirbury, and guardian of the spiritual and temporal interests of the house.

PRIORI DE WORMELEYE PRO CHEREBURY.—Thomas, etc., domino . . .[1] Priori de Wormeleye, salutem, etc. Compacientes infirmitati et impotencie dilecti in Christo filii, domini . . .[1] Prioris de Chyrebury, adjutorem vos damus eidem; custodiam domus de Chyrebury, tam in spiritualibus quam temporalibus, vobis plenarie committentes donec eandem duxerimus revocandam. Datum apud Fromam Episcopi, v Idus Januarii, anno Domini M°CC°LXX° nono.

1—Names omitted in MS.

The Prior of Leominster is called upon to produce documentary evidence of the canonical appropriation of the Church of Eye, which, as well as the Priory, was visited on December 28.

PRIORI LEOMINISTRIE PRO EYA.—Thomas, etc., domino Priori Leoministrie, salutem, etc. Cum ad Prioratum Leoministrie, anno, etc., iij° die Januarii, accederemus visitandi causa, ac eodem die ecclesiam parochialem Leoministrie, secundo die monachos ipsius ecclesie, et tercio ecclesiam parochialem de Eya, quam iidem monachi sibi asseruerunt canonice appropriatam[1], prout consuevimus et de jure debuimus, visitaremus, ac ex deposicione quorundam fidedignorum testimonalium examinatorum in visitacione predicta daretur intelligi quod ecclesiam de Eya minus canonice, colore cujusdam firme, absque auctoritate pontificum teneretis; nos ad supplicacionem vestram in crastino clausi Paschatis terminum peremptorium vobis damus, ad ostendendum coram nobis, etc., jura et munimenta quorum autoritate ipsam ecclesiam in proprios usus tenuistis [h]actenus et tenetis. Valeatis. Datum ut supra proximo.

Jan. 13.—Release of the sequestration of Much Cowarne till mid-Lent.

RELAXACIO SEQUESTRI DE COURA.—Memorandum quod Dominus relaxavit sequestrum, si quod fuerit, interpositum in fructibus ecclesie de Magna Coura usque ad mediam Quadragesimam. Datum apud Duntesburne, Idibus Januarii.

1279.—Bull of Nicholas III. directing the Archbishop of Canterbury to decide the suit between the Bishops of Hereford and St. Asaph, which was referred to the Bishop of Llandaff, with the Archdeacon and Precentor, and by them transferred to the Prior of St. Oswald's, Gloucester, from whom the Bishop of St. Asaph appealed on the ground of the Constitution, ne ultra duas dietas, &c.; *asking that the Priors of Worcester and of Wombridge, and the Archdeacon of Carmarthen might be judges delegate.*

BULLA [NICHOLAI PAPE DIRECTA] ARCHIEPISCOPO PRO EPISCOPO ASSAVENSI.—Nicholaus, etc. [Johanni Peckham], Archiepiscopo Cantuariensi, salutem, etc. Sua nobis Venerabilis Frater noster, Episcopus Assavensis, peticione monstravit quod, licet ville et alia loca in Gordor, Assavensis diocesis, consistencia sint sibi lege

---
[1]—The Priory seems to have made good its claim, for in the Taxatio, a few years later, it is entered as their property and of the value of £45 yearly.

diocesana subjecta, et tam ipse quam predecessores sui, Assavenses Episcopi, qui fuerint pro tempore, in villis et locis predictis Episcopalem jurisdiccionem [h]actenus consueverint exercere a tempore cujus memoria non existit; tamen Venerabilis Frater noster, Herefordensis Episcopus, minus veraciter asserens quod idem Episcopus Assavensis in nonnullis castris et villis terre predicte, Herefordensis diocesis, ut dicebat, Episcopalem jurisdiccionem sibi contra justiciam satagens vendicare, pueros et puellas confirmare, et alia que per solos Episcopos exercentur, dicto Herefordensi invito renitente, in illis exercere presumit, quamvis ab antiquo sibi Herefordensi, ut idem asserebat, et antecessoribus suis, non Assavensibus, competeret contra dicti Assavensis assercionem, super hoc ad Venerabilem fratrem nostrum Episcopum et dilectos filios, Archidiaconum et Precentorem Landavenses, in communi forma litteras Apostolicas impetravit. Quibus Priori Sancti Oswaldi in Gloucestria, Wygorniensis diocesis, committentibus in hac parte vices suas, idem Episcopus Assavensis, ex eo senciens a dicto Priore indebite se gravari quod ipsum ultra duas dietas extra suam diocesim ad judicium evocabat, quamquam id non haberet ex predictarum beneficio litterarum, ad Sedem Apostolicam appellavit, et super sua appellacione ad Wygorniensis Ecclesie ac de Wombrugge, Coventrensis diocesis, Priores, et Archidiaconum de Keyrmerdyn in Ecclesia Menevensi nostras litteras impetravit. Cum itaque dictus Assavensis Episcopus coram diversis judicibus litigare cogatur, in illis partibus in quibus, propter potenciam et maliciam adversariorum suorum nequit tute, ac alias plenarie ut convenit, prosequi jura sua; nobis humiliter supplicavit ut providere super hoc de benignitate Sedis Apostolice curaremus. Nos autem quieti ejusdem Assavensis Episcopi providere volentes, ac precavere sollicite ne occasione aliquorum amfractuum in juribus pertinentibus deperire contingat, Fraternitati tue, de qua plenam in Domino fiduciam optinemus, per Apostolicam [auctoritatem] mandamus quatinus, vocatis qui fuerint evocandi, causam hujusmodi de plano et sine strepitu judiciali per teipsum tantum audias, et appellacione remota, debita fine decidas, faciens, etc.; non obstantibus predictis litteris, etc.; seu si est aliquibus indultum ab eadem Sede quod interdici, suspendi, aut excommunicari non possunt per litteras Apostolicas, si non facit plenam et expressam de indulto hujusmodi mencionem, etc.; dummodo extra regnum Anglie per presentes ad judicium non trahatur. Datum Viterbii, xiiij Kalendas . . . .[1] Pontificatus nostri anno secundo.

1—The month was not named.

Jan. 20.—In pursuance of a letter from the Pope's Penitentiary, Robert de Sapy, of the diocese of Hereford, is granted a dispensation from irregularity in receiving the Order of the Priesthood from the Bishop of Worcester, which he has confessed at Rome.

PRO ROBERTO DE SAPY, PRESBITERO, DE DISPENSACIONE SUPER IRREGULARITATE.—Venerabili in Christo Patri [Thome], Dei gracia Episcopo Herefordensi, frater Gilbertus, Domini Pape Penitenciarius, salutem in Domino. Robertus de Sapi, presbiter, vestre diocesis, lator presencium, sua nobis confessione monstravit quod ipse olim, qui existens diaconus in Wygorniensi diocesi diutinam moram traxerat, vestra licencia non optenta se fecit ibidem per Venerabilem Patrem, Wygorniensem Episcopum, ad presbiteratus Ordinem promoveri; rite tamen alias statutis a jure temporibus, et absque vicio simonie. Et ex hoc teneri non credens, tanquam simplex et juris ignarus, eciam post vestram inhibicionem factam simplici verbo tantum, non tamen in contemptum clavium, in sic suscepto Ordine diucius ministravit, et alias immiscuit se divinis; super quibus Sedem Apostolicam adiens supplicavit humiliter sibi misericorditer provideri. Ad vos igitur presbiterum remittentes, eundem Paternitati vestre auctoritate Domini Pape committimus, quod si est ita, et in tales ante sic suscepti Ordinis recepcionem non fuit excommunicacionis sentencia promulgata; injuncta sibi, debita absolucione previa, penitencia salutari, eoque ad tempus, juxta vestre discrecionis arbitrium, a sic suscepti Ordinis execucione suspenso, super ipsius Ordinis execucione et irregularitate ex premissis contracta secum auctoritate predicta misericorditer dispensetis, prout secundum Deum anime ipsius saluti expedire videritis; dummodo alias sibi merita suffragentur, aliudque canonicum non obsistat. Datum Rome apud Sanctum Petrum, Idibus Novembris, Pontificatus Domini Nicholai Pape Tercii anno secundo, Thomas, etc., Roberto de Sapy, presbitero, salutem, etc. Ut execucionem Ordinis presbiteratus, quem a Venerabili Patre, Domino Wygorniensi Episcopo, absque nostris litteris dimissoriis suscepisti, in posterum possis habere, tibi auctoritate Apostolica indulgemus; non obstante irregularitate quam incurristi, in Ordine sic suscepto, eciam a nobis inhibitus, temere celebrando. Super qua tecum dispensamus auctoritate Sedis ejusdem. Datum Londoniis, xiij Kalendas Februarii, anno Domini MºCCºLXXº nono.

Jan. 25.—Mandate to Walter de Redmarley to cite H. de Manchester, Prior of the Friars Preachers in the Province of England, to appear before the Bishop as arbitrator in a suit between them and the Dean and Chapter of Hereford.

PRO FRATRIBUS PREDICATORIBUS.—Thomas, etc., domino Waltero de Rudmerleye, Canonico Herefordensi, salutem, etc. Citetis peremptorie magne religionis virum, Patrem H. de Mamecestria, Priorem fratrum Predicatorum[1] in Provincia Anglie, quod compareat coram nobis pro se et fratribus sui Ordinis [facturus] responsalem in crastino Dominice qua cantatur *Letare Jerusalem*, ubicunque, etc., in negocio ordinacionis seu arbitratus quod inter eosdem Priorem et fratres, ex parte una, et Decanum et Capitulum nostre Herefordensis Ecclesie, coram nobis ordinatore seu arbitratore sub certa forma vertitur, seu verti speratur, ex altera, etc. Datum apud . . . .[2] viij Kalendas Februarii, anno Domini M°CC°LXX° nono.

Similar mandate to the Dean of Weobley, to cite the Dean and Chapter of Hereford. The citations and questions of the Archbishop were sent to the Prior.

PRO EISDEM.—Item memorandum,—Consimilis citacio exstitit directa Decano de Webbele, ad Decanum et Capitulum Herefordensis Ecclesie citandos pro eodem negocio, et sub data prescripta. Et hee citaciones, atque questiones Archiepiscopi Cantuariensis, transmisse fuerunt fratri H. de Mamecestria, Priori fratrum Ordinis Predicatorum in Provincia Anglie, per suum nuncium proprium.

Letter to Cardinal Matthew deploring the injustice to himself involved in the terms of the Papal Commission issued to the Archbishop to decide the suit with the Bishop of St. Asaph, and begging him to use influence with the Pope that the instructions may be modified.

Reverendo in Christo Patri, Domino predilecto, domino Matheo, Dei gracia Sancte Marie in Porticu Diacono Cardinali, suus Thomas, etc. Tenorem littere Apostolice quam nuper contra nos impetravit

---

1—Innocent IV. had forbidden the settlement of the Black Friars in Hereford on the ground that it would prejudice the support of the Churches, of the Grey Friars, and the charities of the town. They had built a little oratory in Portfield beyond Bye Street Gate, and had grave disputes with the Dean and Chapter, who paid in 1273 what would be now at least three hundred pounds to the Proctor who guarded their interests at Rome in the suit with these Friars. (Documents in the Archives of the D. and C.).

2—Place omitted.

Dominus [Anianus], Assavensis Episcopus, Paternitati vestre transmitto, ut vobis innotescant ipsius aculei qui juris peritorum judicio amare me pungunt. Ipsa enim littera jus meum, quod per longas lites laboresque prolixos onerosis sumptibus adquisivi, sine culpa mea aut causa probata absorbere videtur in totum, quod admodum juri scripto molestum existit; nec super causis in ipsa contentis aliqualiter demandatur, licet falsitatem contineat; set presuppositis tanquam veris principalis articuli diffinicionibus de plano absque judiciali strepitu delegatur; non obstantibus litteris Apostolicis et processibus auctoritate ipsarum [h]actenus habitis super diffinicione articuli memorati. Ad vos igitur tanquam ad singulare refugium meum accurro, devotis precibus obsecrans et requirens quatinus a Domino Papa aliquod remedium opportunum super enervacione littere prelibate mihi amicicia vestra procuret, ut, si uberius haberi non possit, saltem quod Domino [Johanni] Cantuariensi, cui littera memorata dirigitur, vel alicui Eboracensis Provincie non suspecto, non obstante Constitucione de duabus dietis, denuo Dominus Papa scribat quod, nisi cause in littera prefata contente, ob quas concessa videtur, veritate nitantur . . . . . [1] ac processus per eam habitus, in irritum revocetur. Statum Domini Regis, immo vestrum, et Curie Romane, michi vestro, si placet, velitis rescribere per presencium portitorem, unacum vestra in omnibus voluntate.

Directions to the Proctor, John de Bitterley, to induce John de Aquablanca to propose as a suggestion of his own to Peter de Langon that he should agree to some compromise, which the Bishop might be thought willing to accept.

ALIA IN LITTERA MAGISTRI J[OHANNIS].—Insuper tanquam ex vestra propria mocione, excitetis dominum Johannem de Aqua Blanka quod ipse, tanquam media persona erga Petrum de Langone, ante instet, et ipsum, si possit, inducat quod super prebenda de Prestone nobiscum ponat in aliqua forma competenti, ita quod minima prebenda remaneat totaliter possessori; et istud per vos, ut superius est notatum, ante fiat aliquamdiu expectando. Et quod dictus Johannes dicat quod, inclinati precibus aliquorum et timore litis perterriti, pacem cum dicto Petro forsitan uniremus, quod quidem ipse Petrus propter sumptus onerosos, diversa gravamina et pericula, deberet, ut intelleximus, affectare. Vos autem in conspectu dicti [Petri] istud dissimuletis prout videbitis expedire, semper eidem viriliter resistentes.

1—Some phrase seems to have been omitted.

John de Bitterley is informed that Adam de Fileby was collated to the Deanery conditionally, and that nothing should be done to prejudice the claims of John de Aquablanca at Rome. Details of the letter to the Cardinal are reported, and a transcript of the commission to the Archbishop is sent, that he may ascertain the full meaning of certain technical phrases. The Church of Croft has been conferred on him notwithstanding that he has been presented to a benefice by the patroness who has won her suit in Court relating to it.

Thomas, etc., Johanni de Buterleye, Procuratori suo in Romana Curia commoranti, salutem, etc. Non credimus vos latere quod Decanatum Herefordensem contulerimus magistro Ade de Fileby in eventum hujusmodi, si contra Johannem de Aqua Blanka super eodem Decanatu in Romana Curia sentencia ferretur, nusquam gerentes in animo ut sibi adversarium pararemus, nec nos nec dictus Adam, nisi, prout suprascripsimus, quo magis elongaretur a consequendo jus suum; proper quod nolumus, immo pocius inhibemus expresse, ne clam vel palam, per vos aut alios, nostro nomine eidem Johanni in prosecucione juris sui super Decanatu impedimentum aliquod aut resistenciam procuretis afferri. Preterea caveatis ne magistro Ade prefato, procuratoribus, sociis, amicis, seu notis ipsius in Curia in predicto negocio, aut in aliis nos tangentibus aut nostros clericos vel subditos, seu beneficia nostre civitatis seu diocesis, omnino credatis, nisi quatenus de hac vobis scripserimus, vel manifeste videritis utile nobis esse quod dicunt; set sollicite laboretis ne per eos aliqua littera graciam seu communem justiciam continens, et nobis ac nostris prejudicialis existens, de quo timemus, aliqualiter impetretur. Hec tamen in virtute obediencie sint vobis secreta. Ad hec mittimus Domino Matheo Cardinali transcriptum littere quam contra nos jam ultimo impetravit Dominus Assavensis, quod nobis misistis, que nobis admodum injuriosa videtur; ut nobis a Domino Papa aliquod oportunum remedium super ejus enervacione procuret; et vos ipsum ad hoc jugiter excitetis, ut, si uberius remedium non possit haberi, saltem Dominus Papa denuo scribat Domino [Johanni] Cantuariensi, cui littera prelibata dirigitur, vel alicui Eboracensis Provincie non suspecto, non obstante Constitucione de duabus dietis; quod, nisi cause in littera predicta contente, ob quas Dominus Papa induci fertur ad hujusmodi litteram concedendam, veritatem contineant, litteram ipsam reiciat, etc. Prefatum autem transcriptum ex habundanti vobis transmittimus, si quo casu fortuito desieritis illud habere, et transcriptum littere quam mittimus Cardinali. Inquiratis eciam quid tenere consueverit Curia; videlicet ad que hec nomina de plano et absque strepitu judiciali debent extendi; et si excepciones aliquas paciantur, et quas; necnon que de examinandarum causarum solito cursu spernant; et quod inveneritis nobis plenarie rescribatis. Vobis contulimus ecclesiam de Croft, non obstante beneficio de cujus patronatu in Curia Regis, contra Dominum Menevensem, pronunciatum existit pro domina vestra, per quam ad dictum beneficium presentati fuistis.

Jan. 19.—Institution of the Vicar of Caynham on the presentation of the Abbot and Convent of Wigmore.

INSTITUCIO VICARII DE KAYAM.—Memorandum quod dominus de Kayam institutus fuit in vicariam ecclesie de Kayam, xiiij Kalendas Februarii, anno Domini M°CC°LXX° nono, ad presentacionem Abbatis et Conventus de Wygemore. Et mandatur Officiali quod poneret eum, etc.

Jan. 23.—Mandate of induction of William de Bodecote to the Church of Hope Bowdler, on the presentation of Milicent[1] de Montalt, after a pledge from his Proctor that he would receive the Order of subdeacon at the next Ordination.

DE POSSESSIONE ECCLESIE HOPE BULLERS.—Item memorandum quod, x Kalendas Februarii, anno predicto, Londoniis, juravit Procurator magistri Willelmi de Bodecote, presentati ad ecclesiam de Hope Bullers per dominam Milisentam de Munthault, veram ipsius ecclesie patronam, in animam ipsius domini sui quod idem dominus suus in Ordinibus proximis in subdiaconum ordinabitur; quo prestito sacramento, dominus scripsit Officiali quod dictum magistrum W[illelmum], vel ipsum Procuratorem suo nomine, poneret in corporalem possessionem ecclesie memorate.

Jan. 24.—Licence of non-residence to study for one year granted to Robert de Lacy, Rector of Brampton Brian. Release of the sequestration for non-residence and for non-appearance at the Ordination.

LICENCIA STUDENDI ET RELAXACIO SEQUESTRI.—Robertus de Lacy, Rector ecclesie de Bromptone Brian, habet licenciam studendi per unum annum continuum a festo Sancti Michaelis, anno Domini

---

1—Milicent de Cantilupe was a niece of the Bishop, married to John de Montalt, and also to Eudo la Zouche (p. 16).

M°CC°LXXX°. Item dominus relaxavit sequestrum interpositum in fructibus dicti Rectoris quia non resedit, et quia non interfuit Ordinibus; et fuit data utriusque littere Londoniis, ix Kalendas Februarii.

Jan. 31.—Mandate to the Dean of the Forest to cite in the Church of Blaisdon Adam, called Surigitus, to show cause why the said Church should not be treated as void.

CITACIO MAGISTRI [ADE] SURIGITI.—Memorandum quod apud Arleye, ij Kalendas Februarii, anno predicto, emanavit citatorium hujusmodi,—quod Decanus de Foresta citaret magistrum Adam, dictum Surigitum, in ecclesia de Blechedone, quod compareat coram Officiali nostro in secundo Consistorio celebrando in decanatu Foreste post Purificacionem, ostensurus si quid habeat cujus pretextu dicta ecclesia non vacet de jure.

Jan. 31.—Dispensation for illegitimacy granted to John de Longhope.

LEGITIMACIO JOHANNIS DE LONGEHOPE.—Ipsis die et loco dispensavit dominus cum Johanne de Longhope, acolito, super defectu natalium, in forma communi.

Feb. 1.—Mandate of the Archbishop, directed to the Bishop of Llandaff, to cite the Bishops of Hereford and St. Asaph to appear before him with all the documents relating to their suit, and to instruct the judges who have had cognizance of it to transmit to him the record of the proceedings.

CITACIO ARCHIEPISCOPI CANTUARIENSIS AD INSTANCIAM ASSAVENSIS.—Dominus J[ohannes], permissione divina Cantuariensis Ecclesie minister humilis, tocius Anglie Primas, Venerabili in Christo Fratri, Dei gracia Landavensi Episcopo, salutem, etc. Litteras Apostolicas, quas vobis volumus exhiberi, nobis post inspeccionem earum illico remittendas, recepimus in hec verba:— Nicholaus, Episcopus, etc., sicut in secundo precedenti folio continetur. Volentes igitur quod nobis in hac parte injungitur cum celeritate qua convenit expedire, vobis in virtute obediencie firmiter injungendo mandamus quatinus dictos Herefordensem et Assavensem Episcopos, necnon eorum locorum Capitula, peremptorie citetis quod compareant coram nobis, ubicunque, etc., quinto die juridico post Dominicam secundam Quadragesime, cum omnibus instrumentis, etc., sufficienter instructi, in causis ipsis et ipsas contingentibus, juxta mandati Apostolici supradicti tenorem et seriem processuri, etc. Vobis insuper inhibemus, et per vos ceteris judicibus qui in causis cognoverant prenotatis, ne, premissis pendentibus coram nobis, in parcium predictarum seu alterutrius earum prejudicium presumatis, vel presumant, aliquid attemptare quominus possimus auctorite predicta facere quod incumbit, et partes premisse dictarum causarum liberam prosecucionem habeant in hac parte. Moneatis insuper judices qui in premissis cognoverant ut processus super hiis habitos nobis ad dictos diem et locum, plene et sine dilacione, transmittant; copiam eciam dicti mandati Apostolici et citacionis presentis, ut plenius instructe venire possint, fieri faciatis partibus supradictis. De die vero recepcionis presencium et forma mandati nostri presentis nos certis die et loco, per vestras patentes litteras harum seriem continentes, distincte et seriatim certificetis. Datum apud Fuleham, Kalendis Februarii, Consecracionis nostre anno primo.

Oct. 19, 1279.—Collation by lapse of John of Bridgnorth, presented by Geoffrey de Pickford, to the chapelry of Broseley. Institution and mandate of induction.

JOHANNES DE BRUGGE CAPELLE DE BOREWALDESLEYE.—Thomas, etc,, Johanni de Brugge, subdiacono, salutem, etc. Capellam de Borewaldesleye, Herefordensis diocesis, ad nostram provisionem hac vice auctoritate Generalis Concilii devolutam, tibi conferimus intuitu caritatis, te canonice instituentes in ea; salvo tamen jure patronatus in posterum domino Galfrido de Pychforde, qui te presentavit ad eam. Datum apud Bernes, xiiij Kalendas Novembris, anno Domini M°CC°LXX° nono. Et mandavit Officiali quod ipsum Johannem poneret, etc.

Feb. 28, 1280.—Mandate to the Dean of the Forest to send a monition to the Abbot and Convent of Gloucester that they should provide an acre and a half of ground near the Church of Churcham and timber for a Vicarage, or else entertain the Vicar as of old in their manor, it being ascertained at recent Visitations that he lives at a distance. A chalice must be provided; the Vicar must find a lamp and a deacon to assist him; and must build and inhabit a Vicarage house; all this under pain of certain fines. Proportionate reduction of the vicarial stipend may be made for the value of the glebe. The Vicar is further to be cited to appear at the next Consistory Court to answer to a charge of incontinency.

Thomas, etc., Decano de Foresta, salutem, etc. In visitacionibus pluribus hactenus factis in ecclesia parochiali de Chyrchamme invenimus pro constanti vicarium et diaconum ejusdem ecclesie, qui pro tempore fuerunt, ante ultimos dies Andree, quondam vicarii loci ejusdem, in manerio Abbatis et Conventus Gloucestrie juxta prefatam ecclesiam commorantes fuisse, et ad mensam eorum, eoque tempore eandem ecclesiam debitis et devotis obsequiis precellere; et tandem, pro utilitate vicarii et diaconi predictorum ac religiosorum ipsorum, certam porcionem, de earundem parcium mutuo consensu, de bonis ipsorum religiosorum ad opus ejusdem vicarii assignatam fuisse, qua in propria mensa se alerent extra manerium antedictum; propter quod dictus Andreas, et ejus successor qui jam ministrat in ipsa ecclesia, apud ecclesiam de Balleye penitus commorantes, ut magis sibi parcerent, diaconum noluerunt habere, et ipsam ecclesiam matricem de Chyrchhamme absque custodia et debito officio usque nunc, non absque multarum animarum periculo et Dei irreverencia, dimiserunt. Quocirca vobis mandamus districte quatinus dictos religiosos canonice moneatis quod, citra Festum Annunciacionis Dominice, aream competentem prope ecclesiam, acram et dimidiam continentem ad minus, in qua vicarius possit domos facere et morari, vobis assignent, et quod de aliquo meremio ad edificandum competenti vicarium inveniant eundem, aut quod citra idem tempus vicarium et diaconum ad suum manerium et ad mensam, sicut olim consueverunt esse, resumant, porcionis assignacione rescissa, sub pena xl solidorum si usque ad predictum tempus hujus opcionis membrum utrumque effectui neglexerint mancipare. Si tamen, ut dictum est, aream competentem assignent, volumus quod in recompensacionem aree, de porcione vicarii allocacionem deducant; dum tamen porcionis residuum, secundum facultates ecclesie, ad sustentacionem vicarii et diaconi racionabiliter sufficere videatur. Item moneatis dictos religiosos et vicarium quod, citra predictum Festum Annunciacionis, calicem in ecclesia memorata provideant, qui continue ibidem remaneat; ac cum provisus fuerit, coram Officiali nostro postea discuciatur qui eundem calicem debeat acquitare; et hoc injungatur sub pena superius annotata. Item moneatis dictum vicarium quod, si aream infra dictum tempus habuerit, quod eam cum omni festinacione qua potest edificet, et eam citra Festum Beati Michaelis proximo venturum inhabitet, et diaconum sibi provideat in ecclesia commorantem. Crassetumque in ipsa habeat continue ardens de nocte, sub pena privacionis vicarie quo ad edificacionem et inhabitacionem, et pena xx solidorum quo ad provisionem diaconi et crasseti, si premissa neglexerit infra prestituta tempora effectui mancipare. Item citetis peremptorie eundem vicarium quod compareat coram Officiali nostro in proximo Consistorio in Foresta, super incontinencia commissa cum Maydegod de Balleye, de qua diffamatur graviter, responsurus. Quid de hoc nostro mandato feceritis, etc. Datum apud Flaxleye, penultimo die Februarii, anno Consecracionis nostre quinto.

Feb. 17.—Institution of Robert Corbet to the Church of Llandinabo at the presentation of Cecilia de Bereford. Mandate of induction.

INSTITUCIO DE LANDINABO.—Thomas, etc., Roberto Corbet, capellano, salutem, etc. Ad ecclesiam de Landynabo, ad presentacionem domine Cecilie de Bereford, vere patrone ipsius ecclesie, te caritative admittimus, et te Rectorem canonice instituimus in eadem. In cujus rei, etc. Datum apud Lugwarthyn, in crastino Cinerum, anno Domini M°CC°LXX° nono. Et scriptum tunc extitit Officiali quod induceret eum, etc.

Mar. 7.—Dispensation on account of illegitimacy granted to Reginald de Radnor, and letters dimissory for all Holy Orders to be conferred by the Bishop of Llandaff.

DISPENSACIO ET DIMISSORIE REGINALDI DE RADENORE, SCOLARIS. —Memorandum quod, eisdem die et loco et anno, dispensavit Dominus cum Reginaldo de Radenore, scolari, in forma communi, secundum tenorem rescripti Apostolici super defectu natalium quem patitur de subdiacono genitus et soluta. Insuper eidem Reginaldo Dominus, per suas litteras dimissorias, concessit quod a Venerabili Patre, Domino W[illelmo de Bruce], Dei gracia Landavensi Episcopo, possit ad omnes Ordines minores et sacros licite promoveri; dum tamen canonicum, etc.

Mar. 31.—Licence to Simon of Hereford, Rector of More, to put his Church out to farm for a term on the usual conditions.

DE FIRMA ECCLESIE DE MORA.—Thomas, etc., Symoni de Hereforde, Rectori ecclesie de Mora, Herefordensis diocesis, salutem, etc. Ut per terminum continuum a Festo Paschatis, anno Domini M'CC°LXXX°, ecclesiam tuam predictam ad firmam ponere valeas tibi liberam licenciam concedimus per presentes; proviso tamen, etc. Datum apud Bosebury, ultimo die Marcii, anno Domini M°CC°LXXX°.

Lent, 1279.—Memorandum that Richard de Acton was instituted to the Church of Newland, near Monmouth, of which he had possession, on the presentation of the Master of the Knights Templars in England.

NOVA TERRA JUXTA MONEMUTAM.—Memorandum quod dominus Ricardus de Actone, capellanus, in vicariam ecclesie de Nova Terra juxta Monemutam, ad presentacionem Magistri Militum Templi in Anglia, apud Bosebury, in secunda septimana[1] xlme, anno Domini M°CC°LXX° nono, exstitit institutus. Habuit tamen antea possessionem ipsius.

Apr. 4, 1280.—Memorandum that the interdict and sequestration on the Churches of Churchham and Cowarne, caused by the failure to pay procurations, were released after the octave of Easter.

RELAXACIO SEQUESTRI CHYRCHOMME.—Item memorandum quod ij Nonas Aprilis, apud Temedebury, relaxavit Dominus penitus interdicta facta in ecclesiis de Chyrchomme et Coure, et sequestra interposita in fructibus earundem occasione procuracionum non solutarum pro eisdem usibus, ad crastinum clausi Pasche relaxavit dumtaxat, anno Domini, etc., octogesimo.

Apr. 15.—Memorandum that the sequestration of the fruits of Blaisdon, due to the failure of the Rector to present himself for Holy Orders, was released.

RELAXACIO SEQUESTRI DE BLECHEDONE.—Memorandum quod Dominus sequestrum interpositum in fructibus ecclesie de Blechedone, eo quod magister A[dam], Rector ejusdem, non venit ad Ordines, penitus relaxavit; et hoc apud Wyteburne xvij Kalendas Maii, anno Domini, etc., octogesimo.

1—*Ebdomada* added in MS.

Apr. 19.—Collation of Richard de Kimberley to the Church of Ullingswick, resigned at the same time by John de Kemsey; the tithes of corn to be equally divided between the two in the autumn, and all the crops sown by John to be his; Richard to maintain a chaplain and bear all the charges, receiving the altar offerings.

ORDINACIO SUPER ECCLESIA ET FRUCTIBUS DE ULLINGWYKE.—Item quod xiij Kalendas Maii, anno Domini M°CC°LXXX°, apud Wyteburne, Johannes de Kemeseye, clericus, ecclesiam de Ullingwyke oretenus et eciam litteratorie resignavit in manus Venerabilis Patris, Domini Thome, Episcopi Herefordensis, qui eam statim Ricardo de Kyneburle, clerico, intuitu contulit caritatis; ordinans quod dictus Johannes habeat in proximo autumpno futuro fructus terre ad ipsam ecclesiam pertinentis quam severit, unacum medietate decime garbarum dicte ecclesie in eodem autumpno; et quod dictus Ricardus ab illo [tempore] capellanum exhibeat, et omnia onera illi ecclesie incumbencia agnoscat, et alteragium totaliter recipiat, et aliam medietatem decime garbarum eciam percipiat; et quod post illum autumpnum fructus ecclesie sue totaliter sibi remaneant.

Dec. 23.—Mandate of Pope Nicholas III. to the Bishop to grant, after due inquiry and satisfactory results, dispensation on account of illegitimacy to Reginald de . . . .

Nicholaus Episcopus, Servus servorum Dei, Venerabili Fratri Episcopo Herefordensi salutem et Apostolicam benediccionem. Accedens ad presenciam nostram Reginaldus de . . . ,[1] tue diocesis, nobis humiliter supplicavit ut cum ipso, cupiente, ut asserit, ascribi milicie clericali, super defectu natalium quem patitur de subdiacono genitus et soluta, quod, hujusmodi non obstante defectu, ad omnes Ordines promoveri, etc., dispensare curaremus, etc. Datum Rome apud Sanctum Petrum, x Kalendas Januarii, Pontificatus nostri anno secundo.

Apr. 30.—Mandate to the Official to sequestrate all the fruits of the portion of Ledbury and of the office of Archdeacon of Salop that belonged to James de Aquablanca, including any that were in other hands, and to report what had been done.

SEQUESTRUM PORCIONIS CUJUSDAM LEDEBURY ET ARCHIDIACONATUS SALOPIE.—Memorandum quod ij Kalendas Maii, anno

---
1—The corner on which the place-name was written has been torn off.

Domini M°CC°LXXX°, apud Arleye, mandavit Dominus Officiali suo quod porcionem de Lodebury, quam tenuit magister Jacobus de Aqua Blanca, prout magistro Ricardo de Heytone sequestratori suo alias injunxit, unacum Archidiaconatu Salopie, cum omnibus fructibus et obvencionibus, etc., in manus ipsius Domini reciperet; non permittens ipsum aut suos procuratores in ipsis aliqualiter administrare. Et si inveniret aliquos occasione dictorum fructuum sibi obligatos in aliquo, illud in manibus eorundem, dicti Domini nomine, sequestraret; et quod super hiis que fecerit in premissis Dominum prefatum suis litteris redderet cerciorem.

Mandate to sequester also the fruits of the prebend of the aforesaid James.

SEQUESTRUM FRUCTUUM PREBENDE DE CASTRO.—Item dictis die, loco, et anno, mandavit Dominus suo Officiali quod fructus prebende dicte de Castro, quam dictus magister Jacobus tenuit in Ecclesia Herefordensi, in grangia et in terra existentes, teneat sequestratos donec sibi mandaverit aliud de eisdem.

Monition through the Official to Walter de Caple to present immediately to the Church of How Caple; otherwise the Bishop would collate by lapse.

MONICIO PRESENTANDI AD ECCLESIAM DE CAPLE.—Item prescriptis loco, die, et anno, scripsit Dominus Officiali suo quod, quia ecclesia de Caple vacavit a die Beati Michaelis proximo preterito, domino Waltero de Caple, patrono memorate ecclesie, denunciaret quod ad ipsam in brevi personam ydoneam presentaret. Alioquin ipsam, prout fuerit consonum equitati, per temporis lapsum conferret.

Mandate to the Dean of Frome to induct to the Church of Ullingswick Richard de Kimberley in the person of his Proctor.

DE COLLACIONE POSSESSIONEQUE ECCLESIE DE ULLYNGWYKE.— Memoratis die, loco, et anno, mandavit Dominus Decano de Froma quod, quia ecclesiam de Ullingwyke contulit Ricardo de Kyneburleye intuitu caritatis, ipsum per Willelmum de Kyneburleye, quem ad hoc coram eodem Domino Procuratorem suum constituit, in corporalem possessionem ipsius ecclesie induceret, etc.

May 14.—Appointment of Edmund de Warefelde as Proctor for the Bishop in the Court of Rome.

PROCURATORIUM E[DMUNDI] DE WAREFELDE.—Omnibus Christi fidelibus Thomas, etc. Ad impetrandum pro nobis in Romana Curia tam litteras gracie quam communis justicie, etc., dilectum nobis in Christo clericum, magistrum Edmundum de Warefelde, nostrum facimus Procuratorem, etc. Datum Londoniis, ij Idus Maii, anno Domini M°CC°LXXX°.

Memorandum that two letters are transmitted through the Archdeacon of Surrey, one directed to Edmund de Warefelde, and the other to John de Bitterley. Copies of both are sewn to this folio.

DE LITTERIS MISSIS AD CURIAM.—Item eodem tempore emanarunt due littere, quarum una directa fuit prescripto magistro E[dmundo] de Warefelde, et alia directa fuit magistro J[ohanni] de Buterleye. Et tam dicte littere quam suprascriptum procuratorium transmisse fuerunt ad Curiam per dominum . . . Archidiaconum Sureye. Transcripta autem dictarum litterarum huic folio sunt consuta.

May 14.—Institution of Henry de Upavene to the Church of Hope Say, on the presentation of Isabella de Mortimer. Mandate of induction. Injunction to Henry to learn plain-song.

INSTITUCIO ET INDUCCIO DE HOPE SAY.—Memorandum quod die, loco, et anno subscriptis, salvo jure cujusque, admisit Dominus Henricum de Upavene, clericum, ad ecclesiam de Hope Say, secundum Constitucionem Lugdunensem; et ei injunxit quod disceret cantum; et eidem fecit litteram institucionis, cujus tenor talis est,—Thomas, etc., dilecto in Christo filio, Henrico de Upavene, clerico, salutem, etc. Ad ecclesiam de Hope Say vacantem, ad presentacionem Domine Isabelle de Mortuo Mari, Domine de Arundelle, vere ipsius ecclesie patrone, te admittimus intuitu caritatis; et rectorem canonice instituimus in eadem. In cujus rei, etc. Datum Londoniis, xj Kalendas Junii, anno Domini M°CC°LXXX°. Et mandatum exstitit Officiali quod ipsum H[enricum] induceret, etc.

Dec. 26, 1279.—Graut to Robert of Gloucester of the house near the Cathedral, vacated by the death of Henry de Hawkley.

Collacio domorum que fuerunt H[enrici] de Haukeleye.— Thomas, etc., magistro Roberto de Gloucestria, Canonico Herefordensi, salutem, etc. Domos quas nuper tenuit magister Henricus de Hauekleye, juxta nostram Cathedralem Ecclesiam Herefordensem, vacantes, et ad nostram collacionem spectantes, vobis conferimus intuitu caritatis, Datum Herefordie, vij Kalendas Januarii, anno Domini M°CC°LXX° nono.

Adam de Fileby writes that he greatly desired to see the Bishop before his journey to Rome, of which he has just heard; but he is bound to appear before the Justices at York. He will act as desired, but trusts that the Bishop will want only what is just and honourable.

A[dam] de Fileby.—Venerabili in Christo Patri et Domino, Thome, Dei gracia Herefordensi Episcopo, devotus suus Adam de Fileby, salutem, cum omni reverencia et honore. Retulit michi ballivus vester de Ledebury quod eratis in procinctu itineris versus Romam; propter quod turbatus sum vehementer, eo quod ante recessum vestrum vobiscum colloquium habere non possum. Necesse etenim habeo cum omni festinacione adire partes Boriales, et esse apud Eboracum coram Justiciariis pro quodam negocio quod specialiter me contingit. Set de negociis de quibus alias verba fecistis vestram voluntatem faciam. Videat tamen vestra Paternitas quod non petatis nisi quod justum vel quod videatur honestum, et quod cum jactura mea aliis non dicatur. Conservet vos Deus et cum sospitate reducat ad propria, negociis feliciter expeditis.

Transcript of letters patent drawn up before the Bishop crossed the Channel.

Copia litterarum patencium factarum Domino [et ac]torum Herefordie ante transfretacionem Domini.

June 23, 1280.—*Instructions to Roger de Sevenake to give to John de Bitterley the sentence of deprivation which is to be transmitted to the Archdeacon of Salop with the record; to levy before Michaelmas the tenth allowed to the Bishop; to arrange with Adam de Fileby the steps to be taken as to the prebend of Preston, the fruits of which are to be collected by Richard of Clehonger; to provide for the election of a Prior of Chirbury; for the sale for sixty marks of the marriage of James le Poer; for the debt of one hundred marks from Peter de Lacy; and the sale for one hundred pounds of rents in Wiltshire; for confirmation of the same by the Chapter; and for collation to the Church of Stoke Lacy.*

Memorandum quod anno Domini M°CC°LXXX°, in Vigilia Nativitatis Beati Johannis Baptiste, apud Arnleye, in presencia magistrorum Willelmi de Monte Forti, Willelmi de Alboniaco, Roberti de Gloucestria, et Johannis de Buterleye, precepit Episcopus magistro Rogero de Sevenhake quod sentenciam privacionis Archidiconatus Salopesire, cum toto processu, traderet magistro Johanni de Buterleye supradicto, sibi portandum. Item quod dum officium Officialitatis retineret, procuraret decimam Episcopo concessam levari, si potest, ante Festum Sancti Michaelis proximo sequens, ut eam secum possit portare vel tradere mercatoribus, et quod pecunia sit nova quantum poterit procurari. Item quod idem magister Rogerus colloquium habeat cum magistro Ada de Fileby de fine ponendo erga Herefordensem Episcopum de preloqutis negociis inter eos, quod fieri poterit in presencia Precentoris Herefordensis, qui habebit ad hoc faciendum plenam Episcopi potestatem, dum tamen caveat dictus A[dam] de onere agnoscendo prebende de Prestone, in forma sibi alias tradita et ostensa. Item quod per eundem magistrum R[ogerum] ordinetur quod fructus porcionis de Ledebury per ballivum Episcopi colligantur; et eodem modo fiat de fructibus et proventibus Archidiaconatus, nisi per dictum Precentorem aliud, ut supra tactum est, fuerit ordinatum. Item quod justicia fiat Priori Hospitalis de Ledebury quantum ad presentacionem ecclesie de Capeles. Item quod dictus R[ogerus] tradat possessionem prebende de Prestone Ricardo de Clehongre, saltem pro redditibus et fructibus autumpnalibus colligendis, de quibus bene ordinabitur. Item si eleccio Prioris de Chirebury quoquomodo sit viciosa, vel quecunque fiat postulacio, provideatur de domino Johanne, Capellano nostro. Item quod bona securitas capiatur pro maritagio Jacobi de Poer et fiat vendicio ejusdem pro sexaginta marcis cum warda; salvis fructibus autumpnalibus et aliis mobilibus omnibus; set fiat solucio ad minus infra j annum, vel infra annum et dimidium, si fiat vendicio domino Johanni de la Mare. Item memorandum de littera optinenda pro redditu adhuc habendo per annum de domino Petro de Lacy super C marcis sibi debitis. Item memorandum de redditu x librarum de Wyltesira[1] vendendo pro C libris, et compensacione facienda per terras emptas per Episcopum; videlicet per terram de Cloppeleye et terram de Colewelle, et per terram emptam de domino Petro de Salso Marisco; que terre si valeant x li, bene quidem; sin autem, suppleantur usque ad valorem x libratarum terre per Episcopum de C libris quas recipiet de supradicto redditu. Et procuretur confirmacio Capituli per magistros W[illelmum] de Monte Forti, R[obertum] de Gloucestria, W[alterum] de Rudmareleye et J[ohannem] de Bradeham. Cum ecclesia de Stoke Lacy vacaverit a Festo Sancte Trinitatis infra quindecim dies, auctoritate nostra et secundum Constitucionem Concilii Lugdunensis, per Vicarium Episcopi magistro . . . . [2] conferatur.

Memoranda given to the Precentor, the Official, and others of various payments to be made in the Bishop's behalf, and of a sum of six hundred marks to be secretly deposited in the Cathedral as security for the Tenth in case of need.

Articuli quos Dominus domino [Willelmo], Precentori, [Rogero], Officiali, et aliis, ante suam transfretacionem, tradidit exequendos, —Particule denariorum quos Dominus precepit diversis solvere per dominum N[icholaum], thesaurarium suum, dum fuerit in partibus transmarinis, preter denarios quos idem dominus N. domino J[ohanni] de Clare solvebat super compoto dum Dominus abfuit, et preter denarios quos dictus Dominus J[ohannes] eidem domino N. precepit solvere creditoribus Domini et aliis ex parte sua.

Domine Juliane, sorori, x marcas per litteras patentes in parte recompensacionis, etc.

Domino Symoni, presbitero, de elemosinaria pro quodam portitorio, quod quondam fuit W. Rufi, xl solidos.

Item preceptum fuit eidem domino N. quod domino [Willelmo] Precentori solveret illam summam denariorum pro roba cendalle[3] et forura pro clericis et scutiferis in Anglia morantibus ad seysinam

---

1—Land in Wiltshire belonging to the See is valued in the Taxatio Nic. at £10.
2—The name has not been filled in.
3—*Cendalle*, a fine linen stuff or silk.

estivalem, quam summam idem dominus Precentor eidem domino N. dicet.

Item mandatum est eidem domino N. litteratorie quod ad quasdam ordinaciones faciendas Girardo de Ugina, per talliam scriptam contra dominum J[ohannem] de Clare, de redditu solvat D et xx marcas.

Item mandatum est eidem domino N. quod clam, sub sigillo Officialis vel domini Precentoris, omnibus hominibus hoc ignorantibus preter ipsos, tres CC marcas in partem unam in Ecclesia Herefordensi deponat, ad solvendum pro decima si necessitas id exposcat.

Instructions sent to the Seneschal from Lyre[1] for the distribution in the diocese of twelve quarters of corn.

Apud Lyram preceptum fuit Senescallo quod xij quarteria bladi per Episcopatum faceret distribui.

July 25.—Mandate to the Official to adjourn proceedings against the portionists of Bromyard for a full year, allowing such grace as may be legally possible, and asking the Chancellor to state his wishes on the subject in writing.

DE PORCIONARIIS DE BROMYARDE.—Memorandum quod in Festo Sancti Jacobi Apostoli in Julio apud Pontem de Charentone,[2] anno Domini M°CC°LXXX°, scripsit Dominus magistro Roberto de Gloucestria, Officiali suo, quedam, inter que istud inseritur. Mittimus vobis transcriptum ultimorum actorum coram nobis contra Poncium et Petrum, qui se gerunt pro porcionariis ecclesie de Bromyard; mandantes quatinus, ad diem prefixum eisdem, ipsos, vel eorum procuratores, faciatis vocari ad procedendum secundum ipsorum actorum tenorem, illis diem prefigentes, videlicet diem eundem post annum integre revolutum, ad faciendum et subeundum que facere et subire deberent die eis prefixo, omnibus interim in eodem statu permanentibus; potissimum si secundum jura ipsis graciam hujusmodi facere valeamus; sin autem, graciam quam ipsis de jure facere possimus. Nobis per intervenientem proximum rescribatis, domino Cancellario Herefordensi ex parte nostra dicentes quod nobis scribat quam graciam nepotibus suis voluerit nos facere in

---

1—The Bishop spent some time in the Benedictine Abbey in what is now called Vieille-Lyre. The Abbot was *ex officio* a Canon of Hereford; v. Introduction.

2—The Bishop's stay at Charenton seems to have been connected with some property bought there by Bishop Peter, of which we hear more at a later date.

premissis; cui eciam scribimus de eisdem; ita ut, vestro et suo responso recepto, quod erit faciendum facere valeamus. Transcriptum autem actorum predictorum est conscriptum in tercio ultimo proximo quaterno precedente.

July 25.—Letter to the Chancellor asking him to take counsel with his friends and state his desires as to his nephews Peter and Poncius, and to report what he thinks his brother will do as regards the estate at Charenton, where the dilapidations are very grave.

CANCELLARIO HEREFORDENSI.—Thomas, etc., domino E[merico], Cancellario Herefordensi, salutem, etc. Venientibus ad nos nepotibus vestris, Poncio et Petro, nobis supplicarunt quod de porcionibus suis de Bromyarde eisdem ulteriorem graciam faceremus; quibus diximus quod, scita et intellecta super hoc vestra consciencia et voluntate, citra Festum Sancti Michaelis per mensem, velle nostrum eis constare plenius faceremus. Propterea vobis significamus quod, deliberato consilio cum magistris Luca [de Bre] et Roberto de Gloucestria et aliis vestris amicis, nobis super negocio hujusmodi rescribatis quod videritis rescribendum. Ad hoc vobis nuper scripsimus de bonis vestris apud Charentone emendis, vel de eisdem unacum domibus ad firmam recipiendis, habito respectu ad deterioracionem vinearum et domorum, que major est, periculosior, et sumptuosior quam credatis. Necnon vobis significamus quod habito consilio cum vestris nobis rescribatis quod in via composicionis, realiter, vel nobiscum ad tempus, de dicto manerio facere velle creditis fratrem vestrum, ut sic, aliqua prescriptarum viarum electa, que in universo sunt quatuor, possimus nos vel vos ad emendacionem, vel saltem sustentacionem, domorum et vinearum, sumptus securius facere quamvis graves. Et super premissis vestram voluntatem per aliquem intervenientem nobis celeriter rescribatis. Bene valeatis. Datum apud Charentone, in Festo Sancti Jacobi.

Aug. 12.—Mandate to Robert of Gloucester to collate Philip, the nephew of Ardicio, to the prebend of Inkberrow in the same form as in the case of Ralph de Hengham to Morton. He wishes William de Montfort to have the prebend which Ardicio now holds, and desires Robert to have this arrangement accepted. He does not want exotics in his orchard.

MAGISTRO R[OBERTO] DE GLOUCESTRIA, OFFICIALI SUO, PRO MAGISTRO ARDICIONE.—Magister R[oberto de Gloucestria], salutem, etc. Magister Ardicio nobis quandam suam litteram supplicatoriam nuperrime, presentibus interclusam, misit, unacum quadam littera nostra patente vobis et magistro Gifredo de Vezano[1], Cameracensi Canonico, directa conjunctim, prout ex inspeccione ejusdem liquido poterit apparere. Et quoniam, ante nostrum recessum ab Anglia, in mente ordinavimus quod magistro W[illelmo] de Monte Forti proximam vacantem prebendam, sua aliquatenus pinguiorem et Herefordensi Ecclesie propiorem, caritatis intuitu conferremus; ac per eandem viam in non dando petitam, nostram conscienciam illesam melius poterimus conservare; ita videlicet ut is pro quo dictus magister Ardicio porrigit nobis preces, si ydoneus fuerit, prebendam magistri W[illelmi] habeat memorati, ac idem magister Willelmus ipsam quam modo tenet magister Ardicio valeat optinere; vobis mandamus quatinus erga eundem magistrum A[rdicionem] instetis viriliter quod dicte prebende secundum hanc nostram ordinacionem, suo beneplacito mediante, modo annotato superius conferantur. Mallemus verumptamen quod dictus magister A[rdicio] suam prebendam retineret ut prius; ad quam eundem pro viribus inducatis. Arborem enim peregrinam vel non fructificantem non libenter in orto nostro, nisi inviti, sicut nec condecet, plantaremus. Ad hec mittimus vobis transcriptum cujusdam littere quam nobis magister Edmundus de Warefelde, noster Procurator in Curia, destinavit; vobis mandantes quatinus super omnibus et singulis articulis nostras causas in dicta Curia tangentibus, et in ipsa littera contentis, nobis per intervenientem proximum vestrum consilium rescribatis. Ceterum allegaciones vestras, et aliorum sociorum nostrorum, Domino Archiepiscopo utroque die propositas, in quantum eas poteritis recolligere, nobis sub sigillo vestro transmittatis in scriptis. Valeatis. Datum apud Pontem de Charentone, ij Idus Augusti, anno Domini M°CC°LXXX°. Vosque cum supradicto magistro G[ifredo] potestatem nostram habentes de prebendis suprascriptis, cum vacaverint, conferendis vice nostra, prebendam de Inteberge ad instar collacionis nostre de prebenda de Mortone domino Radulfo de Hengham facte, que in tercio precedenti folio registratur, cujus transcriptum vobis transmittimus, Philippo, nepoti dicti primicerii, conferatis. Data ut superius in hac littera.

1—Geoffrey de Vezano was a clerk of the Pope's chamber, Collector of the tenth for the Holy Land in England, afterwards Papal Nuncio, Canon of Chartres and Cambrai, and finally Bishop of Parma.

*Aug. 12.—Powers delegated to Geoffrey, Canon of Cambrai, and
Robert of Gloucester, the Official, to confer the two prebends
and canonries as above described.*

Fol. 65b. OFFICIALI, ET MAGISTRO GIFREDO DE VESANO.—Thomas, etc., magistris Gifredo, Canonico Cameracensi, Camere Domini Pape clerico, et ejus in Anglia Nuncio, et Roberto de Gloucestria, Officiali nostro, salutem, etc. Ut prebendas et canonicatus quos tenent in nostra Ecclesia Herefordensi discreti viri, magister Ardicio de Comite, primicerius Mediolanensis, Domini Pape capellanus et ipsius Nuncius in Anglia, et magister Willelmus de Monte Forti, Precentor dicte Ecclesie nostre, cum domibus, juribus, et aliis pertinentibus ad easdem, cum ipsas de jure vacare contigerit, prefatis magistris Willelmo et Philippo de Comite, nepoti predicti magistri Ardicionis, caritatis intuitu libere conferre et assignare possitis plenarie vice nostra, vobis conjunctim liberam tribuimus tenore presencium facultatem. In cujus rei, etc. Datum apud Pontem de Charentone, ij Idus Augusti, anno Domini M°CC°LXXX°.

*Aug. 15.—Edmund de Warefelde and John de Bitterley are appointed
the Bishop's Proctors at Rome in the suit with P. de Langon,
but the proxy is not to be used except in case of need, and
they are not to delegate.*

PROCURATORIUM CONTRA P[ETRUM] DE LANGONE PER MAGISTRUM R. DE REDEWELLE MISSUM AD CURIAM STATIM POST MORTEM BARDI.—Memorandum quod Dominus constituit magistros E[dmundum] de Warefeud et J[ohannem] de Buterleye, clericos, conjunctim et divisim sub alternacione, Procuratores suos in causa quam movet contra eum P[etrus] de Langone, etc. Datum apud Pontem [de] Charentone, xviij Kalendas Septembris, anno Domini M°CC° octogesimo. Et mandatum est eisdem magistris quod procuratorio non utantur eodem nisi necessitate urgente, et quod ex virtute ejusdem non substituant.

*Apr. 19.—Institution of John de Clare to the Church of Colwall;
and of John de Kemsey to Great Dean, on the presentation
of Henry de Dean.*

INSTITUCIONES DE COLEWELLE ET MAGNA DENE.—Item memorandum quod xix die mensis Aprilis, anno Domini M°CC° octogesimo, apud Wyteburne, dominus [Johannes] de Clare institutus fuit in ecclesia de Colewelle, et J[ohannes] de Kemeseye in ecclesia [de] Magna Dene, ad presentacionem domini Henrici de Dene, veri ipsius ecclesie patroni, scilicet litteratorie, institutus extiterat.

June 5.— Institution of Roger of Weobley to the Church of Almely, on the presentation of Sir Roger Pichard of Stradewy.

INSTITUCIO DE ALMALY.—Item memorandum quod v die Junii, anno Domini MºCCºLXXXº, fuit dominus Rogerus de Webberleye, presbiter, institutus in ecclesia de Almaly, ad presentacionem domini Rogeri Pichard de Straddewy,[1] militis, veri ipsius ecclesie patroni.

June 13.—Institution of W. de la Burkate, deacon, to the Church of Whitbourne, in the gift of the Bishop.

INSTITUCIO DE WYTEBURNE.—Item memorandum quod, Idibus Junii, fuit dominus W. de la Burkate, diaconus, institutus in ecclesia de Wyteburne immediate spectante ad patronatum Domini. Datum apud Prestebury die et anno predictis.

June 16.—Institution of Walter Marsh to the Church of Bromsberrow, on the presentation of R. de Bosco.

INSTITUCIO DE BREMESBERGE.—Memorandum quod Walterus de Marisco institutus fuit in ecclesia de Bremesberge, ad presentacionem domini R. de Bosco, veri ipsius ecclesie patroni. Datum apud Oseneye xvj Kalendas Julii, anno Domini supradicto.

Licence to J., Rector of Croft, to farm out his benefice for three years from Michaelmas, 1280.

DE ECCLESIA DE CROFT PONENDA AD FIRMAM.—Item memorandum quod magister J., Rector ecclesie de Croft, habet licenciam ponendi ecclesiam ipsam ad firmam per triennium a Festo Sancti Michaelis, anno Domini MºCCº octogesimo.

1—Stradewy, where the ruins of the old castle of the Pichards stand, is now called Tretower, near Crickhowell.

July 25.—Instructions to his Official and others to pay all moneys accruing from all sources to Nicholas the Penitentiary, who had been appointed treasurer for the Bishop during his stay in France.

PRO OFFICIO THESAURARIE DUM DOMINUS FUERIT IN PARTIBUS TRANSMARINIS.—Thomas, etc., magistro Willelmo de Monte Forti, Procuratori suo et vicario, ac [Roberto] Officiali, senescallis, sequestratori, decanis, ballivis et prepositis suis, tam in Episcopatu Herefordensi quam extra, salutem, etc. Quoniam dominum Nicholaum, nostrum Penitenciarium in Ecclesia Herefordensi, thesaurarium nostrum constituimus per presentes, ad recipiendum totam pecuniam tam ex spiritualitate quam temporalitate in Episcopatu vel aliunde provenientem nostro nomine quoquo modo, dum fuerimus in partibus Gallicanis; vobis mandamus quatinus totam predictam pecuniam, cum emergat, eidem domino Nicholao nostro nomine liberari per litteras vel tallias faciatis. Et ut securius fiant ista, presentes litteras sigillo nostro fecimus communiri. Datum apud Pontem de Charentone, viij Kalendas Augusti, anno Domini M°CC°LXXX°.

July 25.—Request to Nicholas that he will act as his treasurer and transmit to him the proceeds of the contribution of the clergy.

NOMINACIONIS IPSIUS LITTERE.—Thomas, etc., domino Nicholao, Penitenciario suo, salutem, etc. Quoniam credimus pro constanti quod aliquibus nostris negociis vacaretis, si vos super hoc oraculo vive vocis, aut per nostram epistolam, rogaremus, vestram dileccionem attencius exoramus quatinus secundum consilium et ordinacionem dominorum Precentoris Herefordensis, W [alteri] de Rudmerleye, et nostri senescalli, pecuniam provenientem tam ex spiritualitate quam temporalitate nostri Episcopatus nostro nomine quoquo modo recipiatis, et eam per litteratorium warantum nostrum, aut eorum qui vobis warantum facere habuerint potestatem, prout nobis melius expedire videritis, liberetis; officio thesaurarii nostri fruendo dum abfuerimus a partibus Anglicanis. Et vobis injungimus per presentes quod pecuniam,[1] que ex contribucione proveniet cleri nostri, cum ad vos venerit, magistro Willelmo de Monte Forti vel magistro Roberto de Gloucestria liberetis. Datum ut supra.

[1]—This subsidy appears to have been asked for by the Bishop to meet his expenses at Rome.

Aug. 29.—Requests to the Bishops of Llandaff and Bangor that they will act for him during his absence in dedicating or reconciling churches and cemeteries.

PRO DEDICACIONE ET RECONCILIACIONE ECCLESIARUM DUM DOMINUS FUERIT ABSENS.—Venerabili Patri, amico in Christo karissimo, Domino W[illelmo], Dei gracia Landavensi Episcopo, Thomas, etc. Non sine causa a partibus Anglicanis absentes, ac de vestre caritatis sinceritate plenius confidentes, vos votive requirimus et rogamus quatinus, Episcopale officium exercentes quo ad ecclesias et cimiteria dedicandas seu eciam reconciliandas, in nostra diocesi, dum hac vice abfuerimus a partibus Anglicanis, cum per nostros fueritis requisiti, velitis vos favorabiles reddere et benignos; in consimilibus enim quando hore et tempora se obtulerint vestra faciemus, Domino concedente. Quid autem in hiis vobis placuerit faciendum magistro Willelmo de Monte Forti, nostro Procuratori et Vicario Generali, seu [Roberto], nostro Officiali, constare plenius faciatis. Valeat, etc. Datum apud Pontem Charentone iiij Kalendas Septembris, anno Domini M°CC°LXXX°.

EPISCOPO BANGORENSI SUPER EADEM.—Sub hac forma et data scriptum fuit Domino Episcopo Bangorensi.

Aug. 31.—Authority to William de Montfort, Precentor and Vicar-General, to balance the account of the forty marks due to and from Adam de Fileby, Archdeacon of Salop, and to give a formal discharge of his bond of one hundred marks to the Bishop.

AD CONPENSANDUM CUM ADA DE FILEBI DE XL MARCIS.—Universis, etc., Thomas, etc., salutem, etc. Noveritis quod, cum nos venerabili magistro Ade de Fileby, Archidiacono Salopsire, in xl marcis sterlingorum teneamur, idemque Archidiaconus nobis teneatur in xl marcis aliis vice versa, nos venerabili viro, magistro Willelmo de Monte Forti, Precentori Herefordensi et nostro Vicario Generali, ut cum dicto Archidiacono Salopsire possit debitum ad debitum conpensare, et Archidiacono nostro nomine facere litteras de soluto de obligacione C marcarum dicti Archidiaconi, penes nos residente et sibi minime restituta, facientes specialiter mencionem, plenam tenore presencium tribuimus facultatem. In cujus rei, etc. Datum apud Pontem Charentone, ij Kalendas Septembris, anno Domini M°CC° octogesimo.

Mar. 25.—Bond to Adam de Fileby of forty marks for fruits of the prebend of Ledbury, called Higher Hall, to be repaid at Lady-Day, 1281.

OBLIGACIO DOMINI DE XL MARCIS ERGA DICTUM A[DAM DE FILEBY].—Omnibus Christi fidelibus, etc., Thomas, etc. Noveritis nos teneri magistro A[de] de Fileby, Canonico Herefordensi, in xl marcis sterlingorum, pro fructibus prebende de Ledebury, que appellatur Superior Aula, venditis et liberatis per eundem. Quam pecunie summam solvere et reddere promittimus eidem apud Herefordiam in Festo Annunciacionis Dominice, anno gracie M°CC°LXXXI° intrante. Et ad hoc obligamus nos et omnia bona nostra eidem specialiter et expresse. Datum apud Pontem, etc., sicut in alia littera proximo supra.

Sept. 2.—Letter of institution of Geoffrey de Bradenham, subdeacon, to Stoke Lacy, sent to William de Montford to be executed if the wishes expressed in the Bishop's letter can have effect; if not, he will, when so advised, make another collation.

COLLACIO ECCLESIE DE STOKE LACY.—Thomas, etc., magistro Galfrido de Bradenham, subdiacono, salutem, etc. Ad ecclesiam de Stoke Lacy, ad collacionem nostram auctoritate Constitucionis in Lugdunensi promulgate Concilio spectantem, te caritative admittimus, et rectorem canonice instituimus in eadem. In cujus rei, etc. Datum apud Pontem Charentone, iiij Nonas Septembris. Et memorandum quod Dominus misit hanc litteram magistro W[illelmo] de Monte Forti exequendam, maxime si ea sortirentur effectum que tunc Dominus scripsit eidem. Sin autem, quod cicius ei hoc scribat, ut aliam collacionem ipsius ecclesie possit ad suam facere voluntatem.

June 28.—Appointment of Robert de Gloucester as Official.

COMMISSIO OFFICIALITATIS FACTE MAGISTRO R[OBERTO] DE GLOUCESTRIA.—Thomas, etc., magistro Roberto de Gloucestria salutem, etc. Ad audiendum et terminandum omnes causas et negocia jurisdiccionis nostre, corrigendum excessus subditorum nostrorum, et ad omnia alia facienda et expedienda que ad officium Officialitatis nostre in Herefordensi civitate et diocesi de jure et consuetudine spectare noscuntur, vobis committimus vices nostras cum cohercionis canonice potestate; vos nostrum Officialem tenore presencium facientes, ac ipsam Officialitatem ab aliis quibus eam [h]actenus commisimus penitus revocantes. Datum Londoniis, iiij Kalendas Julii, anno Domini M°CC° octogesimo.

Sept. 3.—Appointment of John de Bitterley as Proctor in the suit against the Bishop of St. Asaph. The deed was committed to the charge of J. Marshall, with a letter of instruction, in which it was enjoined that no substitute was to be named without urgent cause.

PROCURATORIUM J[OHANNIS] DE BUTERLEYE IN CAUSA CONTRA EPISCOPUM ASSAVENSEM IN CURIA ROMANA.—Noverint universi quod nos, Thomas, etc., constituimus, facimus, et ordinamus dilectum nobis in Christo magistrum Johannem de Buterle, clericum, Procuratorem nostrum in causa seu causis, principali et principalibus, appellacionis vel appellacionum que inter nos, ex parte una, et dominum Assavensem Episcopum in Curia Romana vertitur vel vertuntur, seu . . . . verti speratur vel sperantur, ex altera; ad agendum, etc. In cujus rei, etc. Datum apud Poyssi, iij Nonas Septembris, anno Domini M°CC° [octogesimo]. Hoc procuratorium tradidit Dominus apud Poyssi J. Marescallo, Parisius, magistro J[ohanni] de Buterleye fideliter per cursorem transmittendum, unacum quadam littera sua eidem magistro directa, in qua continebantur quedam instructiva ad dictam causam, que patent in littera magistri Roberti de Gloucestria huic registro attachiata. Et per illam litteram injungebatur quod nullum in hac causa sibi substitueret nisi urgens necessitas id exposceret. Datum ut prius.

Feb. 1.—Mandate of the Archbishop to the Official of Worcester to cite the Prior of St. Oswald's, Gloucester, to appear before him, to answer for his contempt in ignoring the appeal to the protection of the Court of Canterbury in the suit of the Bishop of Hereford against the Bishop of St. Asaph and others.

CONTRA PRIOREM SANCTI OSWALDI IN GLOUCESTRIA.—Frater J[ohannes], permissione divina Cantuariensis Ecclesie Minister humilis, tocius Anglie Primas, dilecto in Christo filio Officiali Wygornie salutem, etc. Licet in causa quam Venerabilis frater noster, Herefordensis Episcopus, contra Venerabilem fratrem nostrum, Episcopum Assavensem, et quosdam rectores Assavensis diocesis, coram Priore Sancti Oswaldi Gloucestrie (cui Venerabilis frater noster, Episcopus, et dilecti filii Archidiaconus et Precentor Landavenses, Judices a Sede Apostolica, ut asseritur, deputati, vices suas in solidum commiserunt) movebat ex parte dicti Assavensis, fuisset ab eodem Priore ex certo et sufficienti gravamine ad Sedem Apostolicam et Curie Cantuariensis, prout ab antiquo fieri consueverat, tuicionem legitime appellatum, ac beneficium tuicionis hujusmodi parti appellanti, justicia exigente, fuerit concessum; Prior tamen provocatus, cui mandatum Curie Cantuariensis super hujusmodi tuicione in forma consueta directum extiterat, tam dicte Sedis Apostolice quam Curie Cantuariensis prelibate in contemptum, mandato supradicto parere contempnens, ipsum mandatum cum injuria et offensa non modica respuens et vilipendens, Officialem Curie Cantuariensis de facto presumserat suis litteris inhibere ne [in] tuicionis negocio procederet antedicto; penas non modicas si contra fieret comminando, prout in ipsius Prioris littera vidimus contineri, cujus excessum sine juris offensa dicteque Sedis Apostolice injuria, cui nostra Curia in suis tuicionibus famulatur, dissimulando deserere non possumus impunitum. Quocirca vobis in virtute obediencie firmiter injungendo mandamus quatinus dictum Priorem peremptorie citetis, quod compareat coram nobis quarto die juridico post terciam Dominicam Quadragesime, etc. Datum apud Foleham, Kalendis Februarii, anno Domini M°CC°LXXIX°, Consecracionis nostre anno primo.

Sept. 15.—Letter to the Vicar-General and the Official instructing them not to enforce for a year the claim on the Abbot and Convent of St. Peter's, Gloucester, for procurations due on account of the Visitation of Great Cowarne Church.

LITTERA GRACIE PRO ABBATE GLOUCESTRIE.—Thomas, etc., magistris W[illelmo] de Monte Forti, Precentori Herefordensi et Vicario nostro in Anglia Generali, ac Roberto de Gloucestria, Officiali nostro, salutem, etc. Anno Domini M°CC°LXXX°, in Octabis Nativitatis Beate Marie, Virginis, venientibus ad nos apud Lyram in Abbacia fratre Nicholao de Lanrothal, Monacho Glovernie, et magistro Willelmo de Alesleye, procuratoribus virorum religiosorum, domini Abbatis Sancti Petri Gloucestrie et ejusdem loci Conventus, sufficienter coram nobis comparentibus, prout in eorundem procuratorio, cujus transcriptum de illorum expressa voluntate sub sigillis eorundem penes nos residet, plenius continetur; petentibus quod demandam procuracionis ecclesie de

Magna Coura racione Visitacionis petite quam fecimus in eadem, in respectum poneremus ad tempus. Nos igitur dictis Abbati et Conventui graciam facere cupientes, exaccionem procuracionis ecclesie supradicte racione Visitacionis petite a Festo Sancti Michaelis, anno Domini supradicto, usque ad annum plene completum, vel diucius, secundum quod eisdem per litteras nostras plenius constare faciemus, et vobis, ponimus in respectum; omnia sequestra interposita, et omnimodas sentencias, si que late fuerint racione procuracionis predicte, presentibus relaxantes, salvo jure uniuscujusque, quantum ad acta et eciam munimenta. Quam quidem graciam nostram, quantum ad relaxacionem et omnia alia supradicta, per vos execucioni volumus demandari. Valeatis. Datum in Abbacia de Lyra, xvij Kalendas Octobris, anno Domini supradicto.

Memorandum that the Abbot and Convent of Gloucester objected to official action on the part of Robert of Gloucester as suspected of partiality, but declined to give their reasons. As they had allowed Visitations they had implied consent to procurations, whatever general immunities they may be able to produce.

MEMORANDUM CONTRA DIES FUTUROS CONTRA ABBATEM.—Memorandum quod, ad peticionem domini . . . Abbatis Gloucestrie et ejusdem loci Conventus, quam oretenus recepimus per fratrem Nicholaum de Lanrothal et magistrum Willelmum de Alesleye in Octabis Nativitatis Beate Virginis, anno Domini M°CC°LXXX°, velut superius continetur; et, licet peterent ea vice quod magister Robertus de Gloucestria tanquam suspectus ammoveretur, vel saltem quod non suspectus ei adjungeretur, quantum ad negocium procuracionis petite causa Visitacionis dudum facte in ecclesia de Magna Coura; eis dedimus in responsis quod illud facere nos non decuit, nisi certam causam suspicionis et legitimam allegarent; quod tamen tunc facere recusabant. Et memoriter habeatur quod, sive per dominum sive per suos substitutos negocium debeat terminari, prospiciat sibi judex quod, si in genere fiat peticio de adnullandis omnibus procuracionibus singularum ecclesiarum Abbatis de Gloucestria propter tenorem instrumentorum ejusdem, respondeatur quod illa instrumenta non debent obesse, cum predicta instrumenta absolvant Abbatem a prestacione procuracionis, ut videtur, set non a Visitacione quam bene permittit et permisit dictus Abbas; et ex consequenti permittere debet prestacionem procuracionis, ut videtur, cum una ad aliam necessario consequatur. Iterum si aliquo tempore valuerunt predicta instrumenta, tamen per contrarium actum, tam apud Bromfeld quam alibi, nunc non valent. Iterum etsi in aliis ecclesiis predicta instrumenta robur optineant firmitatis, pro ecclesia tamen de Magna Coura valere non poterunt, cum ipsa diu est ad statum suum redierit primitivum, post quem cessare debuerunt privilegia memorata. Item procuracio illius nunc debetur, ut videtur, expressa concessione Abbatis, que elici potest ex quodam memorando subscripto quod inter ipsum ex parte una, et Vicarium et Officialem nostrum ex altera, extitit nuper factum. Et hec racio breviter tangitur in littera nostra patenti supra, cum dicitur—salvo jure uniuscujusque quantum ad acta, etc.

Aug. 13.—Memorandum of agreement between the Vicar-General and the Official on the one part, and the Abbot and Convent of Gloucester on the other, that corn to the value only of ten marks should remain under sequestration at Cowarne till September 15th; that meantime the claims might be met, or release ordered by the Bishop, or evidence exhibited by the Convent.

Memorandum quod de consensu domini Vicarii et Officialis Herefordensis ex parte una, et venerabilis viri, domini Abbatis Gloucestrie ex alia, remanserunt x marcate dumtaxat de veteri blado ejusdem Abbatis apud Couram in sequestro, ita quod suspensio, racione nunc solute procuracionis prius relaxata, duret relaxata usque ad Octabas Nativitatis Beate Marie; et quod acrior sequestracio non interponatur de novo usque ad diem eundem; et quod interim dictus dominus Abbas de dicta procuracione eisdem Vicario et Officiali satisfaciat, aut litteram Domini Episcopi de relaxacione exaccionis procuracionis hujusmodi eis portet, aut saltem litteram Domini Episcopi portet quod de jure speciali dicti domini Abbatis cur procuracionem racione Visitacionis solvere non debeat cognoscere valeant et hujusmodi negocium terminare de jure. Actum et factum in aula domini Precentoris, tunc Vicarii Episcopi, die Beati Ypoliti, anno Domini M°CC°LXXX°. Hujus vero forme copiam Abbas recepit, sub sigillo Officialitatis Herefordensis.

Oct. 9.—The Bishop requests the Archbishop to suspend proceedings against William Daubeny till his return from abroad.

Fol. 67.   DOMINO CANTUARIENSI ARCHIEPISCOPO DE W[ILLELMO] DE ALBANIACO.—vij Idus Octobris, apud Lyram, anno suprascripto,

Dominus scripsit Domino Cantuariensi Archiepiscopo quedam, inter que exoravit eundem quod negocium quod contra dominum Willelmum de Albaniaco, ut dicebatur, extitit attemptatum velit ponere in suspenso, donec ad partes Anglicanas se duxerit disposicio Salvatoris; quod quidem foret infra annum eodem Salvatore ducente. Et quod tunc et semper idem dominus Willelmus suis mandatis omnibus obediret, et quod idem Dominus Archiepiscopus suam super hiis et aliis rescriberet voluntatem.

Letter to Nicholas de Knovile thanking him for his services in the matter last mentioned, asking him to be present at the delivery of the letter, and to press for the delay requested.

DOMINO N[ICHOLAO] DE KNOVILE, PRO EODEM.—Item, Dominus tunc scripsit domino Nicholao de Knovile, ipsi regracians quod prius erga illos quorum intererat pro negocio institit memorato; ipsum rogans quod exhibicioni pretacte littere interforet, et ipsum erga dictum Dominum suum pro viribus procuraret, et circa dictum respectum habendum instaret.

Memorandum that John de Clare, who had been sent to England, carried with him the letters referred to below.

J[OHANNES] DE CLARE.—Memorandum quod dominus Johannes de Clare, de Lyra in Angliam missus ob diversa, litteras que inferius continguntur secum, prout ei injunxit Dominus, deportabat.

Sept. 27.—Mandate to Robert of Gloucester to collect the money promised by the clergy, and entrust it to bankers or others, as John de Clare will advise. The two hundred marks assigned by Richard of Hereford for the use of his son Roger, on his coming of age, and deposited with Walter de la Bare have been removed, and must be replaced. John will convey further instructions as to the will of Richard and the procurations at Cowarne.

OFFICIALI.—Magistro R[oberto] de Gloucestria, Officiali suo, salutem, etc. Mandamus quatinus pecuniam a clero promissam, cum collecta fuerit, consilio J[ohannis] de Clare in forma quam vobis dixerit, mercatoribus liberetis, vel per alium liberari faceretis. Ad hec cum CC marce quas Ricardus de Herefordia Rogero filio, ad certos usus, cum ad etatem pervenerit, assignasset, eademque pecunia per ballivum nostrum Herefordensem vice nostra, et per executores ipsius R[icardi], in manus Walteri de la Bare fuisset deposita sub sequestro quousque ordinaremus ad comodum dicti pueri de eadem; intellexerimusque quod dicta pecunia, sine nostro aut nostrorum consensu vel consilio, est exacta, et sequestrum nostrum sive depositum violatum; vobis mandamus quod ipsius pecunie exactores ad dictam pecuniam loco quo prius integre reponendam, monicione premissa, censura Ecclesiastica compellatis; remanente dicta pecunia itaque sub sequestro donec aliter vobis de nostra constiterit voluntate. Alia vobis dicet dictus J[ohannes] de racione testamenti dicti R[icardi] audienda; cui credatis, et quatenus de jure poteritis, exequi non tardetis. Ceterum ad peticionem Abbatis Gloucestrie de procuracione ecclesie de Magna Coura vobis nostram rescripsimus voluntatem; quam eciam dictus J[ohannes] vobis scit plenius intimare. Super aliis vobis non scribimus ad presens; tum quia nos ultimo scripsimus vobis ad multa, responsum ad eadem expectantes; tum quia sepedictus J[ohannes] de Clare voluntatem nostram sciens in aliquibus missis vobis respondebit ad plurima, cum fuerit requisitus. Datum apud Lyram, v Kalendas Octobris.

Sept. 27.—Mandate to Nicholas, the Penitentiary, to send him all moneys available, and to assist John de Clare and Gerard de Ugina in auditing the accounts.

PENITENCIARIO.—Domino Nicholao, Penitenciario, salutem, etc. Cum ad diversa debita in partibus Londoniarum diversis mercatoribus persolvenda et ad providencias nostras faciendas, ingressi[1] in partibus ubi sumus, indigeamus non modica pecunie quantitate, vobis mandamus quatinus totam pecuniam super isto compoto prepositorum Herefordensium recipiendam, et eciam post compotum usque ad reditum Johannis de Clare ad nos, cum illa quam recepistis ante compotum undecumque, eidem Johanni de Clare, quem ad partes vestras pro audicione dictorum compotorum et pro aliis transmittimus, per talliam integre liberetis; rogantes quatinus eidem Johanni et Gyrardo de Ugina in audicione dictorum compotorum, cum vacare poteritis, assistatis; maxime cum in recepcione pecunie vestra intersit, racione oneris quod in vobis ad preces nostras nostri gracia assumpsistis. Valeatis. Datum ut supra.

1.—In MS. *ingresso*.

Sept. 27.—*Letter to Maurice de Membury bidding him to act on instructions from John de Clare, who is sent to England to audit the accounts and on other business.*

MAURICIO DE MEMBURY.—Item tunc Dominus scripsit statum suum Mauricio de Membury, et quod dominum Johannem de Clare in Angliam misit ad compotos audiendos et alia negocia facienda; et quod eidem J[ohanni] crederet in hiis que ei diceret ex parte sua. Datum ut supra.

Request to William de la Greve to make out the compotus-rolls for the See, as in the past, and to come to an agreement respecting the tenths of four years with John de Clare, who will have the accounts balanced for that date that the receipts may then be paid out. The question who shall pay what was due in Bishop John's time will be matter for discussion. He is not himself in fault, but he will not blame his predecessor.

W. DE LA GREVE.—Willelmo de la Greve, salutem. Rogamus vos quatinus scripturas rotulorum super compoto nostri Episcopatus, sicut fecistis nostri[1] gracia retroactis temporibus, intendatis. Ad hec, sive magister Lucas absens fuerit in recepcione presencium sive presens, vos ut collector decime, et J[ohannes] de Clare ex parte nostra, coequetis vos de decima quatuor annorum de tempore nostro plenarie completorum, de quo tempore dictus J[ohannes], sicut inceptum est, vobis facere faciet ad plenum; et vos nobis similiter faciatis, sicut incepistis, litteras de soluto. De tempore vero predecessoris nostri in discussionem veniet quis solvet pro eo decimam memoratam; de quo tempore neque iniquitas nostra neque peccatum; quia quidem non ad predecessoris nostri precordialis diffamacionem vel suorum, set ad nostri excusacionem scribimus ista tantum. Valeatis.

Sept. 27.—*Letters of attorney to authorise John de Bradeham, Nicholas the Penitentiary, Gerard de Ugina, and John de Clare to audit the accounts of the See.*

POTESTAS COMPOTORUM AUDITORUM.—Eodem die scripserat Dominus,—Universis, etc., quod magistrum J[ohannem] de Bradeham], senescallum suum, N[icholaum], Penitenciarium et thesaurarium suum, G[irardum] de Ugina, et Johannem de Clare suos attornatos vel procuratores constituit ad compotos audiendos de

1—In MS. vestri.

Episcopatu suo, tam de spiritualitate quam temporalitate, a Festo Sancti Michaelis, anno Domini, etc., LXX°IX° usque ad idem festum anno revoluto, a ballivis, prepositis, et administratoribus quibuscunque; dans eis potestatem allocandi que fuerint allocanda, et ad alia facienda que ad consuetudinem spectant compotorum sive legem; adiciens quod, si non omnes predicti quatuor audicioni dicti compoti interesse poterunt, tres tamen vel duo eorum audicionem terminent antedictam. In cujus rei. Datum ut supra.

Instructions to the same to have exact copies made of the accounts of earlier years and transmitted to him, that the coming audit may start from the end thereof.

PRO J[OHANNE] DE CLARE ET SUIS COAUDITORIBUS COMPOTI EPISCOPATUS.—Domino N[icholao], Penitenciario, magistro J[ohanni], senescallo, et Girardo [de Ugina] salutem. Cum Johannes de Clare erga nos institerit ut suum compotum redderet de administracione bonorum nostrorum per tempus aliquod retroactum, vobis mandamus quatinus, scrutatis rotulis compotorum Episcopatus in quibus compoti dicti Johannis redditi registrantur, copiam dictorum compotorum ipsius J[ohannis] de verbo ad verbum sub sigillo alicujus vestrum nobis transmittatis; ut finis illorum compotorum redditorum possit esse principium compoti jam reddendi.

Letter to the Precentor to tell him that he can place entire confidence in any communications from John de Clare.

DOMINO PRECENTORI.—Domino Precentori Herefordensi salutem, etc. Mittimus Johannem de Clare, clericum nostrum, in Angliam, ad audiendum unacum aliis compotum Episcopatus nostri, et alia negocia faciendum; cui in hiis que ex parte nostra vobis dixerit oretenus fidem indubitatam adhibere velitis, et per eundem rescribere que fuerint rescribenda. Valeatis.

Similar instructions to the Seneschal, who will be detained in the diocese, and must leave the accounts of Somerset and Earley to be audited without him, but can receive instructions from John de Clare.

SENESCALLO.—Senescallo salutem, etc. Mittimus Johannem de Clare ad audiendum compotum Episcopatus nostri una vobiscum, Penitenciario, et Girardo, sicut in littera patente quam exhibebit dictus J[ohannes] apparere poterit intuenti; cui injunximus quod compotum Somersethe et de Arleye audiat solummodo cum Girardo, credentes quod vos Episcopatum non poteritis exire tunc temporis propter vestrum circuitum statim post audicionem compoti faciendum; prefato igitur J[ohanni] in hiis que dixerit ex parte nostra tam compotum tangentibus quam alia credatis. Valeatis. Datum ut supra.

Instructions to Gerard to assist John de Clare.

GIRARDO.—Eadem vice scripsit Girardo quod J[ohanni] de Clare assisteret in compoto audiendo, et sibi crederet in hiis que sibi ex parte sua diceret oraculo vive vocis.

Letter to the Dean of St. Paul's asking that John de Clare might have free access to documents deposited there.

PRO DEPOSITIS IN ECCLESIA LONDONIENSI.—Similiter tunc Dominus scripsit Decano Sancti Pauli Londoniarum de statu quo que voluit, et per eandem scripturam ipsum Decanum rogavit quod ipse et sui Johannem de Clare permitterent libere ingredi et egredi Ecclesiam dicti loci pro rebus Domini deponendis, et de deposito hujusmodi extrahendo quociens illuc veniret ob eandem causam.

July 6, 1281.—Royal letter desiring that the Bishop's Official will not continue to molest a monk sent by the Abbot of Reading to take charge of the Manor of Leominster.

Edwardus, Dei gracia Rex Anglie, etc., Venerabili in Christo Patri, Thome, eadem gracia Herefordensi Episcopo, salutem. Cum dilectus nobis in Christo Abbas Radingie quendam de monachis suis nuper ad custodiam manerii sui de Lemenystria vestre diocesis deputaverit, sicut ipse et predecessores sui, Abbates Radingie, voluntate sua hactenus facere consueverint, Officialis vester predictum monachum, pro eo quod vobis, vel sibi vice vestra, presentatus non extitit, multipliciter inquietare et per suspensionis seu excommunicacionis sentencias molestare non cessat, asserens custodem hujusmodi auctoritate vestra, et per presentacionem vobis factam de . . . . [1] ibidem deputari debere; quod tamen fieri non debet, nec hactenus fieri consuevit, sicut nec de aliis hujusmodi custodibus

[1].—The writing of one or two words is here effaced.

maneriorum suorum, quos Abbates constituunt et destituunt pro sue beneplacito voluntatis. Et quia Abbacia predicta de fundacione progenitorum nostrorum, Regum Anglie, et de predicto manerio ex dono regio specialiter est dotata, propter quod de indempnitate Abbatis et Conventus ac Abbacie predicte, tam in se quam in membris suis, merito sumus solliciti, attendentes quod ex usurpacione et inquietacione predicta magna dissensio et contencionis materia in utriusque partis dispendium poterunt suboriri; Paternitatem vestram affectuose requirimus et rogamus quatinus, viam litibus et incommodis hujusmodi paterna sollicitudine precludentes, Officiali vestro predicto dare velitis in mandatis ut ipse ab omni hujusmodi molestacione et inquietacione nostri contemplacione desistat, et predictos Abbatem et Custodem ipsius, usque ad reditum vestrum in Angliam, super hoc in pace dimittat. Nos enim extunc libenter volumus consilium adhibere qualiter hec omnia pacificum et debitum, auctore Domino, sorciantur effectum. Teste meipso apud Westmonasterium, vj die Julii, anno regni nostri nono.

July 26.—The Bishop, in reply, assures the King that he has been misinformed, but that the proceedings of the Official shall be stayed until the Christmas following.

Excellentissimo Principi ac Domino suo Reverentissimo in Christo, Domino Edwardo, Dei gracia Regi Anglie Illustri, etc., Thomas, Herefordensis Presbiter, talis qualis, cum omni reverencia et subjeccione se totum, in Eo qui est omnium vera salus. Ex suggestione cujusdam data scribere nobis nuper pro Abbate Radingie dominacio vestra curavit, quod gravamina que Officialis noster eidem Abbati pro destitucione unius monachi sui a prioratu Leoministrie in nostra diocesi, missione alterius monachi ad eundem infert multipliciter, ut refertur, usque ad adventum nostrum in Angliam, ducente Domino, relaxari mandavimus, et interim a molestacione cessari. Licet vero salva pace suggerentis, ipsa rei veritas non sit circumquaque vobis expressa, sicut per Dei graciam postmodum apparebit manifeste; tamen excellencie vestre beneplacito, in quantum sine Dei omnipotentis offensa valemus, obedire volentes, dicto Officiali nostro mandamus . . . . . [1] sciatis quod sentencias quas tulit, et alia que contra dictum Abbatem ex natura sui officii attemptavit, usque ad Natale proximo futurum relaxet, ita quod contra dictum Abbatem predicti Officialis incepta in-

1—Writing to faint to be read.

terim conquiescant; circumspectam vestram excellenciam humiliter exorantes quatinus nobis, qualitercunque . . . . . [1] simus vestri, nichil, nisi estimaveritis Deo placens, velitis precipere vel mandare. In isto siquidem facto ipsa veritas tam in principali quam circumstanciis alias lucidius patefiet. Rex Regum et Dominus Dominancium vos conservet et vestros, ad proteccionem Ecclesie sue Sancte per tempora longiora. Datum apud Fontanas[2] in Normannia, vij Kalendas Augusti.

Jan. 13, 1282.—William de Wynton, subprior or subdean of Leominster, cited to appear before the Bishop to answer for alleged incontinence with a nun of Lingebroke, and other women, was represented in court by a Proctor, who undertook that William would, under pain of a fine of one mark, himself appear on the next law-day fixed. This, though irregular, was allowed, but he failed to present himself, and was excommunicated and fined. He demanded protection from the Court of Canterbury on the ground of an appeal to Rome, and the Official of Canterbury intervened to stay proceedings. No notice of appeal had been given, but with due deference the Bishop sent to Rome the record of the proceedings and fixed a day for further action in the Papal Court, of which notice is sent to William the subprior, and to the Prior and monks of the Convent.

DELACIO ET PREFIXIO SUBDECANI LEOMINISTRIE.—In nomine Domini. Amen. Nuper, cum ad nos, Thomam, permissione divina Herefordensis Ecclesie ministrum humilem, frequenti clamore insinuante, pervenisset quod frater Willelmus de Wyntone, monachus de Ordine Sancti Benedicti, supprior in prioratu Leoministrie nostre diocesis, qui a quibusdam subdecanus Leoministrie nominatur, super incontinencia cum Agnete de Avenebury, moniali de Lynggebrok, et aliis certis mulieribus esset multipliciter diffamatus, nolentesque in tanti [s]celeris inmanitate, quod plurimis scandalum generabat, surdis auribus, prout nec decuit, pertransire, super hoc inquisicionem fecimus diligentem; per quam invenimus famam esse hujusmodi vicii multiplicis incontinencie vehementem. Huic igitur morbo canceroso medelam congruam, juxta nostri officii debitum, adhibere curantes, ipsum fecimus legitime evocari quod, die juridico proximo post festum Beati Andree, Apostoli, coram nobis, etc. Quo die quidam Johannes de Gynes, clericus, coram nobis comparens, ad defensionem ejusdem cum instancia petiit se admitti; et licet

1—Writing too faint to be read.
2—Perhaps Fontaine la Sorêt, where there was a cell of the Abbey of Bec, but the name is a common one in Normandy.

in negocio talium correccionum defensor admitti non consueverit, ipsum tamen, quo ad diem illum, ad defensionem admisimus sub caucione; ita videlicet quod proximo die litis dictus frater W[illelmus], ratificaret personaliter sub pena unius marce argenti quicquid illo die suo nomine per illum clericum esset factum. Et cum idem clericus esset ad defensionem prefati monachi sic admissus, petiit nomine ejusdem articulum super ei obiciendis sibi edi; quo optento, prefiximus in persona ejus eidem fratri W[illelmo] diem juridicum proximum post Festum Sancte Lucie, Virginis, ad respondendum, etc. Et quia talis prefixio defensori hujusmodi erat facta ex habundanti, fecimus legitime et peremptorie ipsum citari quod eodem die coram nobis personaliter compareret, veritatem dicturus in premissis; cum de veritate Procuratorem sicuti per ipsum constare non potuit in hac parte, et consuetudo eciam approbata Procuratorem in correccionis negocio non admittit. Quo die adveniente, idem Johannes comparens porrexit quoddam procuratorium prima facie nomine dicti monachi, sigillo tamen incognito sigillatum, in quo ratificavit prius expositam caucionem; et cum super sigillo probando testes ex parte ejusdem [Johannis] fuissent producti, de eodem facere non potuit plenam fidem. Et quia constabat nobis per retroacta caucionem fuisse die ultimo sic emissam, ut isto die factum sui defensoris ratificaturus personaliter compareret, prout in actis separatis que idem J[ohannes] consignari petebat, et que consignata gratis admisit, et quibus expresse consensit, liquide continetur, penam prefatam pronunciavimus esse commissam; attendentes eciam procuratorium non esse probatum, nec procuratorium, eciam si de eodem procuratorio legittime constitisset, fore in tali negocio admittendum, prout superius est expressum, ipsum contumacem reputantes ab ingressu Ecclesie suspendimus justicia exigente; citantes eundem nichilominus legittime quod coram nobis die juridico proximo post Festum Epiphanie Domini compareret, etc. Et cum illo die nullo modo coram nobis comparere curaret, ipsum ex duabus causis, pro eo scilicet quod ipsum ab ingressu ecclesie suspendimus et penam pronunciavimus esse commissam, per magistrum Robertum de Rodewelle, clericum, et collateralem[1] nostrum, cui hoc specialiter commisimus, excommunicavimus, illud sua contumacia exposcente. Post hec vero Henricus dictus Styward, senescallus prioratus Leoministrie, Willelmus de la Hulle, Johannes clericus, servientes ejusdem prioratus, apud Bosebury, die Martis proxima post Festum Epiphanie pre-

1—*Collateralem*, assessor.

dictum, nobis quandam litteram inhibitoriam Officialis Cantuariensis porrexerunt, ex cujus recitacione perpendimus evidenter quod dictus frater W[illelmus] eidem suggesserat se a nobis, propter justas pronunciaciones premissas, directe Sedem Apostolicam, et pro tuicione Sedem Cantuariensem appellasse; et iccirco idem Officialis nobis eadem sua littera inhibebat ne aliquid in partis appellantis prejudicium faceremus, quo minus habere possit appellacionis prosecucionem liberam utriusque. Quamquam igitur nulla appellacio fuisset in nostra presencia recitata, nec Apostoli[1] juxta juris exigenciam requisiti, nec alio modo quam per litteram inhibitoriam predictam nobis de eadem constabat; nos tamen ob reverenciam Sacrosancte Sedis Apostolice, eidem appellacioni, si qua fuit, detulimus reverenter; hunc nostrum processum ad eandem humiliter transmittentes; prefigentes eciam tam nobis quam parti appellanti terminum, videlicet diem juridicum proximum post Dominicam qua cantatur *Quasimodo geniti* ad faciendum in Curia Romana super premissis quod postulaverit ordo juris. Hanc autem delacionem et prefixionem fecimus publice eisdem predictis qui nobis litteram inhibitoriam porrexerunt, injungentes eisdem quod hec notificarent fratri Willelmo, monacho Leoministrie antedicto; et ex habundanti publice in prioratu de Leoministrie, cum ipse frater W[illelmus] sui copiam non faceret set pocius latitaret, fecimus coram Priore et monachis ejusdem loci tam de delacione quam de prefixione eidem notificari. Acta apud Bosebury, die Martis antedicto, anno Domini M°CC° octogesimo primo, in presencia testium infrascriptorum; videlicet magistrorum Roberti de Rodeswelle, Gilberti de Heywode, Johannis de Bradeham, Galfridi de eadem; dominorum Johannis de Clare, Nicholai de Oxonia, et aliorum multorum. Et in premissorum testimonium sigillum nostrum fecimus hiis apponi.

June 23, 1280.—Memorandum of the collation of Anthony Beke to the prebend of Norton, and of mandate of induction.

ol. 67b.   PREBENDA DE NORTONE ANTONIO BEKE.—Item memorandum quod Dominus intuitu caritatis contulit domino Antonio Beke[2] prebendam de Nortone, spectantem ad Ecclesiam Herefordensem, apud Arleye, in Vigilia Nativitatis Beati Johannis Baptiste, anno Domini M°CC°LXXX°. Et ad eundem inducendum scriptum fuit, prout moris est, Ebdomodario Herefordensi.

1—*Apostoli* are the letters in which a judge, from whose sentence there had been appeal, stated the case for the higher court.
2—Antony Beke, or Bek, the King's Secretary and familiar Clerk and Keeper of the Wardrobe, held already much ecclesiastical preferment, and was in 1283 to begin his brilliant and masterful career as Bishop of Durham.

Nov. 1, 1280.—Dispensation for illegitimacy to Hugh de Brocbury.

DISPENSACIO HUGONIS DE BROCBURY, PRESBITERI.—Item quod in Festo Omnium Sanctorum, anno predicto, apud Liram, Dominus dispensavit cum dilecto Hugone de Brocbury, presbitero, super defectu natalium, in communi forma.

Memorandum of the collation of Robert of Gloucester to the house vacated by Henry de Hawkley, and of Walter de Redmarley to that of Luke de Bre in Canons' Row.[1]

DE DOMIBUS R[OBERTI] DE GLOUCESTRIA ET W[ALTERI] DE RUDMERLEYE.—Item memorandum quod Dominus, ante suam transfretacionem, contulit magistro Roberto de Gloucestria domos quas aliquando tenuit magister H[enricus] de Hauekele, et domino W[altero] de Rudmerleye domos quas aliquando tenuit L[ucas] de Bre, in vico Canonicorum.

Dec. 25, 1279.—Collation of Walter de Redmarley to the prebend of Moreton, vacated by the death of Henry de Hawkley. Mandate of induction.

PREBENDA DE MORTONE W[ALTERO] DE RUDMERLEYE.—Thomas, etc., domino W[altero] de Rudmerleye, etc. Prebendam de Mortone, quam magister H[enricus] de Hauekle aliquando tenuit in Ecclesia Herefordensi, vacantem per mortem ipsius magistri, vobis conferimus intuitu caritatis. In cujus rei, etc. Datum apud Herefordiam in Festo Nativitatis Domini, anno Ejusdem M°CC°LXX°IX°.

Feb. 11, 1281.—Collation of Nicholas de Knovile to the prebend held by Richard de Stratford. Mandate of induction.

COLLACIO PREBENDE QUE FUIT R[ICARDI] DE STRATFORDE.—Thomas, etc., Nicholao de Knovyle, clerico, salutem, etc. Prebendam quam nuper tenuit magister Ricardus de Stratforde in Ecclesia Herefordensi, quatinus vacat, vobis per presentes conferimus intuitu caritatis. In cujus rei, etc. Datum apud Cunches,[2] iij Idus Februarii, anno Domini M°CC°LXXX°.

INDUCCIO.—Et scriptum fuit Ebdomodario in forma communi, etc.

1—It appears from very early documents in the archives that the North side of the Close was called Canons' Row.

2—The Benedictine Abbey of Conches was near that of Lyre in the Dept. Eure. It held property in the Diocese of Hereford.

May 23.—Mandate to John de Bitterly to proceed, in pursuance of Papal instructions, to recover any ecclesiastical property that had been alienated in the diocese, giving notice to all concerned, lay or clerical, except to the Bishop's adversaries or ignorant monks.

J[OHANNI] DE BUTERLEYE.— Magistro J[ohanni] de Buterleye salutem. De consilio sapiencium vobis mandamus quatinus, propter aliquam litteram Papalem duplicatam, saltem ea que de bonis Ecclesie Herefordensis sunt alienata in majori forma faciatis quantocicius poteritis impetrari; non caventes aliquo modo alicui de nostro Episcopatu, maxime religiosis, set cicius in judicium conveniatis et locum si per aliquem vel aliquos contradicatur eidem; ita tamen quod alicui Episcopo scribatur, aliis seu alii fidelibus et in jure peritis, adversariis quos nostis dumtaxat exceptis; et ita quod non scribatur religiosis aliquibus, qui penitus sunt ignari, ut patet, in pluribus, et alieno ausu ducuntur. Et quia de Stoke Lacy queritis scire rumores, noveritis quod ea que vobis mandavimus de eadem ex relatu Vicarii nostri in Anglia habuimus; nec adhuc aliam recepimus certitudinem de eo quod mandabatur, nec de ejus contrario, quamvis scripserimus pro habendo finali responso; quod tamen habuerimus vobis per Dei graciam innotescet. De statu et condicione domini Radulfi Pypard[1] sciatis quod, licet idem dominus plurima maneria habeat et diversa in Anglia, nullius tamen manerii nichil magne renominacionis existit. In Hibernia tamen habet castrum quod vocatur Saltus Salmonis; ubi, et in Anglia, habet bene mille libras terre sterlingorum; isque magnus dominus in omni terra poterit nuncupari. Ad hec qualiter Decanus se gerit in nostris negociis promovendis nobis faciatis constare. Et si ex officiali auditoris nobis in premissis Cantuariensis Archiepiscopus judex detur, ipsum nullatenus recusetis. In brevi siquidem speramus vestras recipere litteras, plures articulos continentes: ad quos tamen habuerimus ipsos respondebimus indilate. Valeatis. Datum apud Fontanas, x Kalendas Junii.

May 26.—Mandate to the Official to suspend the sequestration and excommunication of which the Abbot of Reading has complained, if the Prior of Leominster has been removed, and if not, to send a detailed report by the Abbot's messenger, if he still insists.

OFFICIALI PRO LEOMINISTRIA.—Thomas, etc., Officiali salutem. Domino Abbate Radingie de multis molestiis per vos sibi factis, ut

[1]—Ralph Pipard had manors in several counties, especially in Oxfordshire, where Rotherfield-Peppard had its name from the family. (Dugdale, Baronage, p. 9). By exchange of land in Ireland with the King he owned the Manor of Bray. (Mem. de Parl., p. 144. Rolls).

dicitur, nobis nuper suam epistolam transmittente, sibi per litteras nostras respondebamus prout nobis visum [est] respondendum fore de jure sine prejudicio sentencio melioris; cujus responsi transcriptum inferius continetur; mandantes vobis quatinus sequestrum et excommunicaciones quas tulistis solum propter ammocionem Prioris Leoministrie, ut refertur, si ita fuerit, revocetis, si predictum Priorem reducat in pristinum statum; quod si facere hoc recuset, omnes causas sequestri et excommunicacionum vestrarum, nobis, si dictus Abbas erga vos instet, per ipsius nuncium nuncietis distincte pariter et aperte. Si vero coram nostro Vicario procedere voluerit, placet nobis. Valeatis. Datum apud Fontanas, vij Kalendas Junii, anno Domini, etc., LXXX° [primo].

Letter to the Abbot of Reading, appealing to him in the interests of peace, to remove from office the monk who is the cause of the dispute. Failing that let him send particulars, as the Official will do on his side, to the Bishop; or he can bring the matter before the Vicar-General, who will do justice.

ABBATI RADINGIE.—Abbati Radingie salutem. Licet vobis aut privilegiis vestris prejudicium facere nunquam in mente habuimus vel habemus; equa tamen libra factum Officialis nostri sine cause cognicione non debemus (ut nostis) ad alicujus suggestionem simplicem totaliter revocare. Ut igitur utrique parti, quatinus sine juris offensa poterimus, placeamus, vestram caritatem in Domino deprecamur quatinus, propter bonum pacis quod vellemus, sciatis, et vos velle debetis, materiam licium resecantes, monachum vestrum, racione cujus exorta est hec dissensio quam mandastis, velitis ad statum pristinum revocare, usque ad adventum nostrum in Angliam; quod erit in brevi, Domino concedente. Quod si facere volueritis, Officiali nostro mandamus quod omnia que contra vos et ecclesiam vestram attemptaverit . . . . .[1] revocet indilate. Et si istud vobis non placeat usquequaque, eidem Officiali nostro sub disjunccione mandamus quod causas sequestri et excommunicacionum in vestris nobis missis litteris contentarum nobis rescribat per vestrum nuncium si velitis, vosque in hac causa si expedire videritis, pro parte vestra nobis mittatis, una cum dicti Officialis responso, que fuerint transmittenda, ut nos per utriusque responsum veritatem elicere valeamus et facere quod est justum. Quod si utraque dictarum viarum, racione dilacionis, prejudicialis vobis ab aliquibus videatur, ecce Vicarium habemus in Anglia Generalem, virum in jure peritum,

1—Two words are not clear.

magistrum W[illelmum] de Monte Forti, Herefordensis Ecclesie Precentorem ; qui, ut bene novimus, sine dilacione indebita vobis paratus erit facere in predictis justicie complementum, a juris tramite juxta suam conscienciam minime deviando. Has vias vobis scribimus multiformes, ut appareat manifeste quod vobis aut vestris injuste adversari nollemus, nec quod vobis fieret aliquod gravamen aut prejudicium consentire. Valeatis. Datum ut supra proximo.

The Abbot is directed to send the letter addressed to the Official under cover to Richard de Kimberley for transmission, if he is unwilling to forward it directly.

ABBATI RADINGIE.—Postea mandabatur eidem Abbati in quadam alia quod, quia in predicta littera directa Officiali alia negocia Domini continebantur que ipsum Abbatem non tangebant, idem Abbas eandem litteram, si pro negociis propriis eidem Officiali mittere nollet, clausam traderet Ricardo de Kyneburleye transmittendam eidem.

Mandate to the Official to collect without delay the remainder of the clerical subsidy and deposit it in the Treasury at Hereford; surprise is expressed that only £40 has been collected by R. de Heyton.

Fol. 68.

OFFICIALI.—Et dicto Officiali similiter in quadam alia mandabatur quod Dominus mirabatur de tam parvo levato de subsidio cleri, puta de xl libris post domini J[ohannis] de Clare ab Anglia recessum, diligenciam magistri R[icardi] de Heytone minime commendando ; et eidem Officiali mandando quod residuum sollicite levari faceret, quod estimatur ad lx libras, et idem in Thesaurariam Herefordensem cum alia collecta deponeret, quousque Dominus mandaret quod vellet fieri de pecunia memorata.

The Precentor is instructed not to give occasion of appeal to the Abbot of Reading or others, and to ascertain through Antony Beke if the King intends to cross the Channel this summer.

PRECENTORI.—Item mandabatur in quadam littera domino Precentori quod nec domino Abbati Radingie nec alii daret materiam appellandi, et quod mitteret ad dominum A[ntonium] Beke, ubi Dominus Rex foret in quindena Sancte Trinitatis, anno LXXXI°, ad sciendum ab ipso si Rex debeat hac estate transfretare, et super hoc et aliis certificaret Dominum per aliquem de familiaribus, excepto Bruselaunce.

Gerard de Ugina is informed of the letters that have passed as to the clerical subsidy, the whole of which he is to bring over; but this is to be kept secret; the Official has not yet been told.

G. DE BEBURY.—Item mandatum fuit G[irardo] de Ugina quod predictus Officialis de dicta contribucione Cleri levata Domino nunciavit et responsum Domini supradictum, et quod Dominus disposuit ut idem G[irardus] totam illam contribucionem apportaret cum alia pecunia apportanda; et quod super hoc scriberet Officiali predicto, cui modo non scripsit ex causa, ne adhuc dicta apportacio per Girardum innotesceret alicui.

Mandate to Richard de Kimberley to forward immediately the five letters, and two under cover, which the messenger of the Abbot would give him, to the Precentor and Gerard, as well as another to the Official, which the Abbot may be unwilling to send himself.

R[ICARDO] DE KYNEBURLEYE.—Item mandatum fuit R[icardo] de Kyneburleye quod dictas litteras, domino Precentori et Girardo directas, quas reciperet a nuncio dicti Abbatis Radingie per quem Dominus predicta omnia, scilicet v litteras cum ij clausis, destinavit, mitteret cum festinacione eisdem, et tertiam litteram Officiali directam peteret ab Abbate, si Abbas mittere nollet, eam mittens celeriter Officiali predicto.

June 2.—Letter to Peter of Sheppey, the Pope's Penitentiary, asking him to arrange, if possible, for the absolution without the personal presence of some one before commended, and promising his own good offices for the Rector of Munslow, the Penitentiary's kinsman.

FRATRI PETRO DE SHEPEIA PENITENCIARIO DOMINI PAPE.—Viro religioso et, si placet, speciali amico, fratri Petro[1] de Shepeya, Domini Pape Penitenciario, Thomas, etc., salutem. Pro vestris litteris nobis nuper directis, et contentis in ea, grates vobis referimus speciales, et pro dileccione quam habetis erga magistrum J[ohannem] de Buterleye, Procuratorem nostrum in Romana Curia commoran-

---

1—*Petro.* His name is given as Galfridus in the Bollandist Acta, p. 523, in Peckham's Reg. II., 703, and in a document in the Chapter Archives.

tem, potissime in expedicione nostrorum negociorum pendencium in eadem. Verum, quia in litteris vestris nobis mandastis quod litteras absolucionis, vel super irregularitate dispensacionis, absenti non conceditis quoquo modo, vos rogamus quod nobis rescribere dignemini an ille clericus, cujus casum et negocium magister W[illelmus] Brun vobis exposuit non est diu, necesse habeat pro eorum expedicione Curiam memoratam adire; et pro illo vos rogamus quatinus ejusdem clerici negocium, quantum poterit in ejus absencia, velitis nostris precibus promovere in tantum, si placet et fieri possit, ut pro expedicione prelibata ad Curiam eandem accedere minime compellatur; quod quidem eidem feceritis seu procuraveritis in hac parte nobis reputabimus fore factum. Et si pluribus occupati nomen dicti clerici oblivioni dederitis, ipsum dictus magister W[illelmus] vobis iterum revelabit. Ceterum erga consanguineum vestrum, Rectorem ecclesie de Munselowe, paternum affectum habebimus, ut mandastis. Et quia non scimus et factum suum totaliter ignoramus, scribere nostro Officiali decrevimus quod eum in aliquo non molestet. Et cum nobis aliquando scripseritis specialius de eodem, ea pro viribus effectui curabimus mancipare. Valeatis. Datum apud Fontanas, iiij Nonas Junii.

Letters to William Brun and John de Bitterley contained secret instructions, and were not copied.

MEMORANDUM.—Et memorandum quod ipsa vice Dominus propria manu sua scripsit magistris W[illelmo] Brun et J[ohanni] de Buterleye quedam secreta, quorum non habebantur transcripta.

Iste littere subscripte ad Curiam Romanam per P., nuncium, et Pikarde fuerant deportate.

June 16.—Letter to his Proctors on the need of presents to the Cardinals in order to expedite his affairs at Rome. He can only send one hundred pounds, which will suffice but for a few and the most influential. Several modes of distributing the sum are mentioned. He dislikes the proposal to offer money or jewels to the Pope. If absolutely necessary, more must be borrowed for the purpose; if that be not feasible, deductions should be made from the sums proposed.

PROCURATORIBUS IN CURIA ROMANA MORANTIBUS.—Magistris W[illelmo] Brun et J[ohanni] de Buterleye salutem. Licet inter nos sermo extiterit aliquando, et postmodum super eodem fuerit

subsecuta relacio litteralis, scilicet de visitando[1] omnes et singulos
Cardinales; postmodum tamen deliberato consilio perpendimus quod
hoc gravamina debitorum et Episcopatus exilitas non permittunt;
verum, quia intelleximus, immo scimus, quod negocia in Curia
minime promoventur nisi in generali vel speciali fuerit visitata,
propterea ad nostra negocia expedienda per litteras mercatorum
Pistoriensium vobis mittimus centum libras sterlingorum in sterlingis
vel grossis[2] Turonensibus recipiendas; cujus pecunie summa, et si
modica videatur, prodesse tamen poterit caucius distributa, quod
judicio quorumdam fieri poterit in hunc modum; videlicet, quod
dominus Hugo, Anglicus Cardinalis, habeat xxx marcas, Dominus
Gerardus, Cardinalis, auditor noster, x libras et sua familia v marcas,
Dominus Mattheus Ruffus, Cardinalis, x marcas, Dominus Jordanus,[3]
Cardinalis, x marcas, Vicecancellarius xv libras, Auditor contradic-
torum x marcas, B. de Neapoli, et alius notarius magis excellens et
Domino Pape magis specialis, xx marcas pro equali porcione; Cubi-
cularius Domini Pape x marcas, hostiarius Domini Pape xl solidos
sterlingorum. Aliis videtur quod a summa Vicecancellario deputata
possunt detrahi v marce, ita quod habeat x marcas tantum; a
duobus notariis et Cubiculario Pape possunt subtrahi vij marce et
dimidia, ita quod quilibet istorum habeat tantum. Et ita remane-
bunt de C libris xxxiij marce et dimidia.[4] Aliis videtur quod bonum
esset respicere Papam, cui est familiaris Archiepiscopus a quo
appellatur, in xl vel l marcis, tot prius subtrahendo quot essent
summam memoratam pecunie recepturi. Nobis siquidem videtur
quod media via est magis proficua et honesta; dum tamen si necessitas urgeat, Papa in aliquo respiciatur quod sibi placeat a quo
omnis gracia dinoscitur dependere. Hoc tamen quod de Papa
scribimus nobis non est cordi, nisi in defectu illius facti causa
nostra contra Assavensem et alia nostra negocia in periculo existerent manifesto. Quocirca bene vellemus quod prefato Domino
xl vel l marcas vel marcatas in jocalibus presentetis pocius novicio
mutuando quam de supradicta summa partem aliquam subtrahatis;
ad quod mutuum contrahendum vobis non mittimus signetum
nostrum, quia non credimus quod hoc facere nos oporteat ista vice.
Mercatores tamen Pistorienses, cum aliquali obligacione nostra,
credimus ad comodum nostrum nobis summam tante pecunie mutua-

---

1—*Visitare* is the usual euphemism for the offer of the gifts expected by influential personages at Rome from suitors in the Court or candidates for office.

2—*Grossis*. The silver *gros* of Tours was much in use. Fifty-two of these were exchanged for a mark in Swinfield's time (Household Roll, p. 127).

3—Jordanus, cardinal deacon of St. Eustace, had a yearly pension of twenty marks from Peckham. (Reg. 111, 873).

4—There appears to be some mistake in the figures given

bunt. Quod si per eos vel alios amicos nostros nostris necessitatibus non poterit procurari, tunc de C libris quantum videbitis expedire recipiatis ad opus Domini; supradictum residuum pecunie inter alios distribuentes prout ad proficuum cause nostre et aliorum negociorum nostrorum videbitur expedire. In causa contra Assavensem rei regulam principaliter teneamus cujus est causam quantum poterit protelare; in causa tamen supradicta, in qua acceptam habemus appellacionem a Domino Archiepiscopo Cantuariensi legitime nuper factam, nolumus subterfugia querere turpia et suspecta quibus possimus animum judicis commovere, vel talia que erga eundem redderent nos suspectos, vel per que posset nobis periculum iminere si ad priorem judicem remittamur; quod forte a nostro adversario preoptatur. Desideramus quidem pericula plurima evitare dum causa sit in Curia antedicta; dum tamen expense nostre quas fecimus pro missione nuncii simplicis ad impetrandum, antequam is a quo appellatur appellacioni nostre detulerit, nobis primitus refundantur, vel saltem petantur cum instancia competenti; propterea quia in hac via distribucionis, cui, ut suprascripsimus, melius consentimus, restant xxxiij marce et dimidia distribuende, bene volumus quod Dominus noster Hyspanus Cardinalis, cui scribimus, habeat x marcas, et Dominus Benedictus, Cardinalis, et Dominus Jacobus, Cardinalis, vel Willelmus, Gallicus Cardinalis, qui de istis tempore distribucionis amicicior Domino Pape erit, et in promocione negociorum nostrorum nobis poterit plenius valere, habeat x marcas; undecim siquidem marcas. Ad hec residuas vestre mutue relinquimus ordinacioni, pro alio vel aliis visitandis, vel expensis aliis necessario faciendis. Facta siquidem distribucione, vellemus quod ad nos cum summa festinacione nuncii nostri redirent, cum vestris litteris continentibus seriem geste rei et recipiencium voluntates, unacum rumoribus aliis referendis. Quia sumus (benedictus Altissimus), spiritualiter restituti in tantum et corporaliter emendati quod corpus nostrum ad labores et dolores et officii nostri exercicium sufficiat hiis diebus, proponimus circa Festum Sancti Michaelis ad propria remeare, Domino concedente, potissime quia super hoc Dominus Rex jam bis post Pascha suas litteras nobis misit. Et si unum de nostris nunciis ad nunciandum nobis certitudinem cause nostre [vel] alium ad nos remittatis, cum qua festinacione oporteat, ut a Fontanis, ubi tunc erimus, voluntatem nostram ante recessum nostrum vobis per eundem vel alium rescribere valeamus. Nolumus siquidem quod eciam unum de nostris nunciis retineretis tempore nimis longo, quia nuncii satis certi et fideles de Curia redeunt tota die, per quos nobis significare poteritis velle vestrum, et quia nobis per tales hactenus [statum] Curie nunciastis reddimus vobis grates. Mittimus siquidem vobis tenores litterarum quibus scribimus ut petistis; quibus informati loqui caucius poteritis cum eisdem. Magister Adam de Filebi cito ad Curiam, ut audivimus, est venturus. In qua siquidem affeccione sit erga nos penitus ignoramus. Si ultra distribuciones et expensas necessarias solvi poterunt magistro E[mundo] de Warefelde pro salario iiij marce, tunc modis omnibus ita fiat; quod eciam nobis inter alia nuncietis. Et, quia ultra x marcas quas recepistis a nobis, et quas in nostris negociis arduis expendistis, viij solidos sterlingorum et iij solidos j denarium grossorum Turonensium impendistis, prout per quandam vestram cedulam intelleximus nobis missam, bene volumus quod de pecunia vobis missa satisfaciatis, si ad nostrum comodum fieri valeat, vobis ipsis. Si pecuniam memoratam commodius distribuere valeatis quam in dictarum viarum aliqua sit expressum, tunc prout utilius nobis erit in nomine Domini faciatis; dum tamen de hujusmodi facto constet. Valeatis. Datum apud Brynun xvj Kalendas Julii, anno Domini M°CC°LXXX° primo.

June 16, 1281.—Appointment of William Brun and John de Bitterley as Proctors to receive one hundred pounds from Spina and his partners, of Pistoia, and to sign letters of acknowledgment.

PROCURATORIUM AD RECIPIENDUM DICTAM PECUNIAM.—Pateat universis quod nos, Thomas, etc., magistros Willelmum Brun et Johannem de Buterleye nostros Procuratores facimus et constituimus ad recipiendum nostro nomine a Spina et sociis suis, mercatoribus Pistoriensibus, in Curia Romana commorantibus, centum libras sterlingorum, et ad administrandum de eadem pecunia secundum quod eisdem magistris dedimus in mandatis, et ad faciendum dictis mercatoribus in hac parte litteras de soluto; ratum habentes, etc. In cujus rei, etc. Datum ut proximo supra.

June 21.—*Mandate to John de Bitterley to send back in all haste one of the two messengers of the Bishop with full details of the progress of his affairs at Rome; not to press for payment from the Archbishop of expenses caused by his delay to recognise the appeal, if to do so would prejudice the Bishop's interests; to procure from Adam de Fileby reimbursement of moneys due to himself or expended by him or by Edmund de Warefeld. Surprise is expressed at the payment of a mark to Master Cursius, who has not been formally appointed Proctor. In case of opposition from the Archbishop's side, a petition should be presented.*

J[OHANNI] DE BUTERLEYE.—Salutem. In proximo vobis ad Curiam Romanam, cum nostris litteris, misimus duos nuncios nostros similiter et ex causa; et quia nollemus quod ipsi ambo in eadem Curia inutiliter morarentur, mandamus quatinus unum ex eis ad nos cum summa festinancia remittatis, una cum statu Curie, causarum, et aliorum negociorum nostrorum in ea, et impetracionibus, si quas habueritis, et aliis factis vestris, et hiis que speratis agere in premissis aliisque rumoribus referendis; reliquum nuncium retinentes et eciam remittentes, prout nobis videritis expedire; ita quod is quem duxeritis retinere in suo reditu certitudinem nobis portet super articulis per eum et alios vobis scriptis, una cum impetracionibus et ceteris omnibus que nobis videritis nuncianda. Et licet, antequam causa nostra contra Assavensem sit in Curia, peti possit refusio expensarum ab Archiepiscopo, a quo extitit appellatum, eo quod ad Curiam misimus ad impetrandum tantummodo, ipso postmodum deferente eidem; malentes tamen unum adversarium habere quam duos, mandamus quatinus, si perpendere possitis Procuratorem dicti Archiepiscopi, pretextu forte peticionis expensarum dictarum, nobis velle adversari et parti adverse firmius adherere, hujusmodi expensarum peticioni nullatenus insistatis; ita siquidem quod causa propter multas raciones sit in Curia omnimodo; super quo per proximum intervenientem nos curetis reddere cerciores. Ceterum, quia magister A[dam] de Fileby, sicut pro certo didicimus, in proximo ad Curiam est venturus, mandamus quatinus illam marcam quam magistro Thome le Priur pro causa P[etri] de Langone solvistis, et dimidiam marcam magistro Roberto de Braundone pro ipsa solutam, et eciam quicquid vos seu magister E[dmundus] de Warefelde, vel quicunque alius noster amicus in Curia a vj° Idus Aprilis, anno Domini M°CC°LXXX° jam preterito, circa causam apposueritis antedictam, a dicto magistro A[da] petatis instanter, cum idem [Adam] nobis obligatus existat quod a dicto tempore agnoscet omnia onera dicte cause; qua recepta, ab ipsa pecunia nos exoneretis in tantum. Preterea de una marca magistro Cursio persoluta, quem vestrum dicitis comprocuratorem, quamplurimum admiramur, cum nostro memorie non occurrat nos ipsum Cursium nostrum quoquo tempore constituisse Procuratorem, nec fuisse de nostra consciencia constitutum; super hoc igitur nos reddatis inter alia cerciores. Item non obstante quod residuum pecunie, ultra distribucionem expressam nuper in nostra littera vobis missa, vestre et magistri W [illelmi] Brun reliquimus totaliter discrecioni; volumus quod de illo magistro Edmundo de Warefelde de iiij marcis pro salario satisfiat. Alias autem satis computabitur cum eodem de quo tempore salarium sibi solvit antedictum. Finaliter autem scribimus ista—quod, si Procurator Domini Archiepiscopi nobis omni modo voluerit adversari, et firmiter teneatis quod causa erit in Curia, tunc vellemus quod dicta peticio, vel consimilis fieret cum effectu; sic enim jus nostrum manifestius apparebit, et nostra victoria seu inanis gloria erit. Valeatis. Datum apud Cumbisville, xj Kalendas Julii.

Petition of the Bishop of Hereford to be allowed to celebrate in person or by deputy, even in the time of a general Interdict, as also to ordain anywhere outside his diocese, or to celebrate in the presence of persons excommunicated, without the special licence of the Ordinary; and that he should be free from claims for payment of tenths due from Bishop John, who died in debt, while the Crown had the fruits during the vacancy of the See. It is desirable that James de Sabello be informed of all this, and a present offered to him.

Petit Herefordensis quod ubique, dum tamen loco honesto, possit celebrare et facere celebrari. Item quod extra Episcopatum suum suos possit licite ordinare absque Ordinarii licencia speciali. Item quod in generali interdicto, cum suis et paucis aliis, possit celebrare et facere celebrari. Item quod in presencia suspensorum et excommunicatorum, qui tamen notabiliter non sunt excommunicati, possit licite celebrare et facere celebrari. Item petit relaxacionem decime de tempore J[ohannis] predecessoris, etc. Cause relaxacionis possunt esse quod pro facto predecessoris nostri non debemus indebite pregravari; indebite dicimus, quia bona predecessoris nostri non sufficiunt ad sua debita persolvenda. Et Rex per magnum tempus, puta tempore vacacionis Episcopatus, ipsius bona omnia asportavit, pro cujus tempore prelatus qui succedit tenetur, ut videtur, minime respondere. Ita nichil amittet Papa ex tali relaxacione, cum forte alicui vel aliquibus dictam decimam totaliter assignabit. Et non est putanda elemosina, ut dicit canon, rapere ab uno et dare alii. Et utinam, istis in presencia domini Jacobi de Sabello[1] allegatis, idem Dominus ad nostrum comodum inter alios visitetur.

John de Beccles, notary-public, announces in the presence of the Bishop and others that the Archbishop of Canterbury has deferred to the appeal from his judgment as Judge delegate made to the Papal Court by William de Ludlow, the Bishop's Proctor, on the ground that he had unjustly rejected the pleas and defence of the Bishop. The Archbishop fixes a term for the appearance of the Suitors before the Pope or his Auditor, and for the statement of the case for the higher Court. The Proctor of the Bishop of St. Asaph expressed assent. The record is to be duly forwarded, and the Priors of Alberbury and Chirbury are instructed to defend the rights of the Church in Gordwyr and elsewhere.

Ego, notarius infrascriptus, a Reverendo Patre Domino Johanne, Dei gracia Cantuariensi Archiepiscopo, tocius Anglie Primate et Apostolice Sedis Judice delegato in hac parte, nuncius ad hoc specialiter destinatus, in presencia Domini Herefordensis Episcopi antedicti et Willelmi Daubeny, Canonici Herefordensis, magistri Thome de Bisele, Johannis de Clare, et aliorum, et laicorum ipsius Episcopi familiarium et testium constitutus, publice recitavi et distincte legi ac expresse denunciavi eidem Domino Herefordensi in scriptis et forma subscripta, que talis est. In nomine, etc. Amen. Ego, Johannes de Beccles, auctoritate Apostolica publicus notarius, a Venerabili Patre Domino Johanne, Dei gracia, etc., ad vos, Domine Herefordensis, specialiter destinatus, vobis denuncio quod dictus Dominus Archiepiscopus vestre appellacioni, cujus tenor talis est,—Coram vobis, Venerabili Patre Domino Johanne, Archiepiscopo Cantuariensi, qui dicimini Judex a Domino Papa concessus in causa que vertitur inter Venerabiles Patres, Dominum A[nianum], Assavensem Episcopum, actorem, ex parte una, et Dominum Thomam, Herefordensem Episcopum, ex altera, propono ego, Willelmus de Lodelawe, procuratorio nomine dicti Episcopi Herefordensis, quod vos in interlocutoria quam die hesterna, non admissis excepcionibus, defensionibus, et racionibus pro parte dicti

---

[1]—As an influential personage at the Papal Court, James de Sabello received an annual pension of twenty marks faom Peckham. (Reg. III, 873).

Domini Episcopi Herefordensis, quorum tenor inferius continetur, contra prodictum Dominum meum pro dicto Episcopo Assavensi tulistis sub hac forma, me nomine predicto, et dictum Dominum meum, et Ecclesiam Herefordensem injuste gravastis, a dicta interlocutoria injusta et iniqua senciens me nomine predicto, et dictum Dominum meum gravari et gravatos esse, ad Dominum Papam et Sedem Apostolicam appello, et Apostolos instanter peto, et iterum peto, quos si michi denegaveritis, iterum in hiis scriptis appello, et ad Dominum Papam denuo, cum pro tempore recitacionis interlocutorie decem dierum spacium sit a jure concessum, ad convolandum ad appellacionis beneficium; et vos, addentes gravamen gravamini dictum juris beneficium michi contra jus auferre nitentes . . . .[1] ut ego, nomine Domini mei predicti, sive dictus Dominus meus, libellum recipere debemus, et in negocio procedere principali; ex hoc eciam senciens gravari, me nomine predicto et dictum Dominum meum, Ecclesiam Herefordensem, et jura ipsius, proteccioni Domini Pape et Sedis Apostolice subicio et suppono. Gravamina autem illata manifeste apparent in excepcionibus et racionibus propositis, quas raciones et excepciones et defensiones offero me nomine predicto, secundum formam juris in qua teneor, coram competenti Judice probaturum et ostensurum. [Cui appellationi Dominus] ob reverenciam Sedis Apostolice detulit reverenter, et tam nobis quam dicto Assavensi Episcopo terminum prefixit in Curia Romana, videlicet ab viij Kalendas Junii, anno Domini M^{o}CC^{o}LXXX°, ad quatuor menses postea continue numerandos, quo vos et dictus Assavensis Episcopus in eadem Romana Curia, coram Summo Pontifice, vel auditore ab eo deputando sufficienter compareatis, instructi cum omnibus actis, juribus, et munimentis ad causam seu negocium prenotatum spectantibus, processuri. Et ego ex parte dicti Domini Cantuariensis Archiepiscopi premissa vobis denuncians, eundem terminum vobis prefigo in forma superius annotata; et nichilominus cito vos peremptorie, ex parte Domini Archiepiscopi supradicti, ut infra quindecim dies, a dicto viij Kalendas [Junii] continue numerandos, per vos vel per Procuratorem ydoneum, compareatis coram eodem Domino Archiepiscopo, ubicunque, etc., copiam relacionis in dicte appellacionis negocio per ipsum Dominum Archiepiscopum prefatum viij Kalendas Junii facte recepturi, si vobis videbitur expedire. Quibus sic actis, idem magister Anianus, Procurator, procuratorio nomine prefati Patris Domini sui Assavensis Episcopi,

---

1—Here, and in several other places of a page attached to fol. 68b, portions have been torn off and some words are lost.

denunciavit ibidem eidem Domino Herefordensi in scriptis ipsum Dominum suum Assavensem prefate appellacioni detulisse. Et idem Procurator predicte appellacioni, nomine dicti Domini sui, tunc similiter deferens, memorato Domino Herefordensi, juxta mandati sui formam, eundem . . . . . Et ego, notarius publicus, prefati Domini Archiepiscopi Cantuariensis auctoritate et mandato speciali, sepedicto Domino Herefordensi Episcopo, ut suprascriptum est, denunciavi . . . . . eciam denunciacioni, delacioni, et prefixioni dicti Procuratoris, necnon et omnibus aliis, ut superius est expressum, interfui . . . . . ad Procuratoris Episcopi Assavensis instanciam scripsi, publicavi, et meum signum apposui . . . . .
. . . .
. . . .
temporis brevitate, vobis mandamus quatinus, retenta copia eorundem, ipsa transcripta per intervenientem proximum remittatis. Mittimus quidem vobis formam in qua pro magistro R[icardo] de Heytone et dictis Prioribus est in Curia impetratum. Ceterum mandamus quatinus jurisdiccionem nostram de Gordor illesam pro viribus defendatis, Prioribus de Chyrebury et de Albrebury firmiter injungentes quod, maxime in hoc autumpno, libertates et jura ac possessiones ecclesiarum suarum, quo ad decimas et alia, tam in dictis partibus de Gordor quam aliis, viriliter protegant et defendant.

John de Bitterley, substitute named by Edmund de Warefelde, the Bishop's Proctor, lays before Gerard, Bishop of Sabinum, many technical objections to the course of the proceedings taken on the other side, and by the Archbishop of Canterbury, as judge-delegate, in the suit with the Bishop of St. Asaph.

HEC EST COPIA RESPONSIONUM MAGISTRI JOHANNIS DE BUTERLEYE QUAS DEDIT CONTRA INSTRUMENTUM PARTIS ADVERSE.—Coram vobis, Venerabili Patre Domino Gerardo, Dei gracia Sabinensi Episcopo, excipiendo proponit Johannes de Buterleye, Procurator substitutus a magistro Edmundo de Warefelde, Procuratore Venerabilis Domini Thome, Dei gracia Herefordensis Episcopi, in audiencia, quod per ea que producta sunt per partem adversam non constat esse appellatum.

Item quod non constat appellacioni per Venerabilem Patrem, Dominum Cantuariensem Archiepiscopum, esse delatum sub aliqua licencia, forma, vel legitimo tempore.

Item non constat ipsam delacionem denunciatam fuisse Domino suo, Herefordensi Episcopo, cum non constat quod Johannes de Becles nuncius fuerat Domini Archiepiscopi ad denunciandum.

Item non constat quod denunciaverit, cum idem ipse nuncius et denunciator et notarius qui de hiis posset testificari esse vel fuisse non potuerit.

Item non constat quod tempora prefixionis alicujus date sine prejudicio quod delatum esset servata fuerint per partem appellatam.

Item denunciacio Procuratoris Domini Assavensis non obstat; nam, licet Johannes de Becles inseruerit tenorem cujusdam procuratorii in presencia Aniani, ut dicit, concepti, non tamen creditur nisi appareat originale, quod productum non est.

Item esto sine prejudicio quod Procurator fuisset dictus Anianus, non tamen habuit credere Herefordensis Episcopus denunciacioni sue, cum adversario suo quis credere non teneatur.

Item non valuisset delacio Judicis vel partis facta non coram Judice, cum hec cause cognicionum[1] requirunt que in presencia Judicis fieri debent; nam ea que cause cognicionum requirunt per libellum inter absentes expediri non possunt.

Item dato sine prejudicio quod constaret de appellacione interposita pro parte Domini Episcopi Herefordensis, et de prefixione que dicitur facta per illum qui se asserebat Procuratorem Episcopi Assavensis, hujusmodi prefixio nulla esset, cum appellatus non posset prefigere terminum de jure appellanti ad prosequendam appellacionem.

Item littera que impetratur in nullo tangit appellacionem de qua videtur fieri mencio in instrumento, unde dato sine prejudicio quod super appellacione de qua fit mencio in instrumento esset causa in Curia, non tamen deberet littera quam impetrat Procurator Domini Herefordensis in audicione propter hoc retineri.

Per premissa dicit Procurator Domini Episcopi Herefordensis, constitutus ad impetrandum, quod debetis, Reverende Pater, litteram que impetratur remittere ad audicionem absolutam.

1—In MS. *coggnicionum* throughout.

May 27, 1280.—Copy of the instrument in which Anianus, the Proctor of the Bishop of St. Asaph, declares his assent to the appeal made by the Bishop of Hereford from the Court of the Archbishop, and notifies the date fixed for prosecution of the suit before the Pope or his Auditor.

Hec est copia[1] cujusdam instrumenti quod exhibuit nuper pars adversa, ad docendum quod causa inter Episcopum Herefordensem et Episcopum Assavensem fuit ad Curiam Romanam devoluta. In nomine Domini, Amen.—Per presens instrumentum publicum pateat omnibus evidenter quod anno Domini a Nativitate M°CC°LXXX°, Indiccione octava, die Lune xxvij mensis Maii exeuntis, in aula Venerabilis Patris, Domini Thome, Dei gracia Herefordensis Episcopi, apud Erle, presente magistro Aniano Galensi, clerico, et Procuratore Domini Dei gracia Episcopi Assavensis; cujus procuratorii tenor talis est—Pateat universis quod nos, frater A[nianus], permissione divina Episcopus Assavensis dilectum nobis in Christo Anianum Galensem, clericum nostrum, facimus, constituimus, et ordinamus Procuratorem, ad denunciandum nomine nostro Venerabili Patri Domino Thome, Dei gracia Herefordensi Episcopo, quod nos appellacioni quam idem Herefordensis Episcopus sub audicione Venerabilis Patris in Christo et Domini nostri, Domini J[ohannis], Dei gracia Cantuariensis Archiepiscopi, Legati Apostolici, Judicis delegati in causa que inter nos, ex parte una, et eundem Dominum Herefordensem, coram eodem Domino Archiepiscopo movetur seu moveri speratur . . . . ob reverenciam ejusdem Sedis deferimus reverenter, et ad prefigendum eidem Herefordensi Episcopo [quod] coram Summo Pontifice, vel Auditore ab eo deputato sufficienter compareat . . . . . instructus cum omnibus juribus, actis, et instrumentis, ad causam seu ad negocium prenotatum spectantibus, processurus, videlicet ab viij Kalendas Junii, anno Domini M°CC°LXXX° ad quatuor menses postea continue numerandos, ratum habituri et gratum quicquid dominus Procurator noster in premissis nomine nostro duxerit faciendum . . . . . [sigillum] quidem Procuratoris erat appensum . . . . . ac ipsum . . . . . dicti Domini Assavensis . . . . . dicitur . . . . . Episcopi . . . . .cum dextra manu . . . . . in manus . . . . . sigilla hec littere legebantur.

1—This document, much of which has been torn away, should have come before the entry preceding it in the Register.

June 13, 1278.—In the presence of the King's Treasurer, the Bishop of Norwich and others, it was agreed that the dispute between the Bishops of Hereford and St. Asaph should be referred to the arbitration of the Treasurer, Luke de Bre, the Archdeacon of St. Asaph, and Gregory de Keyrwent, who should visit the district in question, and take evidence in English and Welsh; the two Bishops pledging themselves under a penalty of one hundred pounds to observe the conditions laid down.

Fol. 69. COMPROMISSUM INTER DOMINOS HEREFORDENSEM ET ASSAVENSEM.—Sub anno Domini M°CC°LXX° octavo, xiij die mensis Junii, in palacio Regio apud Westmonasterium, in camera Prioris Provincialis Fratrum Predicatorum in Anglia, presentibus Venerabili Patre Domino Willelmo, Norwycensi Episcopo, et discretis viris, magistro Thoma Beke, Domini Regis Thesaurario, domino Priore prefato, domino Francisco de Bononia, Professore Juris Civilis, et aliis clericis et laicis ibidem quampluribus, controversia mota inter Venerabiles Patres Herefordensem et Assavensem Episcopos, super jure et possessione vel quasi exercendi officium Episcopale et jurisdiccionem in patria prelibata, tanquam ad verum ipsius patrie diocesanum debeant pertinere, ad formam compromissi subscriptam de eorundem Episcoporum expresso consensu fuit redacta; videlicet quod Magister Lucas de Bre, Thesaurarius Herefordensis, arbiter electus ex parte dicti Domini Episcopi Herefordensis, et dominus Griffith, Archidiaconus Assavensis, arbiter electus ex parte dicti Domini Episcopi loci ejusdem, et magister Gregorius de Keyrwent, Rector ecclesie de Bokkeleye, tercius arbiter electus communiter et concorditer ab utraque parte, associantes sibi assessores clericos unum vel plures, juratum vel juratos, sicut expedire viderint, linguam Anglicam et Wallicam attendentes, prefatam controversiam in forma juris summarie et de plano, excepcionibus dilatoriis exclusis, fideliter examinabunt et terminabunt citra diem Lune proximum post diem Cinerum, anno predicto; ita tamen quod eandem patriam de Gortwor citra proximum diem juridicum post Festum Beati Petri ad Vincula oculis suis subiceant, ac deinde eodem die juridico, apud Bronretpol, feriis vindemiarum et messium pro juridicis computatis, iidem arbitri de consensu eorundem Episcoporum legittimam potestatem citandi, cohercendi, et omnia alia faciendi que negocium compromissi qualitercumque contingunt habentes, et sicut expedire viderint exercentes, eandem controversiam examinare incipiant memoratam; et quod testes examinentur in lingua quam melius noverint. Et prefati Domini Herefordensis et Assavensis Episcopi dictorum trium arbitrorum, aut saltem duorum ex eis, citacionibus, cohercionibus, preceptis, sentenciis et decretis in qualibet parte, quolibet articulo et puncto ipsius examinis et arbitrii adquiescent penitus et parebunt; reservata semper potestate eisdem Episcopis loco decedencium arbitrorum, seu alia causa legittima impeditorum quominus arbitrium expedire valeant memoratum, substituendi alios quos duxerint eligendos. In hanc formam arbitrii compromissarii sepefati Episcopi consenserunt, promittentes per stipulacionem legitimam se procuraturos ipsam communiri Capitulorum suorum sigillis, integraliterque observaturos bona fide, absque dolo, fraude, et ingenio, omnia et singula contenta in ea pariter, et quod ea modis omnibus fieri et perfici procurabunt, sub pena centum librarum a parte non procurante, non observante, seu non parente, solvendarum parti contrarium facienti. Et si contingat, quod absit, hec premissa, aut eorum aliqua, ita non fieri, ut ob hoc per eosdem tres arbitros, aut duos ex ipsis, eciam quandocunque post ultimum diem finiendi arbitrii pena pronuncietur seu dicatur commissa, lis inchoata coram Priore Beati Oswaldi in Gloucestria suo Marte decurrat, et eedem partes coram eodem Priore, in suo Prioratu, tercio die juridico post diem finiendi arbitrii expressum superius compareant, processuri prout justum fuerit in eadem; salvum tamen sit parti Domini Assavensis Episcopi hoc, quod dicit se non consentire in diem, judices, et loca. In cujus rei testimonium, hujus instrumenti, confecti in modum cyrographi, una pars sigilla Domini Episcopi Assavensis et Capituli loci ejusdem, necnon Venerabilis Patris Domini W[illelmi], Norwycensis Episcopi, magistri Thome Beke, Thesaurarii Domini Regis, Prioris Provincialis prefati sigillis signata remanet penes dictum Herefordensem Episcopum, et altera pars sigillis dicti Domini Episcopi Herefordensis et Capituli loci ejusdem signata, necnon et Venerabilis Domini W[illelmi], Norwycensis Episcopi, magistri Thome Beke, Thesaurarii Domini Regis, et Prioris Provincialis prefati signata remaneat penes dictum Dominum Assavensem.

July 23.—John of Salisbury and Robert de la Grave are appointed Proctors to represent the Bishop before the Arbitrators named above.

Fol. 69b.

PROCURATORIUM AD IDEM NEGOCIUM.—Pateat universis quod nos, Thomas, miseracione divina Herefordensis Episcopus, in causa arbitrii compromissarii que inter nos, ex parte una, et Venerabilem Patrem Dominum Assavensem Episcopum, coram magistro Gregorio de Keyrwent et dominis Thesaurario Herefordensi et Archidiacono Assavensi, arbitris specialiter electis in ea, aut quocunque seu quibuscunque loco eorundem omnium, aut alicujus eorum, secundum formam compromissi substituendis aut substituendo, vertitur seu verti speratur ex altera, dilectos nobis in Christo Johannem de Saresbyry, clericum, et Robertum de la Grave, nostros sub alternacione facimus Procuratores; dantes, eisdem, etc. Datum apud Bedefunte, x Kalendas Augusti, anno gracie M°CC°LXX° octavo.

Aug. 11.—Request that the Bishop of Worcester will publish in his diocese the sentence of excommunication pronounced against Reginald Fitz-Peter, who persists in his contumacy.

CONTRA DOMINUM REGINALDUM FILIUM PETRI.—Venerabili Patri in Christo, Domino G[odefrido], Dei gracia Wygorniensi Episcopo, Thomas, etc. Quoniam dominum Reginaldum filium Petri, subditum et parochianum nostrum, propter suam manifestam offensam excommunicatum denunciari fecimus, justicia mediante, et in eadem sentencia excommunicacionis, sue salutis immemor, perseverare non formidat, claves Ecclesie contempnendo, Paternitatem vestram affectuose requirimus et rogamus quatinus mutua vicissitudine predictum dominum Reginaldum in vestra Ecclesia Cathedrali, et in aliis locis et ecclesiis quibus idem R[eginaldus] terras et possessiones in vestra diocesi habere dinoscitur, excommunicatum similiter jubeatis, si placet, denunciari, ut per hoc rubore confusus Deo et Ecclesie satisfaciat pro commissis, et munus absolucionis sibi impendi procuret in forma juris. Quid autem super hoc rogatu nostro vobis facere placuerit, nobis, si placet, faciatis constare, etc. Valeat Veneranda Paternitas vestra per tempora diuturna. Datum Gloucestrie, iij Idus Augusti, anno gracie M°CC°LXX° octavo.

Nov. 12.—Letter of the Prior of St. Oswald's, Gloucester, commissary of Adam de Fileby, Papal delegate, warning the Official of the Court of Canterbury, Sede vacante, not to interfere with proceedings taken at the instance of the Bishop with regard to the excommunication of certain Rectors, John of Welshpool, Adam de Maynoth, Heilin de Bourton, Griffin the Vicar, and Gregory, Chaplain of Welshpool, and John, Chaplain of Guilsfield.

LITTERA INHIBICIONIS COMMISSARIA MAGISTRI ADE DE FILEBY, OFFICIALI CANTUARIENSI DIRECTA.—Prior Ecclesie Conventualis Beati Oswaldi in Gloucestria, discreti viri magistri Ade de Filebi,

Canonici Sancti Martini Londoniarum, Executoris delegati a Papa, commissarius, discreto viro Officiali Curie Cantuariensis, Sede vacante, salutem, etc. Si Prima Sedes nequeat judicari ab aliquo, quis ita insanus ut delegatum ipsius, in hiis que delegacionem contingunt, credat Curie Cantuariensi subjacere. Derogastis igitur primatui Ecclesie Romane in hoc quod Decano, nostro college, inhibere curastis ne in execucione sentencie excommunicacionis in Johannem de Pola, Adam de Meynoth, Heilinum de Bourtone, ecclesiarum Rectores, Griffinum, Vicarium, et Gregorium ipsius ecclesie de Pola, et Johannem ecclesie de Guildefelde, capellanos perpetuos promulgate, ad instanciam Venerabilis Patris Domini Thome, Herefordensis Episcopi, auctoritate Sedis Apostolice nobis commissa, procederet quod citaret dictum Episcopum quod, in prefato negocio responsurus, coram vobis compareret certis die et loco; cum tamen in hac parte oporteat nos obsequi non imperare. Cujus quidem presumpcionis temerarie ulcionem, ob reverenciam Curie Cantuariensis, pretereuntes adpresens, vobis et omnibus aliis Ordinariis, auctoritate qua fungimur inhibemus, sub pena excommunicacionis majoris, quam exnunc in non parentes proferimus, ne per moniciones, inhibiciones, comminaciones, sentencias, seu qualiacunque precepta nos aut dictum Episcopum directe seu indirecte, clam vel palam, impedire decetero presumatis, aut Ordinarii memorati presumant, quominus mandatum Apostolicum libere valeamus peragere, et dictus Episcopus consequatur justiciam secundum tenorem ejusdem mandati. Quid de presenti mandato duxeritis faciendum, etc. Datum Gloucestrie ij Idus Novembris, anno M°CC°LXX° octavo.

June 1.—Bull of Nicholas III. confirming the sentence of excommunication pronounced against the offenders named in the last entry, who had been guilty of violence and robbery in the lands of the Convents of Chirbury and Alberbury.

BULLA CONTRA PREDICTOS MALEFACTORES IMPETRATA.—Nicholaus, Episcopus, Servus servorum Dei, dilecto filio, magistro Ade de Fileby, Canonico Sancti Martini Londoniarum, salutem, etc. Sua nobis Venerabilis Frater noster, Thomas, Episcopus Herefordensis, peticione monstravit quod Johannes de Pola, Adam de Meynot, et Heylinus de Bourtone, ecclesiarum Rectores, Griffinus, Vicarius, et Gregorius ipsius ecclesie de Pola ac Johannes, ecclesie de Guildeffelde, capellani perpetui, Herefordensis et Assavensis diocesium, associata sibi multitudine armatorum, territorium de Chyrebury, Albrebury monasteriorum, et nonnullarum ecclesiarum et ecclesiasticarum personarum Herefordensis diocesis intrantes hostiliter, captis nonnullis clericis ejusdem diocesis, ausu nephario, et quampluribus animalibus monasteriorum et ecclesiarum predictarum abductis in predam, domos, blada, et alia bona ipsorum nequiter destruxerunt, in prefati Episcopi et Ecclesie Herefordensis prejudicium et gravamen; propter quod dictus Episcopus in eosdem malefactores, dum adhuc infra predictam diocesim existerent, qui moniti diligenter ab eo de injuriis sibi et Herefordensi Ecclesie super premissis illatis satisfacere contumaciter non curarunt, cum nichil racionabile proponerent quare id facere deberent, et hec essent ita notoria quod nulla possent tergiversacione celari, auctoritate ordinaria excommunicacionis sentenciam promulgavit, justicia exigente; quam Apostolico petiit munimine roborari. Quocirca discrecioni tue per Apostolica scripta mandamus quatinus sentenciam ipsam, sicut racionabiliter est prolata, facias auctoritate nostra usque ad satisfaccionem condignam, appellacione remota, inviolabiliter observari. Datum Rome, Kalendis Junii, Pontificatus nostri anno primo.

May 13, 1281.—A notary's transcript from the Register of Gerard, Cardinal of Sabinum, of a letter from the Proctor of the Bishop of St. Asaph, received July 29, 1280, notifying the appeal of the Bishop of Hereford, and requesting the appointment of an Auditor. This letter was transmitted to the Cardinal by instructions from the Pope.

COPIA CUJUSDAM COMMISSIONIS IN CAUSA CONTRA ASSAVENSEM.—In nomine Domini, Amen. Hec est copia cujusdam commissionis facte Reverendo Patri, Domino Gerardo, Dei gracia Episcopo Sabinensi, dum erat Basilice xij Apostolorum presbiter Cardinalis; cujus tenor talis est,—Anno Domini M°CC°LXXX°, Indiccione viij, xxix° die mensis Julii, Pontificatus Domini Nicholai Pape Tercii anno tercio, Viterbii, Sigenbaldus de Parma, ejusdem Domini Pape Cursor, ex parte ipsius Domini Pape presentavit et tradidit Reverendo Patri Domino G[erardo], Basilice xij Apostolorum presbitero Cardinali, quandam cedulam infrascripti tenoris, quam cedulam idem Dominus Cardinalis reverenter recepit, et commissionem sibi factam a Domino Papa in eadem acceptans, predictam cedulam per me Mantuanum notarium suum, in actibus redigi et scribi mandavit. Cujus, quidem, cedule tenor talis est,—Significat Serenitati vestre Procurator Reverendi Patris, Domini A[niani], Episcopi Assavensis, quatinus in causa appellacionis seu appellacionum interpositarum pro parte Domini Herefordensis Episcopi, a quibusdam processibus Domini Cantuariensis Archiepiscopi, inter dictas partes a Sede Apostolica Judicis delegati, super jurisdiccione quorundam castrorum, villarum, et aliorum locorum sive terrarum ac jurisdiccionum Assavensis diocesis, dare sibi dignemini auditorem, qui causam seu causas appellacionis seu appellacionum et negocii principalis audiat, et debito fine decidat, si causa est in Curia, Dominus Gerardus, Cardinalis. Ego Johannes, quondam Oddonis Blanchi, civis Parmensis, Apostolica auctoritate notarius, de mandato predicti Domini Sabinensis, prescriptam commissionem de regestro ipsius Domini Sabinensis transcripsi de verbo ad verbum, et in publicam formam redegi, meoque solito signo signavi, anno Nativitatis Domini M°CC°LXXXI°, Indiccione nona, die xiij mensis Maii, Pontificatus Domini Martini Pape Quarti anno primo.

John de Clare informs the Abbot of Reading that the Bishop has received the King's letter brought by the Abbot's messenger, but is unable to reply, as no answer has been given to his earlier communication suggesting three possible alternatives (v. p. 270).

Abbati Radingensi J[ohannes] de Clare salutem. Ad nuncii vestri, latoris presencium, adventum ad Dominum meum Episcopum, declarandi et vos premuniendi [causa] de omissis aliquibus, ut videtur, Reverencie vestre scribo quod nuncius vester predictus prefato Domino meo Episcopo litteras Domini nostri illustris Regis Anglie apportavit, qui eas gratanter admisit, et legi fecit cum qua decuit reverencia, et relegi. Verum quia idem Dominus Episcopus, satis recenter reducens ad memoriam per registrum quod super eodem facto quo Dominus noster Rex sibi scripsit adpresens suam vobis scripsit per triformem viam alias voluntatem, vosque, sicut vester nuncius asseruit requisitus, nichil eidem Domino Episcopo ad aliquam viarum rescripsistis penitus ista vice, quod aliquibus, si fas est scribere, minus curialiter omissum esse videtur. Iccirco idem Dominus Episcopus, non dedignans, sicut nuncio vestro dixit, set que vobis scribere nesciens ex quo vos sibi nichil scripsistis ad suas priores litteras responsivum, vobis adpresens scribere **non** decrevit.

Oct. 12, 1281.—Institution of Roger Springehose, subdeacon, to the Church of Wistanstow, on the presentation of Robert de Stapellon. Mandate of induction.

WYSTANESTOWE.—iiij Idus Octobris, anno Domini M°CC°LXXXI°, apud Bermundeseye, instituimus Rogerum Springehose, subdiaconum[1], in ecclesia de Wystonestowe, tanquam rectorem perpetuum, et tunc scripsimus Officiali nostro quod ipsum in corporalem possessionem dicte Ecclesie induceret, etc. Dominus autem Robertus de Stepeltone, verus ipsius ecclesie patronus, dictum Rogerum legitime presentavit, ad cujus presentacionem eum admisimus.

Oct. 12.—Licence of non-residence for three years granted to Reginald, Vicar of Lydney, who intends to go to the Holy Land as Crusader.

LYDENEYE.—Omnibus Christi fidelibus, etc., Thomas, etc., salutem, etc. Cum dilectus filius noster in Christo, dominus Reginaldus, perpetuus vicarius de Lydeneye, nostre diocesis, zelo fidei et devocionis accensus, signo vivifice Crucis assumpto, in Terre Sancte subsidium proposuerit proficisci ; nos suis peticionibus benignum prebentes assensum, ut eo facilius et efficacius Deo Omnipotenti reddere valeat votum suum, percipiendi fructus et obvenciones, racione sue vicarie sibi competentes per triennium a Festo Sancti Edwardi Regis, anno Domini M°CC°XXXI°, continuum et completum, secundum Indultum crucesignatis in Lugdunensi Concilio concessum, quo ad suam perigrinacionem dictorum fructuum percepcionem sibi liberam concedimus facultatem; ita quod de animarum cura, obsequiis debitis dicte ecclesie et capellis sibi annexis, per nos interim ordinetur . . . . . Datum apud . . . . . [2] iiij Idus Octobris anno Domini supradicto.

April 20, 1279.—Master Ardicio and John of Darlington, collectors of the Tenth appointed by the Apostolic See, instruct the sub-collectors of the diocese of Worcester not to claim the dues for the Manor of Prestbury, as the Bishop pays the collectors of the See of Hereford for all his property.

Fol. 70b.   Magister Ardicio, Primicerius Mediolanensis, Domini Pape Capellanus, et frater Johannes de Derlingtone, Ordinis Predica-

---

1—Springehose neglected for some years to proceed to higher Orders, notwithstanding the canonical rule, and refused even to give procurations. He came of an influential family in Shropshire.
2—The words are too indistinct to be read.

torum, collectores decime in regno Anglie a Sede Apostolica deputati, discretis viris collectoribus ejusdem decime in diocesi Wygorniensi specialiter constitutis salutem, etc. Cum Venerabilis Pater, Dominus Thomas, Herefordensis Episcopus, memoratam decimam de omnibus proventibus sui Episcopatus, ubicumque in sua diocesi vel aliena consistant, solis collectoribus Herefordensis diocesis hactenus consueverit solvere, nec de ea collectoribus aliarum diocesium respondere, vobis tenore presencium inhibemus ne de proventibus manerii de Prestebyry, quod idem Episcopus habet in Wygorniensi diocesi, exigatis decimam memoratam. Valeatis. Datum Londoniis xij Kalendas Maii, anno Domini M°CC°LXX° nono, Pontificatus Domini Nicholai Pape iij anno secundo.

Apr. 21.—Mandate from the collectors of the Tenth for the Holy Land to ascertain the actual value of the income of the See of Hereford during the last two years of Bishop John le Breton.

Magister Ardicio, Primicerius Mediolanensis, Domini Pape Capellanus, et frater Johannes de Derlingtone, Ordinis Predicatorum, collectores decime Terre Sancte in regno Anglie, discretis viris magistris Henrico de Havekeleye et Luce de Bree, collectoribus ejusdem decime in civitate et diocesi Herefordensi, salutem, etc. Mandamus vobis firmiter injungentes quatinus diligenter et fideliter inquiratis, ab hiis qui melius noverint veritatem, estimacionem communem secundum verum valorem universorum proventuum Episcopatus Herefordensis, per ultimum biennium quo prestacio decime de proventibus memoratis spectare debuit ad Johannem le Bretone, quondam Episcopum Herefordensem, nunc defunctum. Et quod inquisiveritis clausum nobis remittatis sub vestris sigillis. Datum Londoniis xj Kalendas Maii, anno Domini M°CC°LXX° nono.

Dec. 10, 1281.—Admission of Bartholomew of Gloucester, after due inquiry, to the Church of Little Marcle, on the presentation of John de Sollers and John de Marden and his wife Isabella. Mandate for institution and induction.

PARVA MARCLEYA.—x° die Decembris, apud Colewelle, anno Domini M°CC°LXXX° primo, prehabita legitima inquisicione que ad Dominum est reversa, admissus fuit dominus Bartholomeus de Gloucestria, presbiter, ad ecclesiam de Parva Marcleya ad presentacionem Johannis de Solers, Johannis de Maurdyn, et Isabelle uxoris sue. Et eo die scribebatur Officiali quod ipsum institueret corporaliter in eadem.

Dec. 17, 1281.—Beatrice de Gamages, whose election is set aside as irregular, is admitted Prioress of Aconbury, and mandate of induction is sent.

PRIORISSA DE ACORNEBURY.—xvj Kalendas Januarii, anno prescripto, admisit Dominus, apud Stauntone juxta Lodeleye, dominam Beatricem de Gamages, monialem de Acornebury, ad presidendum Prioratui dicte domus, non ad eleccionem et presentacionem commonialium suarum, que minus sufficientes extiterant et inordinate composite; necnon ex officio suo dicte domui providit de eadem, quassata prius eleccione predicta; quam eciam instituit in eadem, Officiali suo demandans quod ipsam corporaliter induceret in eadem, etc.

Dec. 21.—Licence granted to Adam de St. George and Agnes his wife, with the consent of Symon of Hereford, Rector of Chetton, to have divine service in a private chapel within their manor of Endon, saving the rights of the parish church.

CANTARIA DE ENDONE.—Dominus Adam de Sancto Georgio et Agnes, uxor sua, habent licenciam a Domino per assensum magistri Symonis de Herefordia, Rectoris ecclesie de Chetintone, ut possint suo perpetuo facere sibi celebrari divina in aliquo loco honesto in manerio suo de Endone; indempnitate matricis loci ecclesie semper salva. Datum apud Wenloke in Festo Sancti Thome Apostoli, anno Domini suprascripto.

Jan. 1, 1282.—Institution of Geoffrey de Bradenham to the Church of St. Michael, to which the Chapel of Brumley is annexed, on the presentation of Roger Pichard de Stradewy.

SANCTI MICHAELIS ET BRUMLEYE.—Memorandum quod Kalendis Januarii, anno Domini M°CC°LXXXI°, apud Wygemore, admisit Dominus magistrum Galfridum de Bradenham, diaconum, ad ecclesiam Sancti Michaelis, cui tanquam matrici ecclesie capella de Brumleye est annexa, vacantem, ad presentacionem domini Rogeri Pichard de Straddewy, veri patroni ipsarum; et canonice instituit in eadem.

Jan. 1.—Discharge in full of John de Clare for his accounts of the six years preceding, which have been duly audited, on condition of his payment of the balance of £175 8s. 4d. He is not to be held responsible for loans contracted on the Bishop's account as entered in his compotus.

Tangens compotum J[ohannis] de Clare de vi annis.—Universis Christi fidelibus, etc., Thomas, etc., salutem, etc. Cum dilectus clericus et familiaris noster, dominus Johannes de Clare, Rector ecclesie de Colewelle nostre diocesis, de administracione denariorum nostrorum qui ad manus ejus qualitercumque pervenerunt, coram certis auditoribus ad hoc specialiter per nos datis, dignam et fidelem reddiderit racionem a Festo Sancti Michaelis, anno Domini M°CC°LXX° quinto, usque ad idem Festum, anno Domini M°CC°LXX° primo, integre et continue per sex annos, nos eundem Johannem et executores ejusdem, pro nobis, executoribus et successoribus nostris, absolvimus et quietum clamamus a compoti reddicione, de toto tempore memorato, de omnibus receptis, expensis, et libere in memorato compoto allocatis; ita tamen quod idem Johannes nobis respondeat in futurum de centum sexaginta quindecim libris, octo solidis, et quatuor denariis, in quibus nobis in fine compoti sui prestiti, prout continetur in rotulis originalibus ipsius compoti, tenebatur. Et quod idem Johannes de omnibus expensis et libere sibi in dicto compoto allocatis nos contra quoscumque liberet et quietet; hoc excepto quod sepedictus Johannes in mutuis de quibus se onerat in predicto compoto minime teneatur. In cujus rei, etc. Datum apud Wygemore Kalendis Januarii, anno Domini M°CC°LXXX° primo et Consecracionis nostre anno septimo.

Feb. 27.—Grant by Roger Mortimer of the advowson of Pembridge to Emeric the Chancellor for the term of his life only, because of the scanty income of his dignity, and the burdens of charity and hospitality.

Fol. 72.[1]

Penebruge.—Omnibus Christi fidelibus, etc. Rogerus de Mortuo Mari, dominus de Penebruge, salutem in Domino. Noverit universitas vestra quod nos, attendentes exilitatem Cancellarie Majoris Ecclesie Herefordensis, necnon et hospitalitatis et elemosinarum largicionis onera que Emericius[2] de Aqua Blanca, Cancellarius ipsius Ecclesie crebro sustinere dinoscitur, jus patronatus quod habemus in ecclesia parochiali de Penebruge dicto Emericio

---

1—Folio 71 has been cut out.   2—Elsewhere written *Emericus*.

et Cancellarie sue predicte ad totam vitam ipsius Emericii conferimus in puram elemosinam; ita tamen quod hujusmodi concessio seu donacio nostra, postquam prefatus Emoricius eandem Cancellariam dimiserit, nullum robur optineat firmitatis, set extunc ipsius ecclesie patronatus seu advocacio ad nos, et heredes nostros, tanquam ad verum ipsius patronum, sine omni calumpnia, impedimento, aut contradiccione futuri Cancellarii vel alicujus alterius, pure et absolute revertatur, et nobis et heredibus nostris ad sepedictam ecclesiam, tanquam ad nostram presentacionem spectantem, inperpetuum libere liceat presentare. In cujus rei, etc. Datum apud Penebruge, die Veneris proximo post Festum Beati Petri in Cathedra, anno Domini M°CC°LXXX° primo.

Mar. 7.—Confirmation of the grant of Pembridge and its appropriation to the Chancellor.

ITEM PENEBRUGE.—Thomas, etc., domino E[merico] de Aqua Blanka, Cancellario in eadem (Ecclesia Herefordensi), salutem, etc. Morum et sciencie prerogativam ac vite honestatem quibus insignimini, ac dicte dignitatis vestre exilitatem, cujus facultates ad elemosinarum largicionem et hospitalitatem, que a nobis exiguntur, non suppetunt ut deceret, debite ponderantes; ut hiis sustinendis sufficere plenius valeatis, ecclesiam de Penebrugge, nostre diocesis, cujus jus patronatus ex dono nobilis viri, domini Rogeri de Mortuo Mari, noscimini optinere, de ejusdem nobilis voluntate et consensu expressis Cancellarie vestre et vobis, dum vixeritis, auctoritate pontificali conferimus et appropriamus intuitu caritatis. In cujus rei, etc. Datum Londoniis, Nonis Marcii, anno Domini M°CC°LXXX° primo et nostre Consecracionis septimo.

July 10.—Discharge of the accounts of John de Bitterley, the Bishop's Proctor in the Court of Rome, as audited by John de Clare, showing a balance of three marks out of £106 13s. 4d. committed to his charge.

DE REDDICIONE COMPOTI MAGISTRI J[OHANNIS] DE BUTERLEYE DE PECUNIA SIBI LIBERATA.—Omnibus Christi fidelibus, etc., salutem in Domino. Cum nos semel, apud Pontem [de] Charentone prope Parisius, decem marcas sterlingorum pro expedicione nostrorum negociorum in Curia Romana, et alia vice centum libras sterlingorum, per manus mercatorum Pistoriensium, Procuratori nostro in eadem Curia fecimus liberari, idem magister J[ohannes] coram domino Johanne de Clare, quem ad hoc dedimus, de tota dicta pecunia plenam reddidit racionem apud Florentinum juxta Montem Flasconie, x° die mensis Julii, anno Domini M°CC°LXXX° secundo, et dicto J[ohanni] de Clare dicte racionis particulas liberavit; ita quod, allocatis dicto magistro J[ohanni] in eisdem particulis contentis, idem magister J[ohannes] in tribus marcis sterlingorum nobis tenetur in fine; quas in manibus suis dimisimus in partem solucionis versus alia nostra negocia in dicta Curia prosequenda. In cujus rei, etc. Prefatum vero magistrum J[ohannem], et ejus executores, a compoti reddicione de dicta pecunia absolvimus per hoc scriptum. Datum die et loco supradictis et anno.

July 10.—Renewed injunctions to Walter de Redmarley and Nicholas the Penitentiary to send him any of his money in their hands, as he is in a thirsty land, and must not be left destitute while engaged in the interests of his See.

PENITENCIARIO.—Thomas, etc., domino W[altero] de Rudmarleye, Canonico Herefordensi, et domino Nicholao, Penitenciario suo in eadem Ecclesia, salutem, etc. Licet ante recessum nostrum de Anglia ordinaverimus satis plene, et vobis dederimus in mandatis, quod quocienscunque centum libras sterlingorum haberetis in thesauro, vel amplius, eas dilecto nobis Girardo, ballivo nostro de Prestebury, per talliam liberaretis, ut idem G[irardus] hujusmodi pecuniam ad certum locum portaret et certis traderet personis, per quas tam in Curia Romana, quam alibi ubi essemus, posset ad nos venire secure peccunia memorata. Ut tamen sciatis quod in illo proposito, nichil ex eo mutando, firmiter adhuc stamus, vobis iterato mandamus pecuniam nostram dicto G[irardo], omni dubitacione postposita, liberare curetis in forma superius annotata; et maxime isto tempore liberetis eidem totam pecuniam quam habetis, vel potestis habere de nostro; locus enim in quo agimus multum sitit; tantum facias in premissis, ne nos, qui propter commune bonum regnum eximus, simus in extraniis partibus pecunia destituti; et ut vobis ex vestra diligencia teneamur ad merita graciarum. Ut autem de hac nostra prima voluntate plenius vobis constet, has litteras nostras apertas iterato vobis transmittimus. Valeatis. Datum apud Florentinum juxta montem Flasconie, x die mensis Julii, anno Domini M°CC°LXXX° secundo.

May 7.—*The Bishop's official has deposited in the Treasury at Hereford £40, the residue of the subsidy, as no place in London was indicated in his instructions. The Abbot of Reading has deposed the Prior of Leominster and sent him away. The property of the Priory has been sequestrated, and the Abbot of Reading cited to give evidence on oath as to the Church of Eye, and as to the charge of having raised the amount exacted from the Priory, contrary to the canons of the Lateran Council. He reports the opinion of some that it would be more to the Bishop's interest and credit to stay in England than in France.*

Domino suo suus clericus et minister id modicum quod potest obsequii, cum omnimodis obediencia, reverencia, et honore. De residuo subsidii nostri levando, de quo michi semel et iterum demandastis, quantum districcius potui injunxi magistro Ricardo, et quadraginta libras quas fecit levari portassem et deposuissem Londoniis, si locum deponendi specificassetis in litteris quas michi misistis; et ideo eas signatas deposui in Thesauraria Herefordensi quousque beneplacitum vestrum super eodem michi plenius scriberetis. Ad hec, Abbas Radingie Priorem Leoministrie revocavit, et ipsum, sub pena excommunicacionis, ne rediret ad suum Monasterium, in Scociam ire coegit. Ego vero mandatum nostrum litteratorium, Decano loci directum, anno preterito . . . .[1] cum effectu omnia bona spiritualia ejusdem domus in manus nostras accepi, et Priorem de novo missum, post canonicas moniciones, tanquam intrusorem absque canonica admissione, feci denunciari excommunicatum; Abbatem et Conventum predictos citantes peremptorie quod super ecclesia de Eye coram nobis in crastino Beate Trinitatis secundum retroacta processuri venirent. Prefatum siquidem Abbatem citavi peremptorie quod eisdem die et loco personaliter coram nobis compareat, per suum sacramentum veritatem dicturus si antiquum censum Prioratus Leoministrie auxerit isto anno contra Concilium Latranense, prout ab omnibus proclamatur. Alia vobis relacione digna ad presens scribere nescio, nisi quod ab aliquibus dicitur quod honor et comodum vestrum esset pocius morari in Anglia quam in regno Francorum. Bene valeatis. Datum Londoniis die Beati Johannis de Beverlaco.

William de Cantilupe, as Proctor for the Bishop, formally claims a manor at Charenton, bought by Bishop Peter de Aquablanca out of funds, as is alleged, which belonged to the See.

Cum Venerabilis Pater, P[etrus] de Aqua Blanca, bone memorie, quondam Herefordensis Ecclesie in Anglia Episcopus, manerium

1—Illegible.

quoddam in villa de Ponte Charentone situm, cum vineis, terris, et aliis pertinenciis ejusdem, que de feodo vestro esse dicuntur, tempore sue prelacionis et non aliunde quam de bonis Ecclesie[1] sue antedicte emisset, et in possessione eorundem usque ad finem vite[2] et tempore sue mortis exstitisset, Ego, W[illelmus], Procurator Reverendi Patris, Domini Thome, nunc prefate Ecclesie Episcopi, ac ejusdem P[etri] successoris mediati, a vobis dominis feodi dictarum possessionum peto in forma juris quod, cum possessio dicti manerii cum suis pertinenciis ad Dominum meum nomine Ecclesie sue prenotate legitime fuerit devoluta, eandem ad ipsum devolutam declaretis, et in eandem me, nomine procuratorio, de facto mittatis. Et si qui impedientes fuerint seu eandem quoquo modo perturbantes, eos auctoritate vestra amoveatis et a perturbacione tali quiescere faciatis, cum ego, nomine procuratorio Domini mei antedicti, vobis juxta feodi exigenciam in omnibus respondere paratus existam. Hec peto non artans me ad probacionem omnium et singulorum premissorum, vel sub ea forma qua proponuntur; set quatenus sub ea, vel alia competentiori, ea probavero que michi sufficere de jure debeant, eatenus peto quod optineam in premissis.

July 1, 1281.—Appointment of William de Cantilupe as Proctor, invested with full powers to act for the Bishop.

Universis, etc., Thomas, etc., salutem, etc. Noverit universitas vestra quod dilectum nobis in Christo, Willelmum de Cantilupo, clericum nostrum, facimus, constituimus, et ordinamus Procuratorem, nomine nostro et Ecclesie nostre antedicte, in omnibus causis, etc., domos, vineas, terras, vel quccumque alia, sive rustica predia fuerint sive urbana, ad nos nomine nostro vel Ecclesie nostre pertinencia, petendi, et possessionem eorundem admittendi, et eandem nomine nostro tenendi, ac dominis feodi eo [quod] eisdem possessionibus racione feodi seu census quicquam pertinere potest sufficienter nomine nostro respondendi; omnia quoque immobilia, mobilia, seu se movencia, ad Ecclesiam nostram quoquo modo pertinencia, si qua per aliquem predecessorem nostrum qui ante nos mediate vel immediate Ecclesie prefuit antedicte minus juste fuerint abalienata repetendi; insuper et alia omnia et singula faciendi

---
1—There is no evidence to substantiate this claim, which seems inconsistent with the terms of an earlier letter (p. 248).
2—William de Cantilupe, son of John the brother of the Bishop, had long been in close attendance on him, and gave much evidence to the Commission in 1307.

que nos ipsi faceremus vel facere possemus si personaliter intercessemus. Damus eciam eidem Procuratori nostro potestatem, etc. Datum apud Fontanas in Normannia, Kalendis Julii, anno Domini M°CC° octogesimo primo.

Memorandum that the gravamina of the Suffragan Bishops of the Province of Canterbury have been copied on the preceding sheet.

In proximo precedenti quaterno gravamina[1] per Dominum Archiepiscopum Cantuariensem illata suis Suffraganeis Episcopis Provincie Cantuariensis et responsa ad eadem conscribuntur.

Memorandum that certain debts to the Crown, though discharged by Bishop Cantilupe, were paid again by his successor.

Memorandum quod licet hec subscripta debita fuerint soluta tempore sancte memorie Domini Thome de Cantilupo, tamen eadem debita sunt soluta tempore domini Ricardi, Episcopi Herefordensis, et tempore Domini Rogeri de Burghulle, tunc Vicecomitis Herefordie iterato, prout scribitur inferius.

De Episcopo Herefordensi pro duobus scutagiis xli. xs., xv° rotulo regni Regis Edwardi. Rogerus de Burghulle acquietavit.

De Episcopo Herefordensi de prefato xliij s. iiij d., xiiij° rotulo regni Regis Edwardi.

De Episcopo Herefordensi de auxilio vj marcas, xiiij rotulo regni Regis Edwardi.

De Episcopo Herefordensi de auxilio ad filium Regis militem faciendum xx solidos, xiiij° rotulo regni Regis Edwardi. Rogerus de Burghulle, Vicecomes, acquietavit.

1—It seems unnecessary to reprint these *gravamina*, as they can be found in Wilkins' *Concilia*, II. 75, and Peckham's *Reg. Ep.*, I. 328, and have no special connection with the diocese of Hereford.

ORDINATION LISTS.

Sept. 18, 1277.—Ordination at Leominster.

fol. 41b. Subscripti ordinati fuerunt apud Leoministre die Sabbati proximo ante Festum Sancti Mathei, Apostoli, anno Domini [MCC] LXXVIJ°.

SUBDIACONI.—
Willelmus, filius Johannis de Uptone, ad titulum patrimonii.
Willelmus Philippi, de Lodelawe, ad titulum patrimonii.
Johannes de Lodelawe, ad titulum patrimonii; in gracia tamen Episcopi.
Nicholaus de Momele, ad titulum Cantarii de Momele; et fidejusserunt pro eo Decanus de Bureforde et W. de Baytone.
Johannes de Olretone, ad titulum patrimonii.
Philippus de Lodelawe, ad titulum patrimonii sufficientis.
Willelmus Trigeth, ad titulum 1 solidorum; et tradidit cartam.
Henricus de Malleye, ad titulum xl solidorum.
Symon de Clone. ad titulam xxx acrarum terre in Clone.
Adam de Stauntone, ad presentacionem Vicarii de eadem.
Radulfus le Chevaler, ad titulum patrimonii.
David de Sancto Michaele, ad titulum patrimonii, ut testatum est.
Reginaldus de Cucbrittone, ad titulum patrimonii.
Philippus de Sancto Brevello, ad titulum patrimonii.
Bartholomeus de Clynelode, ad titulum patrimonii.
Johannes le Mason, ad titulum patrimonii.
Magister Nicholaus de Lodelowe, ad titulum patrimonii.
Willelmus de Moneclene, ad presentacionem Vicarii Leoministrie.
Ricardus de Aka, ad titulum patrimonii.
Philippus de Inwarthyn, ad titulum patrimonii.
Johannes Bade, ad titulum patrimonii.
Johannes de Orcop, ad titulum patrimonii.
Adam de Wychecote, ad presentacionem Willelmi Brun.
Willelmus de Stauntone, ad titulum patrimonii.
Rogerus de Caple, ad titulum patrimonii.
Hugo Meth de Bromyarde, ad titulum patrimonii.
Nicholaus de Hentone, pro quo cavit officium.
Ricardus de Strettone, ad titulum patrimonii.
Willelmus de Racheforde, ad titulum patrimonii.

Davyd de Clyfforde, ad presentacionem Vicarii de Yavesoure.
Willelmus de Markleye, ad presentacionem Domine Juliane de Tregoz.
Petrus Tadestone, ad presentacionem Roberti Corebott.
Nicholaus de Clone, ad titulum patrimonii.
Ricardus, filius Jacobi de Temedebury, ad presentacionem Vicarii de Racheforde.
Milo de Radenoure, ad titulum patrimonii.

Diaconi.—

Willelmus de Monekelowe, ad titulum patrimonii.
Philippus de Montegomery, ad titulum patrimonii.
Willelmus Gladewyne, ad titulum Sacristarie de Winstane.
Hugo de Stauntone, ad titulum patrimonii.
Thomas de Clone, ad titulum patrimonii, pro quo cavit Magister W. de Lodelawe.
Johannes de Clone, per litteram Domini Walteri de Hoptone.
Symon de Westone, ad presentacionem Magistri Hospitalis Ledebyry.
Willelmus Tuggeford, ad titulum patrimonii.
Rogerus de Ullingwike, ad titulum patrimonii.
Rogerus de Parva Herefordia, ad titulum patrimonii.
Ricardus de Bromyard, ad graciam ut prius.
Gregorius de Langaran, ad titulum ut prius.
Robertus de Leoministre, ad titulum patrimonii.
Walterus de Wenloke, ad titulum patrimonii.
Thomas de Wymfretone, ad titulum patrimonii, et per litteram Domini Rogeri de Mortuo Mari.
Willelmus de Chirchame, ad titulum patrimonii.
Rogerus de Penbrugge, ad titulum plene pixidis litterarum.
Magister Johannis de Bromfelde, ad presentacionem Abbatis Gloucestriensis.
Willelmus de Caple, ad titulum patrimonii sui, ut prius.
Hugo Gerbouch, ad sacristaria[m] de Westbury.
Willelmus de Persore, ad titulum patrimonii, cum litteris.
Radulfus de Bodeham, ad titulum patrimonii.
Walterus de Selretone, ad titulum patrimonii, cujus carta residet penes magistrum R. de Heytone.
Petrus de Brocbury, ad titulum patrimonii qui residet penes dictum R.
Johannes de Gardino, ad presentacionem Cancellarii Herefordensis, pro quo cavit magister Henricus de Lantone.
Adam de Wygmore, ad titulum patrimonii.

Willelmus Aul de Lodelowe ad titulum patrimonii, qui residet penes ipsum R.
Nicholaus de Marcle, ad titulum patrimonii.
Stephanus de Gromville, absolutus.
Willelmus de Kingeslene, ad presentacionem Leulini le Bret.
Johannes de Bosebury, ad presentacionem Vicarii de Ros.
Davyd de Aspertone, ad presentacionem domini Martini, Rectoris ejusdem.
Johannes de Themedebury, ad titulum patrimonii.
Radulfus de Lydum, ad titulum patrimonii.
Adam de Penbrugge, ad titulum patrimonii.
Willelmus de Bedestone, ad titulum patrimonii.
Johannes de Newent, ad titulum patrimonii, et pro sufficiencia cavit Vicarius de Neuwent.

PRESBITERI.—

Ricardus de Lingayne, ad titulum Domus de Lydlec.
Ricardus de Aka, ad titulum l solidorum per cartam Amicie de Camera.
Johannes Judas, ad titulum patrimonii sui, quod est sufficiens.
Willelmus de Momele, ad titulum patrimonii sui, ut prius.
Johannes de Lindrugge, ad presentacionem Cancellarii Herefordensis, ut prius.
Johannes de Donne, ad titulum quo prius, ad presentacionem Vicecomitis Herefordie.
Henricus de Merstone, ad titulum patrimonii.
Thomas de Stauntone Lacy, ad titulum patrimonii.
Stephanus de Bromyarde, ad servicium Beate Marie de eadem.
Johannes de Wiltone, ad titulum patrimonii.
Philippus de Stowia.
Robertus de Clifforde, ad servicium Beate Marie de eadem.
Galfridus de Akle, ad cantariam capelle de Streddowy.
Rogerus de Castro Godriche, ad titulum lx solidorum ut prius.
Thomas de Newent, ad titulum patrimonii.
Johannes dictus Piscator, ad presentacionem Roberti de Mersy et cavit pro eo Magister de Chaundos, prestito juramento ad faciendam litteram suam.
Willelmus de Walford, ad titulum patrimonii sui, ut prius.
Hugo de Racheford, ad titulum patrimonii.
Willelmus de Leyntwarthin, ad presentacionem Abbatis de Wygemore.

Willelmus de Brocbury, ad titulum patrimonii, qui residet penes magistrum Ricardum.
Walterus de Welnythehope, ad cantariam Beate Marie de eadem.
Johannes de Credenhulle, ad presentacionem Domini G. Talebot.
Rogerus de Blakewelle, ad titulum patrimonii, quem habet magister R.
Johannes de Bristolle, de Ross, ad titulum patrimonii, ut prius.
Hugo de Stauntone, ad titulum patrimonii.
Ricardus de Parva Herefordia, ad titulum patrimonii.
Adam de Astone, ad presentacionem Roberti de Monselowe, per litteram.

Fol. 42.

Nomina Rectorum ordinatorum ad Ordines supradictos.

de Credenhulle.	de Lettone.	de Cardestone.	de Caple.
de Kynardeslege.	de Hope Boudlers.	de Staunforde.	de Staunton in foresta.
de Staunton.	de Hanewode.	de Stoke Lacy.	de Birche Sancte Marie.

Nomina non veniencium Leoministre ad Ordines, scilicet, Rectores ecclesiarum de Etone.[1]

de Pipa.	de Sapey.	de Buterleye.	de Parva Wenlake.
de Kinkeshope.	de Ullingwike.	de Silvetone.	de Maddelege.
de Kyngetone.	de Credele.	de Stoke Milburge.	de Bekebury.
de Lenhale.	de Colewelle.	de Wistantowe.	de Burnwarlege.
de Brocbury.	de Witeburne.	de Castro Ricardi.	de Wililege.
de Monetone.	Item rectores de Estenoure et de Stokbles.	de Hopebagarde.	de Actone Rotunda.
de Byforde.		de Colintone.	de Musselawe.
de Bruge.		de Grete.	de Schiptone.
de Biscopestone.	de Wlfrelowe et fuit ordinandus subdiaconus.	Tres Porcionarii de Bureforde.	de Strettone.
de Strettone.			J. et Wi[l]fredus Porcionarii de Holegod.
de Radenore Nova.	de Parva Coure.	de Lindrugge.	
de Kinille.	de Parva Marcle.	de Cornlege.	de Wlfstanstone
de Sernefeld.	de Froma Castri.	de Hoptone Wafre.	de Lidham.
de Grugeslone.	de Aura.	de Estham.	de Mora.
de Crofte.	de Westbury.	de Aka.	de Clungunforde.
de Humbre.	de Blechdone.	de Bolde.	de Bromptone.
Homptone Wafre.	de Huntelege.	de Wethulle.	de Montgomery.
de Stretforde.	de Tabritone.	de Borewartone.	de Pulrebache.
de Peterestowe.	de Rudeforde.	de Neutone.	Domino de Pontesbury.
de Langaran.			
de Lanwaran.	de Bikenore.	de Clebury North.	Porcionarius de Westbury et de Forda.
de Sancta Kayna.	de Astone.	de Middeltone.	

1—The parallel columns are arranged as in the MS. and are to be read downwards.

de Fendenerac.	de Mordeforde.	de Billingelege.	Item rectores de Pyone Regis
de Landinabon.	de Nova Terra.	de Classelege et. Cornlege. de Tasselege.	de Lugwarthin et Welintone.

June 13, 1278.—Ordination at Tottenham.

ORDINATI APUD TOTEHALE.—Infrascripti ordinati fuerunt a Venerabili Patre, Thoma, Dei gracia Herefordensi Episcopo, apud Totenhale, in Episcopatu Londoniensi, per licenciam diocesani litteralem die Sabbati infra Octabas Pentecostes anno Domini M° ducentesimo LXX octavo.

ACOLITI.—

Johannes de Langetone, Lincolniensis diocesis, cum dimissoriis sine titulo.
Willelmus de la Haye, Herefordensis diocesis, sine titulo.
Henricus de Newwent, Herefordensis diocesis.

SUBDIACONI.—

Thomas, filius Gilberti, Rector de Foxcote, Lincolniensis diocesis, per litteram dimissoriam.
Magister Ricardus de Yngham, presentatus ad titulum ecclesie de Yngham, Lincolniensis diocesis, per litteras dimissorias.
Walterus Oliver, Rector ecclesie de Hegham, Lincolniensis diocesis, per litteram dimissoriam.
Robertus Fulconis, Rector ecclesie Castri Richardi, Herefordensis diocesis.
Johannes de Cave, Rector ecclesie de Humbre, Herefordensis diocesis.
Magister Thomas de Linggeyn, ecclesie de Nenesolers, Herefordensis diocesis.
Magister Thomas de Bromptone, Porcionarius ecclesie de Digesyate, Wellensis et Batoniensis diocesis, per litteras dimissorias.

DIACONI.—

Simon Franc, per litteram dimissoriam Lincolniensis diocesis, sine titulo, qui prestitit corporale sacramentum quod numquam Episcopum Herefordensem impetret, petendo titulum racione Ordinacionis.

Magister Gilbertus de Heywode, Rector ecclesie de Coleby, Lincolniensis diocesis, per litteram dimissoriam.

Magister Ricardus de Sancta Fretheswithe, Rector ecclesie de Chirtulie, Lincolniensis diocesis, per litteras dimissorias.

Johannes de Stabelgate, Rector ecclesie de Alremariecherche, Londoniensis diocesis, per litteras dimissorias.

Simon de Wendoure, ad instanciam Domini Londoniensis, per litteras Domini Episcopi Lincolniensis.

PRESBITERI.—

Magister Alanus de Crespingge, Canonicus Herefordensis.

Galfridus de Coltone, Rector ecclesie de Ledewych, Herefordensis diocesis.

Magister Willelmus de Bruere, Vicarius de Rodeleya, Lincolniensis diocesis, per litteram dimissoriam.

Walterus de Silbestone, ad Vicariam de Bradewelle.

Henricus de Farnham, ad titulum Magistri Militum Templi, et per litteras dimissorias Domini Lincolniensis Episcopi.

Rogerus de Ysselham, filius Roberti de la Rive, per litteras dimissorias Domini W. quondam Roffensis Episcopi.

Sept. 1278.—Ordination at Ludlow.

ACOLITI.—

Willelmus de Hope, Johannes de Clone, Ricardus de Bureforde, Ricardus de Tykelwardyn, Ricardus de Asforde, Thomas de Clone, Rogerus Davy de Lodelawe, Willelmus de Moneur, Johannes de Oldebury, Ricardus le Taylur de Lodelawe, Johannes le Tenturer de eadem, Johannes Aboth, Willelmus de Presthemede, Robertus de Erdintone, Johannes de Waterdene, David de Clone, Walterus de Stottesdone, Walterus de Hoptone, Johannes le Chevaler, Thomas de Holicote, Willelmus de Kynlet, Henricus de Clone, Ricardus de Newenham, Hugo de Chetyntone, Willelmus de Kylmeskote, Willelmus de Sancto Egidio, Adam de Monte Gomery, Johannes de Welyntone, Davy de Lanrothan, Johannes de Wlfrelowe, Nicholaus de Prestemede, Johannes de Bolynhope, Robertus de Etone, Willelmus de Welbeleye, Willelmus le Sevene de Almali, Johannes de Wygemore, Ricardus Davy, Willelmus de Rutone, Johannes de More Akeyn, Nicholaus de Sectone, Johannes de Parva Wenlake, Adam de Welyntone, Morice de Lanrathan, Nicholaus le Champion,

Robertus de Totitone, Willelmus Ruter, Adam de Stwochpe, Willelmus de Marcleya, Ricardus de Ribefor, Johannes de Glasleye, Johannes de Laynthole, Willelmus Rector de Pykesleye.

SUBDIACONI.—

Jurati super sufficienti titulo.

Hugo de Clone ad titulum patrimonii sui et servicium Beate Marie de Clone, ad quod presentatur per parochianos ipsius.

Johannes de Bygetone, ad titulum sui patrimonii.

Hugo de Caus, ad titulum sui patrimonii, quod habet per testimonium Decani de Pauncesbury.

Willelmus de Clona, ad titulum patrimonii.

Gregorius de Lodelawe, ad titulum sui patrimonii, quod habet ex testimonio Decani loci et plurimorum aliorum.

Ricardus de Erdintone, juratus, ad titulum sui patrimonii, quod habet per testimonium duorum juratorum, videlicet, Ade de Tuggeford et Henrici, Fratris Hospitalis Sancti Leonardi de Brugge, capellanorum.

Willelmus Berd de Ledebury, non juratus, ad titulum quem sibi dedit Willelmus, Vicarius de Bromyard; qui vicarius repromisit indempnitatem Domini cum sacramento.

Johannes de Clone, dictus Keydor, ad titulum patrimonii quod habet per testimonium duorum fidedignorum juratorum.

Willelmus de Yarepol, ad titulum patrimonii sui, cujus heres est et ipsius cartam exhibuit.

Adam Bard de Redeford, ad titulum sufficientem quem ostendit, et per testimonium plurimorum.

Stephanus de Monemutha, qui prestitit sacramentum quod infra biennium intrabit Religionem ibidem, ad presentacionem Prioris loci ejusdem.

Willelmus de Bysshopestone, ad titulum competentem quem exhibuit, et prestitit sacramentum quod illum credit esse sufficientem ad sustentacionem sacerdotalem.

Ricardus de Kouera, ad presentacionem parochianorum de Kouera, videlicet Rogeri le Venur et Rogeri le Fremon.

Ricardus de Monemutha, juratus super titulo sui patrimonii quod optinet.

Ricardus de Bodeham, ad titulum quem exhibuit.

Simon de Midelhope, juratus super titulo.

Gilbertus de Sancto Petro, juratus super titulo competenti.

Ricardus de Waltone, juratus super titulo patrimonii.
Johannes de la Hale.
Willelmus Bras.
Johannes de Opesay.
Ricardus de Wenloke, ad titulum competentem.
Rogerus de Parva Herefordia, ad presentacionem Cancellarii Herefordensis.
Nicholaus de Croft.
Ricardus de Esthamptone.
Johannes de le Dene.
Willelmus de Spareforde.
Johannes de Bereweky.
Ricardus de Lawerdene.
Johannes de Chetyntone.
Johannes de Tasseleye.
Hugo de Lentwardyn, ad presentacionem et titulum Abbatis de Wygemore.
Gilbertus de Clunbury, ad presentacionem Prioris de Wenlake.
Isti ordines celebrati fuerunt apud Lodelawe, ante Festum Sancti Michaelis, anno Domini M°CC°LXX° octavo.

PRESBITERI jurati super titulo sufficienti.

Rogerus de Ullingwyke, ad titulum sui patrimonii, quod habet ex testimonio Warini de Grendene.
Simon de Westone, ad presentacionem Magistri Hospitalis Ledeburiensis qui, ut promisit prestito sacramento quod in biennium eum in Ordine suo recipiet.
Ricardus de Bromhale, sine titulo, ad instanciam Warini de Grendene, qui alias a Domino sine titulo ordinabatur.
Nicholaus de Marcleye, ad titulum quem juravit se habere, et ad testimonium R. de Heytone.
Walterus de Caple, juratus super titulo.
Johannes Gorwy, ad titulum competentem, quem testatus est habere in villa de Ledebury.
Gervasius de Waterdene, ad titulum quem habet ex testimonio procuratoris Prioris de Wenlake, de Clona.
Ricardus de Dalyleie, ad presentacionem Capituli Herefordensis et sub periculo L[uce de Bre], Thesaurarii loci ipsius.
Willelmus de Castro Holegot, super titulo competenti juratus.
Willelmus de Chirchhomme.

Adam de Wygemore, ad titulum quem habet in Lodelawe, ex testimonio plurimorum.
Johannes de Bosebury, ad presentacionem Vicarii loci ejusdem.
Rogerus de Alberbury, juratus super titulo quem habet ex testimonio.
Thomas de Clune.
Johannes de Newent, ad presentacionem Vicarii de Chirchhomme.
Hugo de Stauntone, juratus super titulo sufficienti.
Radulfus de Bodeham, juratus.
Johannes de Clone.
Walterus de Wenloke, ad presentacionem Prioris de Wenlokc.
Willelmus de Bedestone, juratus super titulo patrimonii.
Philippus de Sancto Brevello.
Stephanus de Hope,
Ricardus de Eytonemeysy.
Walterus de Sceldertone.
Petrus de Brocbury.
Johannes de Gardino.
Rogerus de Penebrugge.

Dec. 17.—Ordination at Whitbourne.

ORDINATI.—Memorandum quod die Sabbati proximo ante Festum Beati Thome Apostoli ordinavit Dominus apud Wyteburne quosdam Fratres Minores de Wygornia et eciam de Herefordia, videlicet quatuor; et duos monachos de Wenloke, et eciam . . . . . de Chanseye, in diaconum, per litteras dimissorias Domini Saresbiriensis, quas exhibuit, et ad instanciam magistri A[de] de Fyleby. Item tunc ordinatus fuit Willelmus de Marcleye, Rector de Pykesleye in presbiteratum, nec plures ordinavit ibidem.

Mar. 1279.—Ordination at Newent.

Nomina ordinatorum apud Newent ante Pascha, anno Domino M°CC°LXX° octavo.

ACOLITI.—

Robertus de Henore, Hugo de Loctone, Walterus de Thornbury, Walterus de Hamptone, Nicholaus de Dene, Ricardus de Bromosburghe, Willelmus de Alvytone, Radulfus de Ledebury, Thomas de Heref orde, Willelmus de Rowardyn, Walterus de Wyse, Willelmus Mustel, Willelmus de la Petite Dene, Nicholaus de Tybertone,

Johannes de la Flodre, Rogerus de Moneketone, Walterus de la Grave, Johannes de Cattele, Johannes de Monesle, Johannes de Alvyntone, Johannes de Prestone, Willelmus de Hatfelde, Frater Johannes de Parisiis, Religiosus.

SUBDIACONI.—

Waltorus de la Le, juratus super sufficienti titulo.
Willelmus de Flinteshame, ad titulum exhibitum.
Henricus de Clona, juratus de sufficienti titulo, quem exhibuit.
Johannes de Westone.
Philippus de Nova Terra, ex presentacione magistri Roberti de Gloucestria.
Johannes de Bromesburghe, ad titulum exhibitum.
Petrus de Lanrothal, ad titulum exhibitum.
Johannes Legat, per titulum exhibitum.
Adam de Syreburne, ad titulum j carucate terre, site apud Bromesburghe.
Adam de Wentenoure, ad titulum exhibitum.
Richardus Acle, ad titulum patrimonii exhibitum.
Johannes de Prestone, ad titulum burgagii et terre que appropriavit ecclesie de Ledebury.
Willelmus Roter, ad titulum patrimonii.
Walterus Evere, ad titulum sui patrimonii quod habet apud Evre.
Nicholaus de Avenebury, ad presentacionem magistri Johannis de Syldresle.
Robertus de la Fonhope, ad hereditatem patris sui.
Adam de Wyltone, ad patrimonium patris sui.
Thomas de Garewy, ad presentacionem Hospitalariorum.
Frater Willelmus de Stanleye, } Religiosi.
Frater Nicholaus de Moneketone, }

DIACONI.—

Hugo de Cloune, juratus super sufficienti titulo, quem prius exhibuit.
Johannes de Bygetone, ad titulum prius exhibitum.
Nicholaus de Acle, ad titulum prius exhibitum.
Henricus Helwy, ad titulum prius exhibitum.
Nicholaus de Ruwardyn, ad titulum prius exhibitum.
Ricardus de Coure, ad titulum prius exhibitum.
Rogerus de Stoke, ad presentacionem Vicarii de Lydeneye.
Ricardus de Actone, ad presentacionem Preceptorii de Opledene.

Stephanus de Monemuta, ad presentacionem Monachatus.
Willelmus de Bissoppestone, ad titulum prius exhibitum.
Robertus Joye, ad titulum patrimonii.
Willelmus de Clone, ad titulum prius exhibitum.
Willelmus Braz, de Caple, ad titulum patrimonii; et est in possessione.
Adam Barbe, ad titulum sufficientem.
Johannes de Ledene, ad presentacionem J., Rectoris de Radaforde.
Ricardus de Bodenham, ad titulum prius exhibitum.
Henricus de Pontesbury.
Johannes de Froma, ad presentacionem domini Jacobi de Bosebury.
Andreas de Coile, ad titulum prius exhibitum.
Frater Johannes de Everslone, et Johannes de Gloucestria, Religiosi.

PRESBITERI.—

Nicholaus de Clone, ad titulum prius exhibitum.
Johannes de Nyutone, ad titulum prius exhibitum.
Willelmus de Persore, ad titulum sacristatus de Bromyarde, alias exhibitum.
Ricardus de Bosebury, ad titulum domini Jacobi de Bosebury.
Howelus de Hergast, juratus super titulo sufficienti.
David de Sancto Michaele, ad titulum patrimonii.
Simon de Clona, ad titulum prius exhibitum.
Frater Walterus de Gloucestria, Religiosus.

Mar. 31, 1280.—Ordination at Ledbury.

Ordines celebrati apud Ledebury die Sabbati qua cantatur *Sicientes*, a Domino Thoma, Herefordensi Episcopo, anno Domini M°CC°LXXX°.

ACOLITI.—

Rogerus de Tibritone, Johannes de Werehun, Hugo de Stanworde, Hugo de Racheforde, Radulfus de la More, Rogerus de Wonechirche, Willelmus de Assetone, Ricardus de Boklyntone, Robertus Oylun, Johannes de Lydebury. Willelmus de Wyggemore, Stephanus de Bromhart, Johannes Pede, Galfridus le Meyh, Walterus de Assetone, Philippus de la Bokse, Hugo de Penecumbe, Hugo de Cradele, Willelmus de Cloune, Willelmus Barbe, Henricus de Bracy, Rogerus de Cloune, Willelmus de Malwarne, Robertus de Hope.

SUBDIACONI.—

Rogerus de Wilhenehope, ad titulum patrimonii, quem exhibuit et resumpsit.
Johannes Beas, ut supra.
Walterus de Snothulle, ut supra.
Ricardus de Newenham, ut supra.
Hugo de Wydemerchs, ad titulum sufficientem, exhibitum et resumptum.
Ricardus de Sapy, ad titulum patrimonii, quem resumpsit.
Robertus Cok de Herefordia, ad presentacionem fratris Johannis Roce.
Hugo de la Barre, ad presentacionem parochianorum Omnium Sanctorum.
Hubertus de Westbury, ad presentacionem Vicarii de eadem, qui portabit bonum titulum ad proximum Consistorium, per sacramentum bonorum prestitum.
Robertus de Erdesle, ad presentacionem parochianorum ejusdem, ad celebrandam missam.
Radulphus de Wyggemore, ad presentacionem Abbatis et titulum Conventus Beate Marie.
Walterus de Garbeye, ad presentacionem Preceptorii de Upledene et titulum Domus.
Henricus de Stikkeford, per litteras dimissorias Episcopi Lincolniensis, ad presentacionem Willelmi de Steyntone.
Brianus de Pedwardin, per litteras dimissorias Domini Menevensis admissus est Rector.
Johannes de Westone, ad titulum patrimonii, exhibitum et resumptum.
Willelmus de Chandoys, ut supra.
Adam de Ledebury, ad presentacionem Rectoris de Wytebourne.
Frater Ricardus de Chadelintone, heremita, per litteras dimissorias Episcopi Lyncolniensis.
Frater Radulphus de Stratforde, Ordinis Beati Augustini.
Frater Willelmus de Hulhamptone.
Frater Johannes de Byseleye.
Frater Walterus de Lodelowe.
Frater Willelmus de Chadelintone.
Frater Alexander, Lantonie Prime.
Frater de Wyttone.
Frater Willelmus de Wavertone.

Episcopi Herefordensis. 311

Diaconi.—

Ricardus de Hactone, ad titulum patrimonii, quem exhibuit et resumpsit.
Hugo Carnobel, ad titulum prius exhibitum et resumptum.
Tudoer de Orkhope, ad titulum prius exhibitum et resumptum.
Walterus de Sancto Dyonisio, ad titulum patrimonii et burgagii in villa Leomenestrie.
Robertus de Bracy, ad presentacionem Cancellarii Herefordensis.
Willelmus de Markle, ad titulum patrimonii prius exhibitum et rehabitum.
Johannes de Markle, ad presentacionem parochianorum ejusdem loci, ad celebrandam missam Beate Marie Virginis. Johannes Joye presentavit eundem.
Adam de Wyltone, ad titulum patrimonii exhibitum et resumptum.
Adam de Wantenovere, ad titulum patrimonii competentis.
Robertus de Etone, ad presentacionem domini Thome le Brettone et magistri Henrici, Subde[cani].
Nicholaus Champiun, ad presentacionem Abbatis et titulum Conventus de Wyggemore.
Rogerus de Henneberue, ad presentacionem Abbatis de Flaxhele.
Thomas de Garewy, ad presentacionem Preceptorii de Garewy, ad titulum Domus.
Henricus de Cloune, ad titulum sufficientem exhibitum et resumptum.
Thomas de Roulestone, Vicarius Chori Herefordensis.
Walterus Poly, Vicarius Chori Herefordensis.
Robertus de Ribesford, ad titulum patrimonii exhibitum et resumptum.
Ricardus Jakes, ad titulum patrimonii exhibitum et resumptum.
Johannes de Wyggemore, ad titulum sufficientem exhibitum et resumptum.
Willelmus de Leynthale, ad titulum patrimonii exhibitum et resumptum.
Adam de Wyggemore, ad titulum patrimonii exhibitum et resumptum.
Gilbertus de Homme, ad titulum patrimonii exhibitum et resumptum.
Frater Willelmus de Hulhamptone.
Frater Philippus de Lodelowe.
Frater Elias de Gloucestria.
Johannes de Dymmoke.

PRESBITERI.—

Dominus Decanus Eboracensis.
Willelmus de Chirebury, ad titulum patrimonii sui xxx acrarum terre, quem exhibuit et resumpsit. Habet eciam torciam partem unius molendini.
Johannes de Berkhamstede, ad presentacionem Magistri fratrum et sororum domus Sancti Jacobi juxta Westmonasterium.
Robertus de Etone, ad presentacionem Domine de eadem, et titulum patrimonii sufficientis.
Radulphus de Boneshulle, ad titulum patrimonii sufficientis.
Johannes de Newenham.
David de Aspertone, ad titulum patrimonii sufficientis.
Adam de Bromesberue, ad titulum patrimonii exhibitum et resumptum.
Johannes de Bosebury, ad presentacionem Vicarii de Frome Canonicorum.
Ricardus de Sancto Petro, ad presentacionem Prioris et Conventus Malvernie, et titulum ecclesie de Northwode.
Johannes de Prestone, ad titulum patrimonii sufficientis.
Johannes de Reccheford, ad titulum exhibitum et resumptum.
Frater Adam de Wychecotte.
Willelmus de Stanleye.
Frater Willelmus de Chyrebury.

DIACONI.—[1]

Rector ecclesie Sancti Pancracii per litteras dimissorias Decani Cicestrensis Ecclesie.
Rector ecclesie de Petrestowe.
Rector ecclesie de Wyteburne.
Rector ecclesie de le Oke.

SUBDIACONUS.—

Rector ecclesie de Hope Boulers.

PRESBITERI.—

Vicarius de Wydintone.
Vicarius de Mortone.

1—These names are added on the back of the folio, but with an indistinct notice as to them.

INDEX.

Archbishops and Bishops are indexed under the names of their sees. When the proper name of an officer and the name of the office are given in the text, the former only is indexed.

Abbad, John, 64, 65.
Abberley, church of, 156.
Abbey Dore, church of, xxxiv.
Abergavenny, ii.; castle of, 215, 216; constable of, 216; manor of, 35, 172, 215.
Abingdon, abbot of, 81; abbot and convent of, xli.
Aboth, John, 304.
Acle, Nicholas de, 308; Richard, 308.
Aconbury, prioress of, 292; prioress and convent of, 107, 108.
Acton, Richard de, 204, 240, 308.
Acton Round, rector of, 302.
Acton Scott, church of, xxxviii, 81, 82.
Aiswelle, 69.
Akle, Geoffrey de, 301.
Albaniaco, William de, *see* William Daubeny.
Albeny, William de, 94.
Alberbury, convent of, 287, 288; prior of, 132, 198, 279, 281; Roger de, 307.
Albertville, xxvi *n*.
Alesleye, William de, 256, 257.
Alexander IV., pope, 203.
Almeley, 304; church of, 251.
Alto Pascio, hospital of, 51.
Alveston, advowson of, lxiii.
Alvyntone, John de, 308.
Alvytone, William de, 307.
Amiens, conference of, xv.
Anagni, 207.
Andrew, John, 90; Robert, 41.
Anianus, *see* Anianus Galensis.
Anianus II, *see* Bishop of St. Asaph.
Apgurwaret, William, 174.
Apparitor, Henry, 117.

Aqua, John de, 173; William de, 171.
Aquabella, St. Catherine's, xxvii, xlix, 84, 85, 86.
Aquablanca, xxvi; Aymon de, xxvi; Emeric de (Chancellor of Hereford), xxvi, xlix, 30, 118, 135, 175, 176, 192, 193, 195, 197, 198, 199, 208, 209, 210, 219, 247, 248, 293, 294, 300, 301, 306, 311; James de (Archdeacon of Salop), xxvi, lxix, 63, 125, 126, 137, 141, 150, 160, 161, 162, 168, 197, 241, 242, 245; John de (Dean of Hereford), xxiv, xxv, xxvi, xlv, 2 *n*., 30, 112, 114, 115, 198, 199, 209, 210, 214, 233, 234; Peter de, *see* Bishop of Hereford.
Apetot, Geoffrey de, *see* Geoffrey Dabitot.
Arblaster, Roger le, 62.
Arcaud, Walter, 174.
Archenfield, dean of, 127.
Arderne, Adam de, lxx; 22.
Ardicio, *see* Ardicio de Comite.
Argentan, xlviii *n*.
Arleye and Arneley, *see* Earley.
Arly, torrent of, xxvi *n*, 184 *n*.
Arras, John de, 188.
Arundel, Countess of, 243; Earl of, 94.
Ashford, Richard de, 304.
Ashperton, chapel of, 27; David de, 301, 312; rector of, 301.
Ashridge, abbey of, lii.
Aspale, Geoffrey de, 203.
Assebache, 69.
Asseforte, Philip de, 116.
Asshe, xliii, 3, 40, 41.

Astley, Reginald de, 143 ; Walter de, 119.
Aston, Adam de, 302 ; chapelry of, 156 ; rector of, 156, 302 ; vill of, xxviii, 10, 29, 31, 42, 97, 103 ; Walter de, 309 ; William de, 309, 104.
Aston Botterell, rector of, 188.
Aston Cantelow, i, xix.
Astwood, 46, 74.
Athelney, abbot of, xlviii.
Avenbury, Agnes de, 265 ; church of, 152, 157, 163 ; Giles de, xxiv, xxv, 2 *n*, 32, 33, 112, 114, 115, 118, 151 ; Nicholas de, 308 ; Osbert de, 62, 152, 157, 163.
Avenel, Stephen, 77, 78,
Aveny, Aumaricus de, 154.
Awre, church of, 158 ; rector of, 302.
Aylton, church of, 82.
Aylun, Geoffrey de, 122.
Aymestrey, church of, 17, 44, 45 ; vicar of, 117.
Ayno, John de, 9, 28.

Ba, Edmund de, 45.
Bacin, Laurence, 172.
Bacon, Roger, ix, lix.
Bade, John, 299.
Baggindene, Richard de, 123.
Baggode, Robert, 24.
Ballingham, Gregory de, 20; rector of, 209.
Balon, Walter de, 143, 144, 154.
Balun, Walter de, 77, 78.
Banaster, Walter, 63.
Bandinus (merchant of Lucca), 15, 18, 19.
Bangor, Bishop of, 103, 253.
Barbe, Adam, 309 ; William, 309.
Barber, Hugh le, vii *n*, lxxi.
Bard, Adam, 305.
Bardi, the, 12 *n*.
Bare, Walter de la, 259, 260.

Barentin, Drew de, 96, 97.
Baret, Henry, 43, 78.
Barking, John of, lxxi, 20, 21.
Barling, xxxiv ; bailiff of, lxxi, 14, 164 ; manor of, lxiii, 25.
Barnes, lxvii, 237.
Baroke, sheriff of, 218.
Barre, Hamo de la, lxx, 22 ; Hugo de la, 310 ; Walter de la, 83.
Barrow, church of, 116, 119, 155.
Barton, John de, lxx, 210 ; manor of, lxi *n*, 96.
Basing, lords of, xx.
Basset, Alan, 94 ; Ralph, 173 ; Robert, 192 ; Thomas, 94.
Bath, Archdeacon of, 164 ; Edmund of, 157 ; Walter of, 134, 155 ; Wliliam of, 129.
Bath and Wells, diocese of, 303 ; bishop of, liv, 164, 175, 185, 186, 194 ; (Robert Burnell) xxxi *n*.
Bayeux, bishop of, 20.
Baysham, church of, xxiv.
Bayton, Robert de, 36 ; W. de, 299.
Beas, John, 310.
Beauchamp (Bello Campo), William de, 96.
Beaufitz, Adam, 117, 118 ; John, 117, 118.
Beaulu, John, 43.
Beauvale, ii.
Bebler, Petronella, xlvi.
Bebury, G. de, 272.
Bec, abbey of, 265 *n* ; priory of, xlviii.
Beccles, John de, lxx, 105, 106, 107, 209, 279, 282.
Beckbury, rector of, 209, 302.
Becket, Thomas à, *see* Archbishop of Canterbury.
Beckington, lxvii, 40.
Bedfont, lxvi, 142, 144, 165, 286.
Bedstone, Richard de, 225 ; William de, 301, 307.
Beke, Anthony, *see* Bishop of Durham ; Thomas, 284, 285.
Beleford, Gonter de, 29.
Belni, John de, 77, 78.

Benedictus, Cardinal of St. Nicholas in Carcere Tulliano, 275.
Berd, William, 305.
Berecroft, Adam de, 121, 122.
Bereford, Cecilia de, 239.
Bereweky, John de, 306.
Berkeley, Giles de, 123.
Berkham, manor of, lxiii, 217, 218.
Berkhamstead, lii; John de, 312.
Berkle, Arnald de, 174.
Berkynge, John de, *see* John of Barking.
Bermondsey, lxvii, 290.
Berner, Richard, 188, 189.
Bettws, chapel of. 132.
Betune, Robert de, *see* Bishop of Hereford.
Beverley, provost of, 155.
Bevil, Matthew, 97.
Bevyle, Raymund de, 137.
Bicknor, lxv, 98; rector of, 302.
Billingsley, rector of, 302.
Birch, Little, rector of, 302.
Bisele, Thomas de, 279.
Bishop's Castle, lxv, lxvi, 82, 108, 110, 137, 138, 139, 146, 149, 165, 183, 188; constable of, lxx, 171; manor of, lxi.
Bishopstone, rector of 302; William de, 305, 309.
Bitterley, John de, lxx, 213, 215, 233, 234, 243, 245, 250, 255, 269, 272, 273, 276, 277, 281, 294; rector of, 212, 302.
Blaisdon, church of, 217, 236, 240; John de, 171; rector of, 177, 302.
Blakewell, Roger de, 302.
Blechingley, 227.
Blont, John le, lxxi, 43, 77, 78.
Bluet, Ralph, 124.
Bocking, Walter de, 170, 176.
Bockleton, church of, lxix.
Bodecote, William de, 235.
Bodenham, Ralph de, 300, 307; Richard de, 197, 305, 309; vicarage of, 149.
Bodro (Canon of Valence), 21.

Bokkeleye, rector of, 284.
Boklyntone, Richard de, 309.
Bokse, Philip de la, 309.
Bokynham, Henry de, 40.
Bolde, portionists of, xxxviii; rector of, 302.
Boleville, Nicholas de, 97.
Bollers, Robert de, xxvii.
Bologna, x, Francis de, 284.
Boltisham, Roger de, 227.
Bone, Henry de la, 174.
Boneshulle, Ralph de, 312; Robert de, 197.
Boniface viii, pope, xxxvii.
Boniface, *see* Archbishop of Canterbury.
Booltone, Thomas de, 174.
Borham, Hervey de (Dean of St. Paul's), xxxvi, 14, 16, 25, 78, 79, 88, 111, 121.
Borhhulle, Roger de, 123.
Bornhill, Gilbert de, 152, 157; *see* Gilbert de Burghill.
Bosbury, xli, lxi, lxvi, lxvii, lxviii, 21, 45, 70, 75, 100, 116, 119, 154, 157, 158, 159, 184, 185, 187, 191, 196, 197, 198, 202, 240, 266, 267; bailiff of, 127; chaplain of, 197; church of, 126, 127; James de, 309; John de, 301, 307, 312; manor of, lxi *n*, 96; Richard de, 309; Roger de, xxiv, 7; vicar of, 197, 307.
Bosco, R. de, 251.
Boston, fair of, 105, 213.
Botterell, Thomas, 69, 71, 73, 188.
Boughton-nnder-Blean, lxv, 12; church of, 11.
Boun, Humphrey de (Earl of Hereford and Essex), 97.
Bourton, Heilin de, *see* Heylin Matthews; rector of, 140.
Bracy, Henry de, 309; Robert de, 311.
Bradeham, Geoffrey de, 267; John de, lxx, lxxi, 3, 17, 20, 25, 108, 114, 115, 208, 246, 261, 262, 267.

Bradele, Henry de, 129, 130.
Bradenham, Geoffrey de, 254, 292.
Bradley, Roger de, 263.
Bradwell, lxv, 1; benefice of, xx; vicarage of, 304.
Bramford, Richard de, xlvi.
Brampton, rector of, 302.
Brampton Brian, church of, 1, 28; rector of, 29, 125, 235.
Brancestre, J. de (Archdeacon of Worcester), 94.
Braose, Eva, ii.; Giles de, *see* Bishop of Hereford.
Bras, Simon, 138; Walter, 77, 78; William, 306.
Braundone, Robert de, 277.
Bray, manor of, 269 *n*; William de, 169, 205, 206.
Braz, William, 309.
Brecon, prior and convent of, 149, 150.
Bredenbury, lxiii, 171.
Bredwardine, vicarage of, 119; Walter de, 69, 71.
Bree, Luke de, xxi, liii, lxix, lxx, lxxi, 1, 25, 26, 83, 88, 112, 113, 114, 115, 116, 120, 151, 168, 169, 171, 195, 212, 221, 222, 223, 248, 261, 268, 291, 306.
Breose, William de, 94.
Bret, Llewellyn le, 301; Robert le, xxix.
Breteuil, xlvii, lordship of, i.
Breton, John le, *see* Bishop of Hereford; Robert le, 25, 262; Thomas le, 199, 311.
Bridgnorth, hospital of St. Leonard's, 305; John of, 185, 186, 237; King's Chapel, xxxviii; rector of, 302; Thomas of, lxxi, 104, 105, 223.
Bridstow, vicarage of, 125.
Brinksty, wood of, xli, 42, 43, 123.
Bristol, 13, 172; John of, 208, 302.
Brittany, 67.
Brocbury, Hugh de, 268; Reginald de, 138; Peter de, 300, 307; rector of, 302; William de, 302.

Brocke, Roger, 77, 78.
Brockhampton, 41.
Bromfield, lxvi, 162, 258; John de, 300.
Bromhale, Richard de, 306.
Bromhart, Stephen de, 309.
Brompton, Brian de, 71; Peter de, 3, 40, 41; Walter de, 71.
Bromsberrow, 308; Adam de, 312; church of, 251; John de, 308; Richard de, 307.
Bromyard, lxv, 81, 82, 86, 87, 91, 92, 299; bailiff of, 6, 123; bailiwick of, 42; canons of, 107, 108; manor of, lxi *n*, 96; manor court of, 17; prebends of, 126; portionists of, xxxviii, lxix, 135, 141, 184, 188, 192, 208, 247, 248; Richard de, 300; sacrist of, 309; Stephen de, 301; vicar of, 305; wood of, 17.
Bronretpol, 284.
Broseley, chapelry of, 237
Bruce, William de, *see* Bishop of Llandaff.
Bruere, William de, 304.
Bruges, lviii.
Brumley, chapel of, 292.
Brun, William, lxx, 101, 134, 135, 273, 276, 278, 279; William le, 185.
Brunhame, Gilbert de, 156,
Bruton, abbot of, xlviii *n*; convent of, ii; Thomas, xxi *n*.
Brynum, lxvii, 276.
Buckland, hospital at, xl, 165, 166, 167, 181, 228.
Bulge, Ralph, 62.
Bullers, Robert de, 69, 71.
Bulley, church of, 238; Magog de, 239.
Bullinghope, chapel of, 30; John de, 304.
Burcote, Walter de la, 196, 251.
Burford, church of, 101; dean of, 102, 299; Geoffrey de, 101 102; portion of, 102, 120; portionists

of, xxxviii, 141, 169, 170, 302 ;
Richard de, 304.
Burghill, Gilbert de, 163, see Gilbert de Bornhill ; Roger de, 298.
Burgundians, the, xxv, xxvii, 13.
Burnell, Hugh, 73, 164, 211 ; Phillip, 164, 165, 194 ; Robert, see Bishop of Bath and Wells.
Burton, Walter de, 125.
Burwarton, rector of, 302.
Bussebrook, 69, 73.
Byford, rector of, 45, 136, 302.
Bygetone, John de, 305, 308.
Byseleye, John de, 310.

Calstone-Willington, lxvii, 227.
Cambrai, canon of, 249, 250.
Cambrensis, Giraldus, v, vi.
Campo Venti, Peter de, 176.
Cantelbere, Stephen de, see Stephen de Kentisbury.
Canterbury, lxv, 7, 84 ; Archbishop of, 26, 145, 222, 274, 275, 277, 278, 279, 280, 281, 282, 289, 298 ; (Thomas à Becket) iv, vii, xxii, xlvii, xlviii *n*, 96 ; (Boniface) xxvii *n*, 103 ; (Robert Kilwardby) xvii, xxii, xxviii, 10, 103, 187 *n* ; (John Peckham) xii, xvii, xxi *n*, xxii *n*, xxxi, xxxiii, xxxv, xxxvi, xxxix, xlvii, xlix, l, li, lii, liv, lvii *n*, lxi, lxix, 12 *n*, 14 *n*, 95 *n*, 105 *n*, 224, 226, 229, 232, 233, 234, 236. 255, 258, 259, 269, 274 *n*, 279 *n*, 283 ; (Walter Reynolds) lvii ; (Warham) li *n* ; Court of, xxv, xlvi, xlix, lxiii, 32, 33, 137, 193, 197, 255, 256. 265, 287 ; official of, xxiv, xlvi, xlvii, 265, 267, ; province of, 1, 56, 100, 123 ; see of, 267.
Cantilupe, Agnes de, iii, xx ; Fulk de, iii *n* ; George de, xxi ; Hugh de, iii, iv, lxii, lxx, 213 ; John de, ii,
iii, xix, 297 *n* ; Juliana de, see Tregoz ; Millicent de, see la Zouche ; Nicholas de, iii, xxi ; Sir R., ii *n* ; Roger de, ii *n* ; Walter de, see Bishop of Worcester ; William de (1st Baron) iii *n* ; William de (2nd Baron) ii, 80 ; William de (3rd Baron), ii, iii, viii ; William de, ii, xvi, 95, 97 ; William de (Proctor), xlix, 296, 297.
Cantoke, Thomas, 209.
Cantorin, xxvi, 6, 7.
Caorsins, the, xxxii.
Caple, 309 ; rector of, 302 ; Roger de, 299 ; Walter de, 185, 242, 306 ; William de, 185, 300.
Cardigan, constable of, 174.
Cardinals, Benedictus (of St. Nicholas in Carcere Tulliano), 275 ; Gerard (of the Basilica of the XII. Apostles), 274, 288, 289 ; Hugh (English Cardinal), 274 ; James, 275 ; Jordanus (of St. Eustace), 187, 274 ; Matthew Rufus (of St. Mary's in Porticu), 214, 223, 232, 234, 274 ; Spanish Cardinal, 275 ; William (French Cardinal), 275.
Cardington, vicarage of, 192.
Cardiston, chapel of, 36 ; rector of, 302 ; William de, 36.
Carlisle, Bishop W. of, 95.
Carletone, W. de, 181.
Carmarthen, archdeacon of, 197, 229, 230 ; burgess of, 172 ; castle of, 174 ; constable of, 174.
Carnobel, Hugh, 311.
Castell, R , 216.
Castille, Blanch of, i *n*.
Castle Goodrich, Roger de, 301.
Castle Holgate, portionists of, xxxviii, 139, 141, 142 ; prebend of, lxix, 242 ; William de, 306.
Cattele, John de, 307.
Cauncy, Joseph de (King's Treasurer and Prior of the Hospital of St. John of Jerusalem), 1, 28, 35, 125, 165, 167, 199.

Caus, 71, 72, 73; Hugh de, 305.
Caus Castle, capelry of, 154.
Caux, pays de, xxix.
Cave, John de, 41, 303,
Caynham, vicar of, 235.
Caytone, John de, 17.
Celestine V, pope, liv.
Chabeham, John de, 199.
Chaddeworth, Thomas de, lxx, 25.
Chadelintone, Richard de, 310; William de, 310.
Chaise, la, xxvii *n*.
Chalbenore, Hugh de, 206.
Chamberlain, William, 43, 77, 78.
Chambers, Amice, 301; John, 51.
Chambéry, Martin de, xxvi, 27.
Champagne, Bernard, prior of, xxiv, 128.
Champion, Nicholas le, 304, 311.
Chandos; John de, 131; master of, 301.
Chandoys, William de, 310.
Chanseye, . . . de, 307.
Chantelou, William of, xlviii.
Charenton, xlix, lx *n*, lxvii, 247, 248, 249, 250, 252, 253, 254, 294; manor at, 296, 297.
Charlecote, bailiff of, lxiii, lxxi, 19.
Chartham, lxv, 7, 9.
Chartres, canon of, 249 *n*.
Chastroke, vill of, xxviii, 10, 29, 31, 42, 97, 103, 104.
Chaumpvent, William de, 204 *n*.
Chauvent, Peter de, 170.
Chavenham, Walter de, 54.
Chaworthes, Thomas de, 65, 66, 67, 73, 74.
Cherlot, Robert, 41; Walter, 41.
Chesney, Robert de, *see* Bishop of Lincoln.
Chester, 97; Peter of, lxii, 155, 213.
Chetton, lvxi, 150, 151, 155; church of, 164, 165, 194, 211; Hugh de, 304; John de, 306; rector of, 292.
Chevaler, John le, 304; Ralph le, 299.
Chichester, bishop of, 203 *n*; dean of, 312; prebend of, xlviii *n*.

Chikewelle, Ives de, 40; Lucy de, 40.
Chiltham, 90.
Chilton, ii *n*.
Chinbern, Philip, 77, 78.
Chippenham, Allan de, 64.
Chirbury, convent of, xxxix, 287, 288; parish church of, 147; prior of, 132, 147, 148, 198, 228, 245, 279, 281; William de, 312.
Chirtulie, rector of, 304.
Church Withington, prebendary of, lxix.
Churcham, church of, 237, 238, 240; vicar of, 307; William de, 300, 306.
Churchstoke, church of, 131, 132.
Chylteham, William de, lxxi, 6, 80, 108.
Civita Vecchia, li *n*.
Clare, Gilbert de (Earl of Gloucester), iii *n*, xxviii, xxxv, lii, 23, 34, 36, 52, 53, 54, 55, 59, 60, 61, 84, 104, 123, 124, 225 *n*, 227; John de, lxii, lxx, lxxi, 15, 19, 20, 88, 117, 171, 182, 195, 196, 213, 216, 219, 246, 247, 250, 259, 260, 261, 262, 263, 267, 271, 279, 289, 293, 294, 295; Richard de, 61.
Claverleye, Richard de, 117.
Clehonger, Richard de, 41, 64, 171, 245.
Clement V., pope, x, liv, lv.
Clement, Walter, 43.
Cleobury North, rector of, 176, 302.
Clifford, David de, 300; Robert de, 301; Roger de, xxiv.
Cloppele, xliii, 40, 41, 246; manor of, lxi *n*; William de, 40.
Clun, lxvi, 159, 306; church of, 132 *n*; David de, 304; dean of, 46, 97, 131; Henry de, 304, 308, 311; Hugh de, 305, 308; John de, 300, 304, 305, 307; Nicholas de, 300, 309; rector of, 135, 302; Roger de, 309; Simon de, 299, 309; Stephen de, 135; Thomas de, 300, 304, 307; William de, 305, 309.

Clunbury, church of, 159 ; Gilbert de, 306.
Clungunford, rector of, 135, 302.
Clyf, Peter de, 171.
Clynelode, Bartholomew de, 299.
Coberley, Geoffrey de, xxxiv, 106, 107.
Coblenz, 8 *n*.
Coco, Thomas, 77.
Coddington, 40 *n*; rector of, 127 ; Robert de, 100.
Cœur, xxvi.
Coile, Andrew de, 309.
Cok, Robert, 310.
Cokkel, William, 77, 78,
Coleby, church of, 26 ; rector of, 304.
Colevile, Roger de, 172.
Collington, rector of, 302.
Collington Minor, chapelry of, 116.
Colne, St. Aylwin, lxv, 102.
Coltone, Geoffrey de, 304.
Colwall, lxvii, 43, 55, 227, 246 ; chase of, xxviii, 23, 59, 60, 62 ; church of, 195, 196, 250, 251 ; John de, 102 ; manor of, lxi *n*, 96 ; park of, 43, 76, 77 ; parson of, 86 ; rector of, xxvi, lxx, 216, 293, 302.
Comite, Ardicio de, 208, 220, 221, 248, 249, 250, 290, 291 ; Philip de, 249, 250 ; William de, 250.
Conches, xlviii, lxi, 268 ; Abbey of, 194 *n*.
Condover, hundred of, ii *n* ; portionists of, xxxviii.
Conflens, xxvi *n* ; Margaret de, xxi *n* ; William de (Archdeacon of Hereford), xxi, xxvi, lxix, 7, 8, 29.
Constantinople, v.
Corbet, Robert, 36, 239, 299 ; Peter, xxix, xxx, 67, 68, 69, 70, 71, 72, 73 ; Thomas, xxx, 67, 156.
Coreley, rector of, 151, 302, 303.
Cormeilles, abbot of, xlviii *n*.
Cornwall, xliv ; Richard, Earl of, lii.
Cors, Peter de, x *n*, xxvi, 126, 141, 184, 188, 192, 247, 248 ; Poncius de, xxvi, 126, 141, 184, 188, 192, 247, 248.

Corsham, lxvi, 150.
Corve, 227.
Costentyn, Joanna, 41 ; Thomas, 41.
Coutances, canon of, xlviii *n*.
Coventry and Lichfield, bishop of, 161.
Cowarne, Richard de, 305.
Cowarne, Little, church of, 102, 103 ; rector of, 302.
Cowarne, Much, church of, xliii, 49, 50, 229, 240, 256, 257. 260.
Cradley, Hugh de, 309 ; manor of, 96 ; rector of, 302.
Craswell, prior and convent of, 128, 129.
Credenhill, church of, 135 ; John de, 302 ; rector of. 302.
Creppinge, Alan de, 7, 198, 217, 304.
Crivile, Bertram de, 95, 97.
Croft, church of, lxx, 234, 235 ; John de, 88 ; Nicholas de, 306, rector of, 251, 302,
Cropthorne, Adam de, 62 ; Michael de, 188.
Cucbrittone, Reginald de, 299.
Cultellarius, Nicholas, 117.
Cumbisville, xvii, 278.
Cumin, Margaret, ii, xix.
Curceles, John de, 75.
Cursius, Master, 277, 278.
Cuysele, Richard de, 119.

Dabitot, Geoffrey, 62, 70 ; John, 69, 70 ; Lawrence, 171 ; Robert, 69 ; Richard, 69.
Dale, Hamo de, lxxi, 170, 171.
Daleham, J. de, 182.
Dalyleie, Richard de, 306.
Darlington, John de, *see* Archbishop of Dublin.
Daubeny, William, 63, 120, 213, 219, 245, 258, 259, 279.
Davy, Geoffrey, 90 ; Richard, 304 ; Roger, 304.

Dean, forest of, 96, 135, 211, 212; Henry de, 250, 251.
Dene, John de le, 306; Nicholas de, 307; Walter de la, 40, 77.
Deighton, ii, xix.
Denham, lxvi, 164.
Derby, earl of, 94.
Derbyshire, sheriff of, 65, 66.
Despenser, Geoffrey le, 95.
Deuxhill, chapel of, 191; rector of, 151.
Deynte, Robert, lxxi.
Diddlebury, vicarage of, 161.
Dilwyn, lxvi, 160.
Ditcheat, portionist of, 303.
Dixton, church of, 8; incumbent of, lxix.
Dodderhill, lxv, 7, 19, 20; rector of, xx n; rectory of, xix, 19.
Donne, John de, 301.
Dorsington, rector of, 195.
Drayton, lxv, 13, 14.
Droitwich, 19 n.
Drokensford, bishop, lxii.
Dublin, 33; Archbishop of (John de Darlington), 208, 219, 220, 221, 290, 291.
Dudmaston, Richard de, 69, 71.
Duntisborne, lxvii, 229.
Durham, bishop of (Anthony Beke), liv, 267, 271; (N. de Farnham), 95.
Dychesdone, Andrew de, 40.
Dyer, Reginald, 77.
Dymock, church of, 88; John de, 311.
Dynecourt, Edmund de, lxiii.

Eardisland, 194 n; vicarage of, 70.
Eardisley, lxvi, 161; castle of, xv, xxiv; parishioners of, 310; Robert de, 310.
Earley, lxv, lxvi, lxvii, 113, 118, 121, 122, 123, 141, 142, 155, 185, 211, 213, 217, 218, 225, 226, 236, 242, 245, 262, 263, 267, 283; Henry de, xl, 178, 179, 180; John de, 178, 179; manor of, xl, xli, xlvii, lxii, lxiii, 178, 180; Philip de, xl, xli, 165, 166, 167, 178, 179, 181, 182, 228; Robert de, 205.
Eastham, rector of, 302
Easthampton, 67, 68, 69; Richard de, 306.
Easthope, John de, 69.
Eastleach, 117, 118.
Eastnor, 55; chase of, xxviii, 23, 59, 60, 62; manor of, lxi n, 96; parishioners of, 7; rector of, xxvi, 6, 302.
Eastrington, dean of, 189, 190.
Eastwood, wood of, 74.
Eaton, lord of, 312; Robert de, 304, 311, 312; Thomas de, 171.
Eaton-juxta-Leominster, lxvi, 189.
Eaton Bishop, manor of, lxi n, 96; rector of, 302.
Ebulo, John de, 99, 100.
Edward I., xiv, xvi, xxviii, liv, 1, 23, 24, etc.
Edward III., liii n.
Eleanor (Queen of England), 18, 203.
Elmerugge, Adam de, 73.
Ely, bishop of, liv; (Nigel) 96.
Endon, manor of, 292.
English Channel, i, 244, 271.
Ercall, John de, 69, 71, 73.
Erdington, Richard de, 305; Robert de, 304.
Eston, lxi.
Estormy, John le, 62.
Eugines (Ogina), Gerard of, xxvi, 86.
Eure, i, 268 n.
Everle, Geoffrey de, 124.
Everslone, John de, 309.
Evesham, battle of, iii, xvi, xxviii; Roger de, 42, 65, 80, 123.
Evreux, i, xlvii.
Ewias Lacy, 140 n.
Exeter, bishop of (Brownescombe) xxii; (Grandisson) xliv; (Oldham) lii.
Eye, lxii, church of, 229, 296.

Eymer, Peter, 141, 142, 186, 197, 198, 225; Robert de, 153.
Eyton, Madoc de, lxxi, 146.
Eytonemeysy, Richard de, 307.

Faber, Thomas, 117; William, 43.
Facon, 174.
Fairford, 36.
Fairstead, John de, lxxi, 164.
Fareleye, William de, 108.
Farnham, Henry de, 304; N. de, *see* Bishop of Durham.
Faukeburne, William de, 117, 171, 182, 183, 197.
Fekham, Symon de, 51.
Felde, Cecil de la, 78; John de la, 78.
Fendenerac, rector of, 303.
Fenne, William de la, 123.
Ferre, John, 173.
Fikeldene, Robert de, 116.
Fileby, Adam de, lxix, lxx, 13, 14, 17, 63, 112, 113, 116, 136, 137, 138, 140, 150, 160, 161, 162, 168, 186, 187, 208, 209, 225, 234, 244, 245, 253, 254, 276, 277, 286, 306.
Firmario, Hugh de, 117.
Fisher, John, 301.
Fitz-Aere, John, 69, 73.
Fitz-Geoffry, Hugh, 183; John, 95.
Fitz-Gerald, Warin, 94.
Fitz-Gilbert, Thomas, 177, 303.
Fitz-Martin, Nicholas, 174.
Fitz-Osborn, Adelisia, xlviii; William, xlviii.
Fitz-Otes, Thomas, 38.
Fitz-Peter, Reginald, 142, 143, 153, 154, 188, 286.
Fitz-Reginald, Walter, 142, 143, 159, 163, 188, 189, 191, 193.
Fitz-Warin, Henry, lxx, 1, 2.
Flaxley, lxvii, 239; abbot of, 157, 311; abbot and monks of, 206, 207.
Flinteshame, William de, 308.
Flitelefiche, 69.

Flodre, John de la, 308.
Florence, xxxiv, 12 *n*, 295; canon of St. Pancras, 74; merchants of, 223.
Flytenetone, 170.
Folet, Robert, 23.
Foliot, Gilbert, *see* Bishop of Hereford; Thomas, 38.
Folye, Robert de la, 62.
Fonhope, Robert de la, 308.
Fontaine, xlviii, lxvii, 265, 269, 270, 273, 275, 298.
Ford, portionist of, 302.
Forest, dean of the, 139, 236, 237, 238.
Fownhope, 129 *n*.
Foxcote, church of, 177; rector of, 303.
Franc, Simon, 303.
France, parliament of, 11 *n*.
Fraunceys, Ralph, 90.
Fraxino, Simon de, v *n*.
Frederick II. (Emperor of Germany), vii, viii.
Fremon, Roger le, 305.
Freningham, Ralph de, 66.
Fresne, 89.
Friars Minor (Grey Friars), 203, 232 *n*, 307.
Friars Preachers (Black Friars), xi; prior of, 232, 284, 285.
Frome, dean of, 126, 138, 159, 196, 242; John de, 128 *n*, 309.
Frome, Bishop lxvii, 227, 228; manor lxi *n*, 96.
Frome Canon, vicar of, 312.
Frome Castle, rector of, 302.
Fulge, Robert, 158, 303.
Fulham, lxv, 107, 108, 110, 111, 112, 114, 115, 116, 237, 256.
Furches, Robert de, lxxi, 108.

Galensis, Anianus, 280, 282, 283.
Gamages, Beatrice de, 292.
Gamion, constable of, 174.

Garbeye, Walter de, 310.
Gardino, John de, 300, 307.
Garshirche, Roger de, 20
Garway, preceptory of, 311; Thomas de, 308, 311.
Gascony, ii, 128 *n*; seneschal of, iii.
Gatley, park of, 45.
Gaye, Martin de, xxvi, 154, 204, 210, 211.
Gebanon, bishop of (William de Conflens), lxix.
Genevile, Geoffrey de, 141; Matilda de, 141.
Genoa, xxxiv.
Gerard (cardinal of Basilica of XII. Apostles), *see* Bishop of Sabinum.
Gerbouch, Hugh, 300.
Giffard, Godfrey, *see* Bishop of Worcester; Walter, *see* Archbishop of York.
Gillingham, 38.
Gladewyne, William, 300.
Glazeley, John de, 305; rector of, 151, 303.
Gloucester, lxv, lxvi, 13, 36, 53, 101, 286, 287; abbey of St. Peter's, xliii, 30 *n*, 49, 50; abbot of, 13, 258, 260, 300; abbot and convent of, 49, 50, 51, 102, 208, 237, 238, 256, 257; archdeacon of, iii, 213; Bartholomew of, 291; Earl of, *see* Gilbert de Clare; Ellis of, 311; John of, 309; prior of, 6; prior of St. Oswald's, 229, 230, 255, 256, 285, 286; Robert of, xi, xiv *n*, xxiv, lxix, lxx, 63, 159, 163, 171, 197, 224, 244, 245, 246, 247, 248, 250, 252, 253, 254, 255, 256, 257, 259, 268, 308; sheriff of, 52, 53, 55, 170, 176; Walter of, 309; William of, 50.
Gloucestershire, 211; sheriff of, 32, 84, 134.
Godmon, John, 77.
Goldhulle, Thomas de, 54.
Gordwr, xxxi, 229, 279, 281, 284.
Gorwy, John, 306.

Gournay, xlvii; Hugh de, i.
Grave. Robert de la, 286, 287; Walter de la, 308
Greete, rector of, 143, 153, 154, 302.
Gregonet, Robert, iii.
Gregory X, pope, xviii, xxiv *n*, 36, 64, 74.
Grendene, Warin de, 171, 306.
Grendon Bishop, manor of, lxi *n*, 96.
Gresley, ii.
Grestein, abbot of, xlviii *n*.
Grete, Peter de, 73.
Greve, William de la, lxx, 261.
Grey, W. de, *see* Archbishop of York.
Griffin (Vicar of Welshpool), 140, 286, 287.
Griffith (Archdeacon of St. Asaph), 284, 286.
Grosmont, 173.
Grosseteste, Robert, *see* Bishop of Lincoln.
Grugeslone, rector of, 302.
Gruyère, William de, xxvi.
Grys, William, 216.
Guido, professor, x.
Guilsfield, chaplain of, 140, 286, 287.
Gynes, John, 117, 265, 266.

Hactone, Richard de, 311.
Haddestone, Peter de, 117.
Hale, John de la, 306.
Hales, abbey of, lii *n*.
Hall, William, 301.
Halton, Robert de, 176.
Hamildene, manor of, iii.
Hampton, John de, lxx, 52; Nicholas de, lxxi, 19; rector of, 106, 107; Walter de, 307
Hampton Bishop, manor of, lxi *n*, 96.
Hampton Episcopi, church of xix.
Hampton Meysey, church of, 131.
Hanley Castle, 124.
Hanwood, rector of, 153, 302.
Hardel, John, 20.

Haringworth, xxi.
Harley, Sir Roland de, 37.
Harpyn, Adam, lxxi, 26, 77.
Hartlebury, 205.
Hasleye, lxvii, 212.
Hastings, Henry, lord, xxi.
Hatfield, William de, 308.
Haumon, Raymond de, 82.
Haverberge, Walter de, 40, 41.
Hawkley, Henry de, xlix, 105, 226, 244, 268, 291.
Haycrust, 170.
Haye, Wlliam de la, 88, 121, 303.
Haywood, Gilbert de, 99, 100, 159.
Helion, Walter de, 123.
Helyon, Walter de, 60, 61, 62.
Helwy, Henry, 308.
Hempston, ii n,
Hemyhoke, Thomas, 171.
Hengham, Ralph de, xx, lx, 34, 53, 60, 61, 62, 78, 84, 225, 248, 249; Roger de, 185.
Henneberue, Roger de, 311.
Henore, Robert de, 307.
Henry II., 96.
Henry III., ii, xii, xiii, xiv, xv, xvi, xix, xxiii, xlvii, 5, 11, etc.
Henry VIII., li n.
Henseshelde, covert of, 170.
Hentone, Nicholas de, 299.
Hereford, xi, xxiii, xlv, liv, lxv, lxvi, lxvii, 7, 21, 29, 36, 37, 40, 51, 64, 93, 120, 129, 131, 155, 156, 174, 183, 213, 218, 244, 254, 268, 310; All Saints, xxvi, 30, 310; Archdeacon of, xliii, lxix, 81, 136, 154; *see* William de Conflens and Henry de Schorne; bailiffs of, lxxi, 17, 83, 259; bishop of; (Peter de Aquablanca) xiv n, xv, xxii, xxiii, xxv, xxvi, xxvii, xxx, xxxvii, xliii, xlix, lvi, lx, 5, 13 n, 30 n, 54, 61, 67, 84 n, 91, 92, 93, 96, 128, 146, 175, 176, 195, 198, 199, 247 n, 296, 297; (Robert de Betune) xxi n; (Giles de Braose) xxvii, 5, 93, 94; (John le Breton) xxi, xxv, xxvii, xxviii, xliii, 3, 5, 17, 21, 32, 33, 35, 40, 50, 65, 66, 67, 107, 135, 139, 158, 159, 170, 172, 174, 175, 176, 190, 199, 208, 215, 261, 278, 291; (Thomas de Cantilupe) i, ii, x, etc.; (Gilbert Foliot) 49, 50, 96; (Hugh Foliot) xxvii, 38, 43, 50, 170; (Ralph de Maydenstan) xxii, xli, xliii, lxi, 5, 38, 54, 61; (John Scory), xli; (Richard de Swinfield) xxxix, xli, liii, liv, lv, lvii, lx, lxi, lxiii, lxix, 63, 155. 171 n, 178, 179, 204, 210, 211, 298; Bye Gate Street, 232 n; Canons of, xxv, xlviii n; 13, 91, 92, 93, 130, 247 n, *see* Aymon de Aquablanca, John le Breton, Luke de Bree, Thomas Bruton, Peter of Chester, William de Conflens, Alan de Creppinge, William Daubeny, Peter Eymer, Adam de Fileby, Simon de Fraxino, Martin de Gaye, Robert of Gloucester, William de Gruyère, Nicholas de Hereford, H. de Neuwerc, Thomas de St. Omer, Walter de Redmarley, William le Rous, Henry de Schorne, Roger de Sevenake; Canons Row, 268; castle of, iii, 39; Castle Street, xlviii; cathedral church, xv, xxiii, xxiv, xxv, li, lii, lv, lvi, lvii, lix, 87, 128, 130, 133, 152, 163, 212, 213, 244, 246, 247; cathedral school, v; chancellor of, lxix, *see* Emeric de Aquablanca; chapter of, xxii, xxiii, xxvii, xlv, xlviii, liv, lxii, 1, 2, 3, 5, 8, 50, 112, 113, 114, 118, 161, 219, 220, 236, 246, 285, 306; chapter-house of, xlii, 40, 41; choristers of, 206 n; church of, 22, 40, 91, 92, 94; the Close, xxx; citizens of, 91, 92, 93, 113; city of, xxiii, xxv, 4, 5, 7, 83; city and diocese of, 168, 220, 254, 291; dean of, xxiv, 8 n, 38, 50, 128, 195, *see* Merewether; dean and chapter of, xxi, xxii, xxix, l,

liii, lvii, 5, 21, 38, 39, 49, 50, 91, 92, 93, 105 n, 128, 129, 130, 232; deanery of, xxii, xxiii, lxix, 2, 4, 33, 112, 113, 114, 115, 118, 214, 324; earl of, xlvii, 51, 97, 206; fair of, xxxi, 83; friars minor of, 202, 307; hebdomadary of, xliii, 8, etc.; Henry of, 62; manor of, lxi n; mayor of, xxx, 6, 113; Nicholas of, lxii, lxx, 34, 186 n, 252. 260, 261, 262, 295; official of, xxxi, xlv, xlix, lxix, l, 1, etc.; palace at, xxiv, xlii, xlv, 129; penitentiary of, lxii, 1, 2, 34, etc.; Portfield, 232 n; precentor of, lxix, 247, 258, 262, 272, see Henry de Borham and William de Montfort; precentorship, 111, 119; Richard of, 35, 212, 259, 260; Roger of, 259; St. Catherine's chapel, lv; St. Gutlac priory, 129; St. John's, lii n; St. Martin's, xxvi, 30; St. Mary Magdalene chapel, xxiv; St. Peter's, xxvi, 30 n; sheriff of, 35, etc.; Simon of, 239, 292; subdean of, xlvi, 2; succentor of, 88; Thomas de, 307; treasurer of, liii, lxix, 38, 142, 155; treasurership of, xxiv, 32, 33, 120; treasury of, lxii, 118, 271, 296; vicar choral, 311; vicar general, lxix, 221, 222, 252, 253, 256, 258, 269, 270.

Hereford, Little, manor of, 51; Richard de, 306; Roger de, 36, 300, 306.

Herefordshire, sheriff of, 23, 32, etc.

Hergast, Howel de, 309.

Hertford, earl of, see Gilbert de Clare.

Heyton, Richard de, lxx, 27, 177, 194, 195, 242, 271, 281, 300, 306; W. de, 27.

Heywood, Gilbert de, lxxi, 88, 116, 171, 197, 267, 304.

Higham Ferrers (Hegham), rector of, 303.

Hillhampton, William de, 310, 311.

Hindlip, 62.

Hodenet, John de, 24, 36; Nicholas de, 171.

Hodinet, Nicholas de, lxxi.

Holdgate, portionists of, 302.

Holicote, Thomas de, 304.

Holme Lacy, xliii; parish of, 128, 129.

Holy Land, viii, xviii, 6, 107, 219, 220, 221, 249 n, 290, 291.

Homme, Gilbert de, 311.

Honorius III., pope, ix.

Hope, Robert de, 309; Stephen de, 307; William de, 304.

Hope Bagot, rector of, 302.

Hope Bowdler, 171 n; church of, 16, 28, 185, 235; rector of, 302, 312.

Hope Mansell, rector of, 136, 139, 141, 142, 184, 188, 190.

Hopesay, church of, 243; John de, 306.

Hopton, Walter de, 54, 70, 215, 216, 300, 305.

Hopton Wafers, church of, 196, 205; rector of, 302.

Hore, William le, 90.

Horsnede, John de, 64.

Hospitallers, 308; prior of, see Joseph de Cauncy.

Houghton, John de, lxx, 22.

How Caple, church of, 185, 242.

Hudynton, William de, 43.

Hugeford, William de, 69, 71, 70.

Hugh, English Cardinal, 274.

Hughley, vicarage of, 202, 203.

Hulle, Richard de la, 43, 77, 78; William atte, 117; William de la, 266.

Humber, chapel of, 41; rector of, 302, 303.

Huntingdon, prebend of, 155, 213 n.

Huntley, rector of, 302.

Husser, Richard le, 83.

Hyda, manor of, 49.

Hynetone, Philip de, 153.

Hyntlesham, Roger de, 3, 40, 41.

Ightham, xlvi, lxvii, 221, 222, 223.
Ilkeston, ii.
Ingelthorp, Thomas de (Dean of St. Paul's), 127.
Ingham, church of, 303; Richard de, 303.
Inkberrow, prebend of, xxvii, lxix, 84, 86, 87, 122, 248, 249.
Innocent II., pope, xxviii.
Innocent IV., pope, vii, viii, ix, 203, 206, 232 n.
Innocent V., pope, 126.
Inwarthyn, Philip de, 299.
Ireland, lxiii, 24, 25, 33, 269.
Isère, xxvi n.
Isleham, Roger de, 304.

Jakes, Richard, 311.
John (King of England), i, 91, 93, 95.
John XX., pope, 57.
John XXI., pope, 124. 191.
John XXII., pope, xxxvi., lviii.
Jordan (cardinal of St. Eustace), 187.
Joye, John, 311; Robert, 311.
Judas, John, 301.
Jurbain, Philip, 43.

Kanne, Hugh, 117.
Kempsey, lxv, 6; church of, xix; John de, lxx, lxxi, 16, 117, 197, 241, 250, 251; rector of, 106, 107; Robert de, lxx, 52; Walter de, 124.
Kendal, Hugh de, 157, 175; Michael de, 24, 152.
Kenington, 70.
Kensington, xli, lxv, lxvi, 24, 26, 80, 81, 121; church of, 78.
Kentchurch (St. Keyne), rector of, 134, 155, 302.
Kentisbury, Stephen de, xl, 166, 167.

Keydor, John called, 305.
Keyrdif, Henry de, 63.
Keyrwent, Gregory de, 284, 285.
Kilpeck, Joanna de, 80 n.
Kilwardby, Robert, see Archbishop of Canterbury.
Kimberley, Richard de, lxxi, 31, 217, 241, 242, 271, 272; William de, 242.
Kingesemede, Henry de, 81.
Kingsland, rector of, 194; William de, 301.
Kingsley, 22, 23.
Kingston, William de, 122.
Kington, church of, 206; John de, 117; rector of, 302.
Kinkeshope, rector of, 302.
Kinlet, William de, 304.
Kinnersley, Philip de, 88, 117; rector of, 302.
Kirkton, Roger de, 217.
Knights Templars, master of, 192, 240, 304.
Knighton, lxvi, 160.
Knill, rector of, 302.
Knovile, Hugh de, 73; John de, 73; Nicholas de, 259, 268.
Kylmeskote, William de, 304.

Lacy, Peter de, 151, 245, 246; Richard de, 96; Robert de, l, 1, 28, 29, 125, 235; Walter de, 140 n, 141.
Lacu, Henry de, lxxi, 76, 77.
Lambeth, l.
Lambourn, lxv, 31.
Langele, Geoffrey, 174; Walter de, 173, 174.
Langon, Peter de, xxiv, xxv, xxxi, lxii, lxiii, 7, 12, 18, 187, 209, 213, 214, 233, 250, 277.
Langton, John de, 303; William de, see William de Rotherfield.
Lanrothan, Davy de, 304; Morice de, 304.

Laon, 99 *n.*
Lateran the, 127; council of the, xxxv, 296.
Lausanne, bishop of, 204; chancellor of, 138; precentor of, xxvi; treasurer of, 136.
Lavenden, abbot and convent of, 129.
Lawerdene, Richard de, 306.
Le, Walter de la, 308.
Ledbury, xlv, lxi, lxv, lxvi, lxvii, lxxi, 28, 29, 31, 63, 110, 191. 211, 305, 309; Adam de, 310; bailiff of, lxxi, 26, 244, 245; church of, 126, 127, 308; hospital, 245, 300, 306; John de, 27, 30; manor of, lxi *n*, 96, 163; park of, 43, 76, 77; park of Dulingwode, 69; portion of, 241, 242, 245; portionists of, xxxviii, lxix, 141, 142, 185; prebend of, 63, 125, 126, 254; Ralph de, 307; vill of, 91, 92, 306.
Ledene, John de, 309.
Ledewych, church of, 304.
Legat, John, 43, 77, 78, 308.
Leghe, John de la, 77, 78.
Leiburne, Roger de, 174.
Leicester, countess of, xvi; earl of, xvi.
Leinthall, John de, 305; William de, 311.
Leinthall Earles, 44, 45.
Leintwardine, Adam de, 138; Hugh de, 306; William de, 301.
Leominster, xlv, lii, lxv, lxvi, lxvii, 42, 156, 184, 229; chapter-house of, 87; church of, 47, 88, 89, 137, 139, 229; Forbury, xxxix; manor of, 263; prior of, 116, 218, 229, 269, 270, 296; priory and convent of, 46, 47, 79, 87, 88, 95, 265; prior of, xxxviii, xxxix, 37, 48, 264, 266, 267; Robert de, 300; subprior of, xxxix, 116, 265; Thomas de, 17; vicar of, 117, 299; vill of, 311.
Letton, rector of, 302.
Lewes, battle of, xv.

Ley, Nicholas de, 161.
Leyes, John de, 66.
Leyter, Roger de, 66.
Lichfield, 99 *n*; canon of, xix.
Lincoln, bishop of, xii, xiii, 177, 304, 310; (Robert de Chesney) 96; (Robert Grosseteste) iii, viii, xxxii; canon of, xlix 105 *n*; chancellor of, 63; dean of, 11 *n*.
Lindridge, John de, 301; rector of, lxx, 302; vicarage of, 124.
Lingayne, Richard de, 301.
Linggeyn, Thomas de, 303.
Linleye, John de, 132; Walter de, 132.
Lisieux, 99 *n*; hospital at. xlviii *n*.
Littledean, William de, 307.
Llandaff, archdeacon of, 229, 230, 256; bishop of, 229, 230. 236, 239, 253, 256; precentor of, 229, 230, 256.
Llandinabo, church of, 239; rector of, 303.
Llangarran, Gregory de, 300; rector of, 302.
Llanrothal, Nicholas de, 256, 257; Peter de, 124, 191, 308.
Llanthony, Henry de, 300; St. Mary of, 206 *n*.
Llanthony Prima, 310; prior and convent of, 27, 29, 51, 122, 123, 190.
Llanwarne, portion of, 27; portionists of, xxxviii; rector of, 302.
Llewellyn (prince of Wales), xxii, xxvii, xxviii, xxix, xxxi, 9, 10, 29, 31, 42, 103.
Loctone, Hugh de, 307.
Loges, William de, 74, 75.
Lombard, Peter, xvii.
Londesborough, 190; church of, 159, 160, 183, 189, 190.
London, xvi, xl, xli, lxi, lxv, lxvi, lxvii, lxviii, 14, 15, 17, 18, 19, 20, 21, 22, 25, 27, 45, 51, 61, 75, 79, 102, 103, 169, 173, 177, 178 *n*, 186, 203, 204, 206, 208, 210, 215, 216, 217, 218, 219, 224, 231, 235, 236, 243, 254, 260, 291, 294, 296; Ald-

gate, prior and canons of Holy Trinity within, xli, lxiii; bishop of, xx, xxii, l, lii, liv, 174, 304; chapter-house, liv; citizens of, 20; Clerkenwell, hospital of, 173; dean of, 263; (Hervey de Borham) xxxvi, 14, 16, 25, 78, 79, 88, 111, 121; (Cantilupe) ii *n*; (Thomas de Ingelthorpe) 127; (William de Montfort) 111 *n*; dean and chapter, xxxiv, 14, 16; J. of, 157, 158; New Temple, 21, 87, 100, 213, 216; prebend of Cantlers, ii *n*; prebendary of St. Paul's, xix; St. Martin's, canon of, lxix, 287; St. Martin-le-Grand, dean of, 204 *n*; St. Mary Aldermary, 304; St. Paul's, xlii, liv, 182, 263; tower of, 60.

Longhope, John de, 236.

Longmynd, xxix, 69, 73.

Longtown Castle, 140.

Louis IX., king of France, xi, xv.

Lovetot, John de, 66.

Lucca, xxxiv, 51 *n*; Lucas of, xxxiii, 25; merchants of, 13, 15, 18, 19.

Ludlow, 299, 301, 304, 306, 307; church of, 140, 158, 209; dean of, 305; Gregory de, 305; John de, 299; Nicholas de, 299; Philip de, 299, 311; Roger de, 117, 120, 205; W. de, 300: Walter de, 161, 310; William de, lxx, 117, 143, 153, 154, 279.

Luggebrugge, mill of, 22.

Lugwardine, lii, lvii, 175, 227, 239; rector of, 303.

Luvetot, William, 64.

Lydbury, John de, 309.

Lydbury North, 70, 72, 73; castle of, 31, 42, 46, 74, 98, 104; deanery of, 46; forest of, lxxi, 20, 21; manor of, xxix, lxi, 9, 10, 29, 97, 170.

Lydham, Ralph de, 301; rector of, 302.

Lydlee, house of, 301.

Lydney, benefice of, xlviii; church of, 219, vicar of, 290, 308.

Lyngebroke, church of, 219; convent of, xxxix, 200, 201, 202; nun of, xxxix, 265.

Lyons, 65, 152; 1st council of, vii; 2nd council of, xvii, xviii, xix, xxxv, 1 *n*, etc.

Lyonshall, church of, 212, 213; rector of, 302.

Lyre, lxvii, 247, 258, 259, 260, 268; abbey of, xlviii, 194 *n*, 256, 257; abbot of, xlviii *n*, 143, 144; abbot and convent of, 7, 70, 153, 154.

Macclesfield, 64.

Maddelege, rector of, 302.

Maddok, 131.

Madine, Robert de, 54.

Madresfield, lxiii, 171.

Malcolm, Sir (canon of Wells), 211.

Malleye, Henry de, 299.

Malvern, 96; chase of, 52, 227; forest of, 23; foresters of, lxxi, 159; hills of, 62; prior and convent of, 312.

Malwarne, William de, 309.

Mamble, chantry of, 299; Nicholas de, 299; Wiliiam de, 301.

Manchester, H. de, 232.

Maniworde, Reginald, 83.

Mantua, notary of, 288.

Marches, the, 108, 110.

Marcle, lxv, 45; forester of, 77; John de, 30, 311; Nicholas de, 301, 306; parishioners of, 311; William de 161, 300, 305, 307, 311.

Marcle, Little, church of, 24, 291; rector of,, 152, 157, 302.

Marcle, Much, advowson of, 143, 144, 153, 154.

Marden, 175; Isabella de, 291; John de, 62, 291.

Mare, John de la, 246.

Marescallus, J., 255.
Marmion, John, 80 ; Philip, 80, 81 ; William, 80.
Marsh, Walter, 251.
Marshall, W., earl of Pembroke, 94.
Marshalsea, 173.
Martin IV., pope, 289.
Martin, papal agent, viii.
Masingtone (Messyntone), John de, 43, 78 ; Philip de, 43, 77, 78 ; Walter de, 78 ; William de, 43.
Mason, John le, 299.
Mathew, Heylin ab, 140, 286, 287.
Maurthy, Walter de, 190.
Maydenstan, Ralph de, *see* Bishop of Hereford.
Mayfield, lxv, 11.
Maynoth (Meyboth), 140 ; Adam de, *see* Adam ab Meurike.
Mazim, Reginald le, 77.
Medruth, king, xxviii.
Mellington, *see* Muleton.
Melton Mowbray, Robert de, xxix.
Membury, Maurice de, lxx, 205, 228, 261.
Mende, bishop of, liv.
Meole Brace, vicarage of, 121, 122, 138.
Meopham, Richard de, 11.
Mercer, Adam le, 77.
Merdis, William de, 117.
Mere, John de la, 77, 78.
Merewether, dean, lvii *n*, lviii.
Merhokes, 170.
Merstone, Henry de, 301.
Mersy, Robert de, 301.
Meth, Hugh, 299.
Mettingham, John de, 158.
Meudon, John de, 141 *n*, 158.
Meurike, Adam ab, 140, 286, 287 ; John ab, 140.
Meyh, Geoffrey le, 309.
Micheldean (Great Dean), 250, 251.
Midelhope, Simon de, 305.
Middleton, chapel of, 191 ; rector of, 151, 302 ; Richard de, 54 ; Walter de, 54, 119.

Milan, archpresbyter of, 220, 221, 250, 290, 291.
Mill, Walter at the, 77.
Modena, bishop of, 208 *n*.
Moigne, Ralph le, 171.
Monesle, John de, 308.
Moneur, William de, 304.
Monitone, Walter de, 62.
Monkelowe, William de, 300.
Monkland, William de, 299.
Monkton, Nicholas de, 308 ; Roger de, 308 ; William de, 195.
Monmouth, 8 *n*, 240 ; John of, 107, 108, 123 ; prior of, 305 ; prior and convent of, 27 ; Richard of, 305 ; Stephen of, 305, 308.
Mont Ferrand, Stephen de, 173.
Montacute, convent of, ii.
Montalt, John de, 235 *n*; Milicent de, 235.
Monte Fiascone, li, liv, lxviii, 295.
Montfort, Peter de, 215, 216 ; Simon de, iii, xv, 11 *n* ; William de, lxix, 111, 119, 122, 221, 222, 245, 246, 248, 249, 250, 252, 253, 254, 256, 271.
Montgomery, Adam de, 304 ; castle of, 110, 171 *n* : church of, 131, 132, 134, 168 ; constable of, xxvii ; earl, xxix ; garrison of, 108 ; Philip de, 300 ; rector of, 137, 302.
Mordiford, rector of, 303.
More, John de la, 55 ; Ralph de la, 309 ; rector of, 239, 302.
More Akeyn, John de, 304.
Moreton, church of, 141, 186, 225 ; prebend of, 225, 248, 249, 268 ; vicar of, 312.
Morville, church of, 156 ; manor of, xxxviii ; 161 *n*.
Moubray, Adam de, 40, 41 ; Pain de, 41.
Moutiers, xxvi *n*.
Muchelney, abbot of, xlviii *n*.
Mudle, Robert de, 191.
Muleton, vill of, xxviii, 10, 29, 31, 42, 97, 104.

Multone, Jordan de, 116.
Mungomery, Adam de, 71.
Munslow, 203 n; rector of, 41, 272, 273, 302; Robert de, 302.
Munt Virun, Richard de, 62.
Muntosin, John, 174.
Musard, Ralph, 3, 89, 90.
Muscegros, Robert 97,
Mustel, William, 307.
Mynd, Roger de, 170.

Nannan, Anianus of, see Bishop of St. Asaph.
Naves, Gonter de, 45, 136, 162.
Neapoli, B. de, 274.
Neen Solers, rector of, 303.
Neenton, rector of, 188.
Neuwerc, H. de, 17.
Nevyle, William de, lxiii, lxxi, 26, 217, 218.
Newenham, John de, 312; Richard de, 304, 310.
Newent, xlv, lxvi, lxvii, 163, 307; Henry de, 303; John de, 301, 307; Thomas de, 301; vicar of, 301.
Newland, church of, 210, 240; Philip de, 308; rector of, 157, 303.
Newmarch, Bernard de, 49.
Newton, lxvi, 187; church of, 226; Hugh de, 81, 82; Johanna de, 226; rector of, 302.
Nicholas III., pope, 56, 203, 229, 231, 236, 241, 287, 288, 291.
Nicholas IV., pope, li, liv.
Nicholas de N, canon of Hereford, 186.
Norfolk, deaneries of, lvii; sheriff of, 172.
Normandy, xlvii, xlix, 265, 298.
North Petherton, see Petherton North.
Northampton, fair of, 173.
Northwood, church of, 312; Roger de, 35, 134, 199, 200, 216.

Norton, prebend of, 267.
Norton-under-Bredon, xvii.
Norwich, bishop of, 31, 284, 285.
Notteclive, John de, 40, 41; William de, 40, 41.
Nutbatch, 170.
Nyutone, John de, 309.

Oddo Blanchus, 289.
Odiham, 179.
Offa, king, xli.
Old Church Moor, 170.
Oldbury, John de, 304.
Onibury, rector of, 120.
Orcop, John de, 299.
Orkhope Tudor de, 311.
Orleton, John de, 299.
Orleans, university of, iv, ix, x, xii.
Orvieto, (Urbs Vetus), li, liv; Peter de, 14.
Oseney, 251; abbey of, viii.
Osgot, William, 54.
Ostia, bishop of, 187.
Otho, papal legate, iv, xxxv.
Othobon, constitution of, xlii.
Oxford, archdeacon of, 11 n; chancellor of, xiii, xiv, xv, xvii, xxxv; John of, 117; mayor of, xiv; Nicholas of, lxxi, 117, 202, 203, 267; provisions of, xiv, xv; sheriff of, xx; university of, iv, xi, xii, xxii, xxxvii, lxxi, 45.
Oylun, Robert, 309.

Padua, university of, x.
Pancefot, Grimbald, 24.
Paris, 94, 255; John of, 308; Matthew, ii, ix, x, xii, xxiii; university of, iv, v, vi, vii, ix, x, xi, xii, xvi, xvii, xx, xxxvii, l, lxxi, 45, 135, 156, 157, 213 n.

Park Chapel, vicarage of, 185.
Parker, John le, 17.
Parliament, the, 32, 186, 216.
Parma, bishop of, 249 *n*; Sigenbald de, 288.
Paterake, Richard, 28.
Paulyn, Hugh, 117.
Pauntone, Hugh de, 123.
Pecche, Bartholomew, 97.
Peckham, John *see* Archbishop of Canterbury.
Pede, John, 309.
Pedwardin, Brian de, 310.
Pembridge, 294; Adam de, 301; advowson of, 293, 294; church of, 195; Roger de, 300, 307.
Pembroke, earl of, xxi, 94.
Pencombe, church of, 131; Hugh de, 300, 309.
Penebroke, John de, 30, 31.
Persore, William de, 300, 309.
Peterstow, rector of, 302, 312.
Petherton North, farm of, 228; manor of, xl, 165, 166, 167, 181, 182.
Philip, William, 299.
Pichard, Roger, 71, 72, 77, 78, 251, 292.
Picheford, John de, 69.
Pickarde, 273.
Pickford, Geoffrey de, 237.
Pipard, Ralph, 269.
Pipe, rector of, 302.
Pistoia 51 *n*; merchants of, li, liii *n*, 274, 276, 294.
Pistor, Robert, 116.
Pixley, chapel of, 161; rector of, 305, 307.
Poer, Dionisia le, 65, 66, 67; James le, 245; Margery le, 65, 66, 67; Ranulf le, 65, 66, 67, 74.
Poggibonzi, Bardus de, xxxiii, lxx, 12, 13, 15, 18, 19, 213, 250.
Poissy, xlix, lxvii, 255.
Pola, *see* Welshpool.
Poly, Walter, 311.
Pontesbury, lxvi, 140, 143; chaplain of, 143, 153; church of, 160; dean of, 24, 46, 131, 132, 134,

137, 145, 150, 152, 153, 154, 160, 163, 189, 305; Geoffrey de, 160, 163; Henry de, 309 Hugh de, 160, 163; lord of, 302; manor of, 142; Philip de, 154; portionists of, xxxviii, 142, 143, 152, 153, 159, 163, 183, 188, 189, 190, 191, 193; rector of, 145, 150.
Pontigny, xlvii, xlviii *n*.
Pope, the, 106, 107, 273, 274, 275, 279, 280, 283; *see* Alexander IV., Boniface VIII., Celestine V., Clement V., Gregory X., Honorius III., Innocent II., IV., V., John XX., XXI., XXII., Martin V., Nicholas III., IV.; auditor of, 283; chaplain of, vii, 250, 291; legate of, iv, viii, xxxv; nuncio of, 249 *n*, 250; penitentiary of, 231, 272; usher of, 274; valet-de-chambre of, 274
Porcher, Richard le, 117.
Porto, cardinal bishop of (Robert Kilwardby), 187.
Potel, Henry, 43.
Powick, xxxv; parson of, 123, 124.
Prestbury, lxi, lxv, lxvi, lxvii, 3, 4, 5, 6, 25, 26, 27, 30, 41, 46, 81, 86, 89, 90, 109, 133, 155, 156, 185, 198, 251; bailiff of, lxxi, 25, 26, 90, 176, 295; bishop's court of, 3; manor of, 97, 208, 290, 291; reeve of, 109; vill of, 40.
Prestescroftinge, 73.
Presthemede, Nicholas de, 304; William de, 304.
Preston, lxvi, 119; John de, 308, 312; market of, 93; prebend of, xxvii, lxii, lxiii, 8, 12, 16, 18, 187, 209, 233, 245; vill of, 91, 92.
Priur, Thomas le, 277.
Prynne, xxvi.
Pulcomb, lxi.
Pull, la, 22.
Pulverbatch, rector of, 302.
Putte, Robert de la, 43, 77, 78; Walter de la, 43, 77, 78.

Pykestone, Griffin, 140.
Pyon Kings, rector of, 303.
Pyte, William, 77.

Radlow, hundred of, 43.
Radnor, Miles de, 300 ; Peter de, 83 ; Reginald de, 239.
Radnor, New, rector of, 302.
Raone, Thomas de, 171.
Rayleigh, 84.
Rea, valley of the, xxix.
Reading, abbey of, xxxviii, 37, 264 ; abbot of, xxxix, 5, 263, 269, 270, 271, 272, 289, 296.
Reccheford, John de, 312.
Redcliff, Hugh de, 27, 29.
Rede, John le, 227.
Redeford, 305.
Redewelle, R. de, 250.
Redmarley, 70 ; Walter de, lxix, lxx, 17, 63, 171, 211, 216, 217, 222, 232, 246, 252, 268, 295.
Reshale, 22.
Revipele, 78.
Rhuddlan, prior of, xxxi *n*; rector of, 188.
Ribefor, Richard de, 305.
Ribesford, Robert de, 311.
Richard's Castle, church of, 158, 159 ; rector of, 302, 303.
Rigaud, Eudes, *see* Archbishop of Rouen.
Ripple, church of, xix.
Risle, the, xlviii
Rive, Robert de la, 299, 301.
Roce, John, 310.
Roches, Peter des, *see* Bishop of Winchester.
Rochester, bishop of, xxii, lii, 304.
Rochford, Hugh de, 301, 309 ; Richard de, 299 ; vicar of, 300 ; William de, 299.
Rock (Aka), lxvi, 161 ; rector of, 101, 134, 135, 302 ; Richard de, 299, 301.

Rodeford, rector of, 309.
Rodele, manor of, 49.
Rodeleya, vicar of, 304.
Rodewelle, Robert de, 266, 267.
Roger, earl, xxvii.
Rome, xii, lxii, 244, 252 *n*, 288 ; apostolic see, 11, 20, 33, 42, 75, 99, 107, 220, 256, 267, 287, 289, 290, 291 ; court of, xxv, xxvii, xxxi. xxxii, xxxiii, xxxiv, xlvii, xlix, l, li, lv, lvii, lxi, lxiii, lxx, 8, 12, 14 *n*, 15, 19, 84, 85, 86, 106, 140, 186, 187, 197, 209, 210, 213, 215, 233, 234, 242, 250, 255, 265, 267, 272, 273, 276, 277, 280, 283, 264, 294 ; Lateran, the, 127 ; Lateran Council, xxxv, 296 ; St. Peter's, 59, 204, 231, 241.
Romsey, John de, 82.
Romuley, Ralph de, 7.
Ross, lxv, lxvi, 49, 109, 302 ; bailiff of, lxxi, 26, 108 ; church of, 120 ; John de, 199 ; manor of, xli *n*, 76, 77, 97 ; manor house of, xliv *n*; Robert de, 78, 79 ; vicar of, xlix, 301 ; vill of, 76, 77, 91, 92.
Ross Foreign, manor of, lxi *n*.
Roter, William, 308.
Rotherfield, William de, lxii, 105.
Rotherfield-Peppard, 269 *n*.
Rothley, vicar of, 304.
Rouen, i *n*, 94 ; archbishop of, xviii, li *n*.
Rous, Matthew le, *see* Matthew de Ursinis ; William le, 32, 33, 120, 121.
Rowardyn, William de, 307.
Rowleston, Thomas de, 311.
Rudford, rector of, 302.
Rudolph III, xxvi *n*.
Rufus, William, 84, 85, 86, 87.
Ruffus, Matthew, *see* Matthew de Ursinis ; W., 246 ; William, xxvii, 88.
Rushbury, rector of, 212.
Russell, lxxi, 159.
Ruter, William, 305.
Rynweye, Geoffrey de, 106,

Ryton, Luke de, 69, 71; William de, 304.

Sabello, James de, 278, 279.
Sabinum, bishop of (Cardinal Gerard), 274, 281, 288, 289.
St. Asaph, archdeacon of, 284, 286; bishop of (Anianus II), xxxi, lxii, 11, 42, 140, 197, 198 *n*, 209, 229, 230, 232, 233, 234, 236, 255, 274, 275, 277, 279, 280, 281, 282, 283, 284, 285, 288, 289; cathedral of, xxxi *n*; chapter of, 236, 285.
St. Briavels, Philip de, 299, 307.
St. David, bishop of, xxxiv, 235, 310.
St. Dyonisius, Walter de, 311.
St. Edmund, Michael de, 174.
St. Frideswide, Richard de, 304.
St. George, Adam de, 292; Agnes de, 292; Stephen de, 141, 169.
St. Gilles, Thomas de, 127, 131; William de, 304.
St. Ives, fair of, 173.
St. John, baron, iii; William de, 121, 187.
St. John of Jerusalem, prior of the hospital of, 1, 28, 165, 167, 181, 199.
St. Keyne, *see*, Kentchurch.
St. Michael, church of, 292; David de, 299, 309.
St. Omer, college of, lviii; Petronella, de, 156; Thomas de, xxi, 143, 154; William de, 156.
St. Pancras, rector of, 312.
St. Peter, Gilbert de, 305; Richard de, 312.
Salculke, Thomas de, 117.
Salinis, Peter de, 126 *n*; Pontius de, 126 *n*.
Salisbury, xvi; bishop of, 193, 307; earl of, 94; John of, vi, lxx, 65, 66, 171, 285, 286.

Salop, archdeacon of (James de Aquablanca), xxvi, xliii, 125, 137, 150, 160, 161, 162, 197, 241, 242, 245; (Adam de Fileby) 14 *n*, 253; (John de Swinfield) x *n*; (Richard de Swinfield) 63.
Saltmarsh, Peter de, 246.
San Severo, abbey of, li.
Sandford-juxta-Oxford, lxvi, 121.
Sandwich, Ralph de, 165, 167.
Sapey, rector of, 302.
Sapy, Richard de, 310; Robert de, 231.
Sarnesfield, rector of, 302.
Sarreta, xxvi *n*, 136, 138.
Saumun, John, 90.
Savoy, 8 *n*; count of, xxvii *n*; Peter of, 95.
Say, Geoffrey, de, 94; John de, lxxi, 117.
Sceldertone, Walter de, 307.
Schorne, Henry de, lvii.
Scotland, 296.
Scot, Reginald le, 81.
Scudamore, John, 129 *n*.
Sechtone, lxv, 9.
Sectone, Nicholas de, 304.
Seculer, Walter le, 81.
Segrave, Stephen de, 95, 97.
Selretone, Walter de, 300.
Senis, Michael de, 173.
Sevene, William le, 304.
Seys, Griffin, 140; Maredyit, 140.
Seytone, Roger de, 26, 66, 71, 144.
Sevenake, Roger de, lxix, lxx, 63, 88, 171, 221, 222, 245, 246.
Sevenhampton, lxi, 3, 40, 41, 89; manor of, 97.
Sevenoaks, lxvii, 219.
Shakbeard, Egwin, xxix.
Shefhangre, Walter de, 174.
Sheldesley, John de, 101, 102.
Shelwick, manor of, lxi *n*, 22, 96; vill of, 22, 23.
Shepe, Robert de, 41.
Sheppy, Peter of, 272.
Sherborne Decani, xix, lxv, lxvii, 3, 12, 13, 15, 16, 26, 27, 34, 35, 211; prior of, xli.

Shinfield, benefice of, xlviii, lvii; tithes of, lvi.
Shipton, chapel of, 9, 28; Henry de, 40; rector of, 302; Robert de, 40.
Shorham, Henry de, 63.
Shorley, 44.
Shrewsbury, 55, 134, 140.
Shropshire, sheriff of, 67, 68, 70, 72, 73, 74, 135, 140.
Sienna, xxxiv.
Silbestone, Walter de, 304.
Silvington, rector of, 302.
Sinningfeude, Adam de, 66.
Skenfrith, 173.
Snitterfield, ii, xix.
Snothulle, Walter de, 310.
Sobedone, Herbert de, 117.
Sollers, John de, 291.
Somerset, lxiii, 165, 262, 263.
Spareforde, William de, 306.
Spina, 276.
Sponford, 170.
Springehose, Roger, 69, 71, 73, 290.
Spygurnel, Richard, 63.
Stabelgate, John de, 304.
Stafford, archdeacon of, xvi, xix.
Stakebache, John de, 117.
Stamford fair, 75, 173.
Stanford, R. de, 153; rector of, 194, 302; Robert de, 156.
Stanley, William de, 308, 312.
Stanton, lxv, 100; church of, 193.
Stanton-Lacy, Thomas de, 301,
Stanworde, Hugh de, 309.
Stapleton, Robert de, 16, 290.
Staunton, Adam de, 299; Hugh de, 300, 302, 307; rector of, 302; vicar of, 299; William de, 299.
Staunton (Forest of Dean), rector of, 134, 135, 302.
Staunton-juxta-Ludlow, lxvii, 292.
Steyntone, William de, 310.
Stikkeford, Henry de, 310.
Stokas, Roger de, 174.
Stoke, Robert de, 150; Roger de, 308.
Stoke Bliss, rector of, 302.
Stoke Edith, church of, 219.

Stoke Lacy, 269; church of, 208, 245, 246, 254; rector of, 302.
Stoke St. Milburgh, rector of, 302.
Stoke Say, vicarage of, 119.
Stonyhurst, lviii.
Stottesdon, dean of, 151, 202, 203; Walter de, 305.
Stowe, Henry de, 117; Philip de, 117, 301; William de, lxx, 22.
Stradewy, 251, 292; chapel of, 301.
Stratford, Ralph de, 310; Richard de, 83, 84, 102, 155, 268.
Stratford-on-Avon, xix.
Stratton, Adam de, 35.
Stretford, rector of, 302.
Stretton, church of, 119, 120, 121, 190; rector of, 302; Richard de, 299; Robert de, 81.
Stretton Dale, 120, 121.
Stretton Grandison, church of, 27.
Studeley, xvi; priory of, ii.
Stwochpe, Adam de, 305.
Styward, Henry, 266.
Sugwas, xli, liii *n*, lxv, lxvi, lxvii, 38, 95, 109, 110, 120, 124, 125, 126, 127, 131, 132, 135, 137, 139, 149, 153, 154, 171, 188, 189, 190, 193, 194, 195, 228; manor of, lxi *n*; manor house of, xlii; park of, 76, 77.
Suntyngge, Bartholomew de, 197.
Surigitus, Adam called, 236.
Surrey, Archdeacon of, 243.
Susa, Thaddeus of, viii.
Sutton, church of, 24, 36.
Suyndone, 40.
Suysken, father, lv.
Sweynestone, John de, 62.
Swinfield, John de, x *n*, liv; Richard de, *see* Bishop of Hereford.
Syflewast, N., 110.
Syldresle, John de, 308.
Symmynfeuld, Adam de, 64.
Symon, William, 41.
Symond, William, 90.
Syreburne, Adam de, 308.

Tabritone, rector of, 302.
Tadestone, Peter, 300.
Talbot, G., 302; Gilbert, 173, 174; Philip, 135; Richard 135.
Tamworth, 80 n.
Tardebigge, Richard de, 149.
Tasley, church of, 156; John de, 306; rector of, 302.
Taylur, Richard le, 304.
Tedestile, Richard de, 226.
Tenbury, lxvii, 240; Jacob de, 300; John de, 301; Richard de, 300; Roger de, 7; vicarage of, 7.
Tenturer, John le, 304.
Testa, William de, liv.
Tewkesbury, xxiv; liberties of, 34, 52, 53, 84; monks of, xviii.
Thonglonde, chapelry of, 203; Roger de, 203.
Thornbury, church of, 30; Walter de, 307.
Thornbury (Gloucestershire), liberties of, 84.
Tibritone, Roger de, 309.
Ticheseye, lxvi, 186, 187.
Tintern, abbot of, 174.
Titley, cell of, 206 n.
Todenham, church of, 219.
Totitone, Robert de, 305.
Tottenham, xli, xlv, lxiii, lxvi, lxvii, 67, 73, 164, 168, 170, 177, 194, 205, 208, 210, 216, 220, 303.
Tournon, Hugh de, xxvi, 126, 136, 138, 142, 184.
Tours, xxv, 274, 276.
Tower, Nicholas of the, 93.
Tregoz, baron, xxxiv; Juliana de, i n, iii, lxiii, 178, 246, 300; Robert de, iii.
Trenot, Thomas, 166, 167.
Tretire, rector of, 127.
Tretower, 251 n.
Treye, David de, 43, 77, 78.
Trigeth, William, 299.
Trussebut, Agatha, xix.
Tudyntone, John de, 116.
Tuggeford, Adam de, 305; William, 300.

Tupsley, manor of, lxi n, 96.
Turbeville, Thomas xxiv.
Tureville, Robert de, 192.
Turpyn, William, 173.
Turner, Silas, lvii n.
Tyberton, Nicholas de, 307.
Tykelwardyn, Richard de, 304.
Tyrel, Roger, 24.
Tyrone, abbot and convent of, 206.

Ugina, Gerard de, lxx, lxxi, 247, 260, 261, 262, 263, 272.
Ullingswick, church of, 241, 242; rector of, 126, 136, 138, 141, 142, 302; Roger de, 300, 306.
Upavene, Henry de, 243.
Upleadon, preceptory of, 308, 310.
Upton, John de, 299; park of, 76, 77; William de, 299.
Upton Bishop, manor of, lxi n, 96.
Ursinis, Matthew de, 214, 223, 232, 234, 274.

Valence, canon of, 21.
Vaux, Adam, 173.
Venice, xxxiv.
Venur, Roger le, 305.
Verdun, bishop of, 84, 85, 86; Theobald de, 140, 141, 158.
Verney, Walter de, 185.
Vesino, Peter de, xxvi.
Vezano, Geoffrey de, 249, 250.
Vezelai, xlvii n.
Vicini, John, xxvii, 184.
Vienne, hospital of St. Anthony, 30 n.
Virieux, Geoffrey de, xxvii, 136, 139, 142.
Viterbo, 56, 57, 124, 230, 288; church of, 57.
Vitri, James de, xxvi n.

Waleron, Robert, 93.
Wales, 55, 56, 123, 175.
Waleys, John, lxx, 105, 106, 107; Philip le, 120, 121.
Waldringeham, Peter de, 173.
Walford, William de, 301.
Wallissnede, Alice de, 205; Ellis de, 205; Robert de, 205; vill of. 205.
Walkynham, Alan de, lxx, 22.
Walney, 22, 23.
Walton, Richard de, 306.
Wantenovere, Adam de, 311.
Warefelde, Edmund de, lxx, 12, 13, 14, 15, 18, 210, 243, 249, 250, 276, 277, 278, 281; Gervase de, 306.
Waterden, John de, 304.
Wattone, Stephen de (Prior of Leominster), 161, 218.
Wautone, William de, 173.
Wavertone, William de, 310.
Wayte, William le, lxxi.
Welbatch, lxvi, 138, 143, 152, 162.
Wellington, Adam de, 304; John de, 304; rector of, 303.
Wells, canon of, 211; prebends of, xlviii n.
Welsh, the, 110.
Welsh Bicknor, church of, 27.
Welshpool (Pola), chaplain of, 286, 287; John of, *see* John Wennonwyn; rector of, 140, 198; vicar of, 140, 286, 287.
Wendour, Simon de, 304.
Wenlock, lxv, lxvii, 42, 292; church of, 119; dean of, 139, 203; Holy Trinity, 227; Luke de, 156; monks of, 307; prior of, 36, 306, 307; prior and convent of, 9, 28, 119, 185, 186, 191; Richard de, 306; subprior of, 36; Walter de, 300, 307.
Wenlock, Little, church of, 82, 185; John de, 304; rector of, 302.
Wenlond, Thomas, 66.
Wennonwyn, Griffin, 140; John, 140, 197, 286, 287.
Wentnor, 68, 69; Adam de, 308; Stephen de, 117

Weobley, dean of, 232; Roger de, 251; William de, 304.
Were, Stephen de la, 171.
Werehun, John de, 309.
Westbury, Hubert de, 310; portionists of, 150, 302; rector of, 45, 145, 157, 302; sacristy of, 300; vicar of, 310.
Westhope, rector of, 151.
Westminster, lxv, lxvi, lxvii, 22, 23, 24, 33, 35, 52, 54, 64, 65, 66, 67, 68, 70, 71, 72, 73, 74, 75, 80, 96, 105, 111 n, 121, 134, 141, 144, 166, 169, 175, 176, 177, 181, 182, 198, 199, 200, 205, 216, 264, 284; abbot of, 79; prior of, 140, 284; St. James, 312.
Weston, John de, 308, 310; Odo of, 38; Simon de, 300, 306.
Westwood, copses of, lxxi, 146.
Weylonde, T. de, 72, 73.
Whaddon, lxvii, 224; chapelry of, 225.
Wheathill, Adam de, 82; rector of, 302.
Whitbourne, xli, xliii, lxv, lxvi, lxvii, 88, 89, 123, 124, 240, 241, 250, 306; bailiff of, lxxi, 80, 108; church of, 196, 251; manor of, lxi n, 43, 96, 123; rector of, 126 136, 138, 141, 142, 184, 302 310, 312.
White Castle, 173.
Whitney, Eustace de, 123, 131.
Wichford, church of, 99, 100; Thomas de, 99, 100.
Wickham, Ralph de, 164.
Wigmore, lxv, lxviii, 82, 293; Adam de, 300, 307, 311; abbot of, 122, 301, 306; abbot and convent of, 17, 36, 44, 45, 138, 196, 197, 202, 203, 205, 235, 310, 311; Ralph de, 227, 310; William de, 309.
Wilhenhope. Roger de, 310.
Willey, church of, 82, 138; rector of, 302.
Wilton, Adam de, 308, 311; ferry of, 76; John de, 301.
Wimbledon, John de, 88, 117, 171, 245.

Wiltshire, 245, 246.
Winchcombe, John de, 49.
Winchester, lxv, 30, 32, 33, 52 ; Adam de, 35, 172, 174, 175 ; bishop of, xxii *n* ; (Foxe) li *n* ; (Peter des Roches) xxii *n*, 39 *n* ; fair of, 173, see of, lxi.
Windsor, lxv, 2, 3, 16.
Winforton, Thomas de, 300.
Winstone, sacristy of, 300.
Wintringham, benefice of, vii, xix.
Wistanesbache, 73.
Wistanstow, Adam de, 82 ; church of, 290 ; rector of, 302.
Witbred, Richard, 117.
Witloc, lxxi, 159.
Wokingham, lxv, 14.
Wolferlow, church of, 107, 108 ; John de, 304 ; rector of, 302.
Wollaston, church of, 219.
Wombridge, prior of, 197, 229, 230.
Wonechirche, Roger de, 309.
Woodarton, 44.
Woodstock, 96 ; Henry de, xxv, 8, 16, 18, 19.
Wooler's Batch, 170.
Woolhope (Welnythehope), chantry of, 302 ; Walter de, 302.
Woolstaston, rector of, 302.
Worcester, lxvi, 13, 55, 61, 96, 111, 123, 166 ; archdeacon of, 94 ; bishop of, xliv, 20, 106, 231 ; (Alfred) 96 ; (Walter de Cantilupe) ii *n*, iii, vi, viii, xix, xx, xxxv, 134 ; (Godfrey Giffard) xxii, lii, 20. 99, 117, 118, 122, 134, 204, 225, 286 ; cathedral church of, 286 ; diocese of, xvii, 106, 107, 117, 118, 208, 230, 290, 291 ; friars-minor of, 307 ; official of, 140, 255 ; prior of, 13, 229, 230 ; prior and convent of, xix ; priory of, xliv.
Worcestershire, 69 ; sheriff of, 70, 76, 78, 84.
Wormesley, convent of, xxxix ; prior of, 228 ; prior and convent of, 144, 212.

Worthen, church of, 189 ; rector of, 145, 150, 198.
Wrokestone, prior and convent of, 74, 75.
Wulonkelowe, Hugh de, 11 *n*.
Wych, deanery of, 19.
Wychecote, Adam de, 299, 312.
Wycombe, John de, 116, 119, 155.
Wydemerchs, Hugh de, 310.
Wye, Richard de, 70 ; river, 30, 96.
Wyketone, Richard de, 174.
Wyndiate, 62.
Wyne, Ralph le, 64 ; Robert le, 39.
Wyntewelle, 41.
Wynton, Adam de, 172, 174, 175 ; Richard de, 116 ; Thomas de, 142, 143, 153 ; William de, 116, 265, 266, 267.
Wytacre, Robert de, lxxi.
Wytloe, Robert, 227.
Wyse, Robert le, vii, xiv *n*, xlix, lx ; Walter de, 307.
Wyttone, 310.

Yadefen, Ralph de, 71.
Yanua, Humbert de, xxvii, 84, 85, 86, 87.
Yarkhill, church of, 49.
Yarpole, William de, 305.
Yazor, church of, 51, 122 ; vicar of, 300.
Yeovil, xlvi.
York, 244 ; archbishop of (W. de Grey), 95, 105 *n* ; (Walter Giffard) xxxiii, 14 *n*, 177, 190 ; dean of, lxii, 105, 312 ; diocese of, xxxviii, 159, 160, 183 ; precentor of, xix ; province of, 233.
Yvetens, Philip des, 90.

Zouche, Sir Eudo la, 16, 28, 185, 235 *n* ; Milicent la, iii *n*, xxi, 235 *n*.